BREAKING
THE
PHALANX

BREAKING THE PHALANX

A New Design for Landpower in the 21st Century

DOUGLAS A. MACGREGOR

Foreword by Donald Kagan

Published in cooperation with the
Center for Strategic and International Studies

Westport, Connecticut
London

Library of Congress Cataloging-in-Publication Data

Macgregor, Douglas A.
    Breaking the phalanx : a new design for landpower in the 21st
century / Douglas A. Macgregor : foreword by Donald Kagan.
       p.   cm.
    "Published in cooperation with the Center for Strategic and
International Studies."
    Includes bibliographical references and index.
    ISBN 0–275–95793–4 (alk. paper).—ISBN 0–275–95794–2 (PB : alk.
paper)
    1. United States. Army—Reorganization. 2. Twenty-first century.
I. Center for Strategic and International Studies (Washington, D.C.)
II. Title.
UA25.M13   1997
355′.02′09730905—dc20   96–34012

British Library Cataloguing in Publication Data is available.

Library of Congress Catalog Card Number: 96–34012
ISBN: 0–275–95793–4
      0–275–95794–2 (pbk.)

First published in 1997

Praeger Publishers, 88 Post Road West, Westport, CT 06881
An imprint of Greenwood Publishing Group, Inc.

Printed in the United States of America

The paper used in this book complies with the
Permanent Paper Standard issued by the National
Information Standards Organization (Z39.48–1984).

10 9 8 7 6 5 4 3 2 1

For
Major General Edward C. O'Connor, USA (Retired)
and his wife
Charley

Contents

Illustrations

Foreword

The end of the Cold War has not brought an end to the need for careful thought about the defense of peace and security in the world. On the contrary, the collapse of the system on which international relations were based for a half-century, the rapid development of new military technology, and the predictable demand in the United States and among its allies for sharp reductions in expenditure for defense together require the most serious and penetrating consideration of what should be the shape and character of the forces needed to preserve the peace and defend American interests in the years to come.

There is broad agreement that we are probably in the midst of what is called a revolution in military affairs that is rapidly altering the character of warfare. Because this has been driven largely by the availability of new or greatly improved technologies, the tendency has been to look primarily to the application of advanced technology as the answer to current and future military challenges. The temptation is to seek victory through the use of accurate and deadly bombs and missiles fired from aircraft far above the ground or from ships far out at sea, to find a "silver bullet" that will achieve the goals of war without casualties and without, for the most part, any serious use of ground forces.

The development and use of such weapons will certainly be important, but it is wrong and dangerous to imagine they can do the job alone. The Gulf War showed the potentiality of such weapons, but they were no silver bullet. Bombardment at a distance played an important role in the victory over Iraq, but it did not defeat Saddam Hussein's army. That crucial task was accomplished chiefly by ground forces, and it would be reckless to imagine that such forces will not be vital to success in wars of the future.

Ground forces must be equipped with the best weapons and equipment of the new era, but that will not be adequate if the new devices are merely grafted onto a military organization that is not designed specifically to use them to best effect. True revolutions in military affairs depend on the reconfiguration of forces to meet new conditions, and they require new fighting doctrines. Lieutenant Colonel (P) Douglas A. Macgregor's study *Breaking the Phalanx* economically and convincingly makes the case for the inescapable importance of land forces in wars of the future and, no less important, in deterrence of wars.

Colonel Macgregor brings a remarkable panoply of training, education, and experience to the task. A professional soldier, he is a graduate of West Point and an experienced leader of American combat troops in action during the Gulf War. Beyond that, he is a student of history and a scholar of the military art of the first rank. This rare combination allows him to understand current events and developments with the wisdom provided by a knowledge of previous human experience. His use of the victory of the Roman Legion over the less flexible Greek hoplite phalanx as an illuminating analogy to his own proposal for a new military organization is a good example, as are his analyses of military events from the 18th through the 20th centuries that show the special tasks for which landpower is required. This historical knowledge and understanding is tested and reinforced by Colonel Macgregor's direct experience with the latest weapons and tactics and the character of modern warfare. Few analysts of our current and future military needs bring to bear credentials of such value.

His study shows a deep knowledge and appreciation of the value of other forces, air, surface, and undersea, and fairly evaluates their strengths and weaknesses, but his focus is on ground forces. Having demonstrated their continuing essential role, he goes on to recommend a strikingly new organization for ground combat power, more flexible, mobile and self-sufficient, versatile and powerful, structured to operate as part of a Joint Task Force. Its purpose is not only to make the best use of the new technology, but also to unleash the potentialities of the human beings who use them. The new unit is meant to be a "smarter, smaller, faster and more technologically advanced warfighting organization," a central feature of a doctrinal engine on the joint level empowered to develop a unified warfighting doctrine at the strategic and operational levels of war. That is the sort of thinking desperately needed, but not yet evident in the government's plans for the future of its military forces. Those interested in the defense of American security and the pursuit of its interest cannot afford to ignore Colonel Macgregor's innovative proposals and stimulating ideas presented in this study.

Donald Kagan

Acknowledgments

A great many people and organizations have helped me in researching and writing this book. I am indebted to the Department of the Army for the opportunity to spend my war college year as a military fellow at the Center for Strategic and International Studies in Washington, D.C. I also want to thank Dr. William Taylor, senior vice president, International Security Affairs, and director of Political–Military Studies at the Center for Strategic and International Studies (CSIS), for providing me with the facilities and support to write this book. I am equally indebted to Dr. Dan Gouré, Dr. Ahmed Hashim, Mr. Dave Earnest, Mr. Ed Peartree, and Ms. Meg Keough—all of CSIS—for their helpful comments and suggestions. They made the year at CSIS a special pleasure for me.

I am further indebted to a host of friends and associates in the Department of Defense. This list includes Brigadier General Bill Lay, USAF; Colonel V. J. Warner, USA; Colonel Tom Davis, USA; Colonel Mark Kimmitt, USA; Lieutenant Colonel Mike Ford, USAF; Lieutenant Colonel Reggie Gillis, USA; Lieutenant Colonel Mike DeMayo, USA; Lieutenant Colonel John Gordon, USA; Lieutenant Colonel Steven Scroggs, USA (ret.); Commander J. Novarro, USN; Commander Doug Smith, USN; and Major Darrin Irvine, USA. I am equally indebted to Dr. Craig College, deputy director of Program Evaluation and Assessment, Department of the Army, and to his colleague Colonel Tony Hermes, USA, for their assistance with the cost estimates of the current and proposed Army force designs. I also owe thanks to Dr. John Hillen, Defense Analyst at the Heritage Foundation, for his advice and support.

The ideas and professional accomplishments of Army Captains Bill Prior, Chris Hoffman, John Gifford, Steve Pinette, Eric Wang, Jim Gentile, and David Jones, along with CSM Charles "Landshark" Smith, USA (ret.); CSM Roger Stradley, USA; SFC William Burns, USA; and SFC Scott Pear, USA; and numerous others were vital to this work. I also owe thanks to Dr. Fred Kagan, assistant professor of military history, and Major H. R. McMaster, USA, in the Department of History at the U.S. Military Academy. I am most indebted to Colonel David Shanahan, USA, and Lieutenant Colonel Frank Finelli, USA, for their insights and friendship. Without their interest, encouragement, support, and patience, this book would never have been completed.

Because the book had its genesis during my command of the 1st Squadron, 4th U.S. Cavalry in the 1st Infantry Division (Mech) at Fort Riley, Kansas, I owe special thanks to Colonel Mike Crews, USA; Colonel Tom Metz, USA; Brigadier General Michael Dodson, USA; Brigadier General Huba Wass de Czege, USA (ret.); Major General David Ohle, USA; and General William Hartzog, USA, all of whom allowed me and my subordinate officers and noncommissioned officers to put into practice at Fort Riley and the National Training Center the tactical theory which underpins much of the thinking in this book. As always, I can never sufficiently thank all of the junior officers, noncommissioned officers, and soldiers whose selfless service and devotion to the Army and the nation inspired me throughout this effort. However, the customary disclaimer that a book's errors and shortcomings are the author's alone applies with particular force in this instance. The responsibility for this analysis and interpretation is, for better or worse, truly my own.

1

Introduction

In the perspective of history, there are very few models for a 21st century American Army designed to dominate areas of American strategic interest, convey ideas, exert influence, and control the pace of human events through superior organization, leadership, discipline, and technology. However, one stands out.

In 200 B.C., the Macedonians in alliance with Sparta and Syria set out to regain control of Greece and the Aegean coast of Asia Minor from Rome's Greek allies. After two years of inconclusive fighting, the Roman and Macedonian armies finally met in the hill country of Thessaly. When the two armies collided in battle, the Macedonian right wing drove back the Roman left, but while the Macedonian left was deploying from march column on uneven ground, it was struck in the flank and routed by the Roman right. Part of the advancing Roman right suddenly swung around— apparently without orders—hitting the Macedonian right wing and driving it from the field in confusion. Macedonian losses were about 13,000; Roman, a few hundred. Without the means to continue the war, the Macedonians renounced all claims to Greece and the Aegean coast. Rome's victory made Greece and the Eastern Mediterranean an integral part of the Roman Empire for half a millennium. And the Phalanx, the backbone of the Macdeonian military system, was broken.

Until the smaller, more agile Roman Legions (4,500–6,000 men) deployed in checkerboard formation destroyed it, the ancient world regarded the Macedonian Phalanx as invincible. In a typical Phalanx nearly 10,000 heavily armed soldiers stood sixteen deep. Their tactic was simple and deadly: a perfectly aligned charge at a dead run against the enemy's weak point. But these tactics failed in action against the Roman Legions, which could maneuver more easily without fear of losing alignment and without the need for concern about gaps in the line—the gaps were built in!

For efficiency in attacking, subduing, occupying, administering, and pacifying hostile territory, the Roman Legion has seldom been equaled by another military organization. The same legions who routed the enemy in battle could handle disarmament control, police patrol, and general administrative supervision.[1] For almost 500 years, the arrival of the Roman Legion on foreign soil was synonymous with the presence of order, stability, and civilization. This is because however fierce the urge to dominate may have been, the Roman desire for an international system embodying Roman principles of justice and order was greater.

Like it or not, the logic of international relations that positioned Rome at the center of world affairs also compels the United States to remain engaged in the world at a time when America's economic dominance is substantially reduced from what it was just after World War II. There is no going back, in other words, to the assumption on which the traditional American nation-state was founded: that a small army, augmented by large numbers of reservists, is all that is needed to hold the enemy at bay while civilian economic facilities are converted to wartime production.[2] This was tried after World War II with tragic consequences for the U.S. Army and the American people in the Korean conflict.[3] At the same time, America cannot afford to enter the new millennium as a nostalgic posthegemon with expensive industrial age armed forces that simply do not fit the new strategic environment. In practical terms, this involves replacing old military structures and concepts—the contemporary equivalent of the Phalanx—with new structures: the modern American military equivalent of the Roman Legion.

For strategic planners, though, rethinking warfare is not easy. The end of the Cold War saw the beginning of the end of another, equally significant era in world history—that of industrial age warfare. That era opened in the 19th century with the first appearance of mass-produced modern artillery weapons and culminated with the American-led coalition's victory over Iraq in the Gulf War. Iraq's dramatic defeat suggested new ways in which the United States could attack an opponent technologically.[4] As a result, analysts in both the public and private sectors began applying the term "information age warfare" to a new, as yet undiscovered era of human conflict.[5]

Focusing primarily on the role of technology in military affairs entails great risk, however. The passion for new military technology and the desire for quantum leaps in capability that it can provide often lead policymakers to overlook the importance of the right organization for combat within a coherent doctrinal framework. The deterrent value of forward-stationed ground forces is overlooked. Moreover, the never-ending search for elusive silver bullet weaponry ignores the fact that once any military technology is known to exist and its characteristics are understood, it is possible to devise countermeasures that will reduce or completely negate its effectiveness.[6]

Recognizing that the evolution of the United States Army into a new form will depend on more than the incorporation of new technology, this book seeks answers to questions which confront the United States Army today: Is landpower essential to American strategic dominance? Can the Army's elected and appointed leaders shape warfighting organizations that are skilled enough, smart enough, and enduring enough to maneuver within a joint framework through the treacherous environment of contemporary and future conflict? How do political and military leaders ensure crisp execution of complex operations and winning performance in battle without restricting human potential and suffocating the American soldier's individual brains and initiative? Answers to these questions must be found before key choices are made by defense planners.

The first step in the process of finding answers to these questions, however, is that policymakers understand that future control of events on land in areas of pivotal strategic interest cannot be achieved without a substantial American army. In this connection, the most important factor in evaluating the importance of landpower to American strategic dominance is not being blinded by the immediate consequences—successful or not—of a single event.[7] The current period of adjustment in international politics will eventually end as new political authority structures fill the vacuum created by the end of the Cold War. To the extent that American policymakers contemplate the use of force to influence events in pivotal areas— Europe, the Middle East, North Africa, Southwest Asia, and Northeast Asia—landpower will be an essential feature of statecraft and deterrence. Today, historians remind Americans that the refusal of the United States and Great Britain to maintain armies capable of presenting real resistance to fascism on the Eurasian landmass was an important source of encouragement to the aggressors, who concluded that they could achieve their aims without American interference even though America possessed enormous sea- and airpower.[8]

What is needed today is a vision for the role the Army will play in national military strategy, and a description of how the Army will achieve that role. This description must encompass guidelines for the design and use of landpower within a joint military structure. The guidelines outlined in this work suggest an American military strategy based on action by Joint Task Forces (JTFs) either to preempt or to win conflict quickly. This concept for the use of Army Ground Forces links the Army's capability to dominate the strategic landscape to a military strategy focused on areas of the world where economic progress and political stability directly benefit American security.

Desert Storm demonstrated for the first time, really, that American land-based air and rapidly deployable Army heavy ground forces are global weapons like the legions of the ancient world.[9] The reorganization outlined in this work envisions an information age American Army rendered distinctly more mobile and effective by cooperation with American airpower and unchallenged American control of the sea.[10] Rather than relying on the cumbersome mobilization and massed firepower arrangements of the Cold War, this work suggests reorganizing the Army into mobile combat groups positioned on the frontiers of American security, ready to act quickly and decisively, primed to move with a minimum of preparation. Because the fighting power of an Army lies in its organization for combat, this means reorganizing American Ground Forces to "break the Phalanx."[11]

Because it is fashionable to speak of the decisive role technology plays in the "revolution in military affairs" (RMA), much less attention is paid in military circles to the complex set of relationships that actually link technology's military potential to strategy and organization for combat (doctrine) in the broader context of change. As a result, one finds little discussion of this topic in the Defense Department's Bottom-Up Review (BUR) or in the literature of the Army's *Force XXI* program.[12] To date, warfighting organizations for the Army of the future look much like the force structures in the past and present. For instance, the options under consideration for a new Army division range from retaining today's basic structure while inserting new technologies to the adoption of a flexible brigade-based division structure that can be tailored to specific missions.[13]

Yet, historical experience suggests that measures to incorporate potentially revolutionary technology in lethal or nonlethal forms will not make much difference if the warfighting organizations and the methods of application remain unchanged. Technology alone does not bring about a revolution in military affairs.[14] Increasingly lethal weapons lead to greater dispersion of combat forces and to increases in individual unit mobility. The necessity for command, control, and sustainment of dispersed formations increases reliance on subordinate officers' and soldiers' judgment, intelligence, and character. Organizational change in directions that capitalize on these human qualities works to the benefit of armies with high quality manpower that encourage initiative and develop more flexible and adaptive fighting formations.[15] The combination of innovative technology and human ingenuity finds its way through obstacles and obsolescence.[16]

Even if reasonable and promising strategies for the near-term adaptation of existing warfighting structures achieve an incremental improvement in the Army's warfighting capabilities, today's military leaders will want to develop new warfighting formations that can effectively exploit both new technology and increased human potential. Whether there is a current revolution in military affairs is still being debated. What is certain, however, is that organizational change in armies can produce revolutionary change in warfare.[17]

In many ways, the observations about the Roman Legions with which this introduction began throw into sharp relief those key features which should characterize America's information age Army. Like Caesar's Legions, Joint Task Forces (JTFs) will need an Army component that is composed of highly mobile, self-contained, independent "all-arms" combat forces-in-being. These Army forces will have to be structured within an evolving joint military framework to exploit new technology and increased human potential for rapid and decisive action[18] and provide the foundation on land for coherent joint military operations in a new and uncertain strategic environment. When the national command authorities decide in the future to project a JTF capable of exerting direct and enduring influence over an opponent, the Army component must be organized within that JTF to provide the American people with an agile, responsive, and effective tool of statecraft.

On the grounds of logic, politics, and the absence of an impending war, many will dispute the notion that fielding a new, reorganized Army within a joint strategic framework is at least as important to the nation as welfare reform, deficit reduction, and health care. Many defense analysts are already suggesting that reducing the Army to eight or even six divisions would produce quick savings that could be plowed into the high technology areas of electronic warfare, aircraft, and missiles.[19] It is quite possible that the effects of budgetary pressures, service competition for limited resources, and private sector scientific–industrial interests could produce an American force structure without the mix of military means to influence events decisively on the Eurasian and African landmasses.[20] Devoid of a strategically significant objective, an American military strategy based primarily on ships, planes, and precision-guided missiles potentially forfeits military flexibility and courts strategic irrelevance in the 21st century.[21]

Unfortunately, because this approach promises American influence abroad without U.S. forces on the ground it appeals to a rising tide of isolationist sentiment in America's domestic politics and reduces national defense to its raw economic rewards.[22] This helps explain why many elected leaders are ready to channel large portions of shrinking national resources into a few costly, specialized programs with uncertain prospects for success and why this emphasis creates a preference for both airpower and nonengaged sea-based forces over American landpower.[23] Computer-based simulated warfare rewards this focus by elevating old concepts of attrition warfare to new levels of sophistication because quantitative analysis cannot model the positional political and military advantages attained through ground force maneuver.[24]

The pattern is all too familiar. General Malin Craig, whom General George Marshall succeeded as Chief of Staff in 1939, warned in his final annual report that it might be too late to reorganize, retrain, and reequip the U.S. Army for war.

> What transpires on prospective battlefields is influenced vitally years before in the councils of the staff and in the legislative halls of Congress. Time is the only thing that may be irrevocably lost, and it is the first thing lost sight of in the seductive false security of peaceful times. . . . The sums appropriated this year will not be fully transformed into military power for two years. Persons who state that they see no threat to the peace of the United States would hesitate to make that forecast through a two year period.[25]

A senior fellow at the Brookings Institution observed recently that this is a time in American history when the nation's leaders "ought to be thinking more about where we are going."[26] This is true, and it includes thinking about America's participation in future conflict. History tells us that while peaceful times should be cherished, peace is not a permanent condition in world affairs. But recent events suggest that the time and opportunity to prepare for future conflict may not last as long as many had hoped 5 years ago. Even small nations can no longer be prevented from building total war capacity—whether nuclear or conventional.[27] Thus, today's U.S. Army is in a race against time to be ready to fight jointly and win the next conflict wherever and whenever it occurs.

Reshaping the Army force structure to reconcile trends in the technology of warfare and the new strategic environment with the Army's immediate need to preserve its readiness to fight and win today is easy in theory. In practice, reorganizing the Army for future missions in peace and war has never been easy and no new strategy will make it easier. But even if defense planners underestimate the scope of the necessary organizational changes or their short-term consequences, this will not in itself be sufficient grounds to reject organizational change unless the consequences of inaction are also taken into account.[28] If it can be demonstrated to the American people and to the Congress that the kind of deliberate and pragmatic reorganization outlined in this monograph will make better use of the resources the U.S. Army is given and result in landpower that is more potent and economically efficient, then America's Army will win its current race to be ready for the 21st century.

NOTES

1. R. E. Dupuy and T. N. Dupuy, *The Encyclopedia of Military History from 3500 B.C. to the Present* (New York: Harper & Row, Publishers, 1970), 84. The two armies were roughly equal in strength; 26,000 men. In war, for each Roman Legion, there was one identically organized allied legion.

2. Peter F. Drucker, *Post-Capitalist Society* (New York: HarperCollins 1993), 138.

3. Russell F. Weigley, *The American Way of War: A History of United States Military Strategy and Policy* (Bloomington: Indiana University Press, 1977), 392–93.

4. C. Kenneth Allard, "The Future of Command and Control: Toward a Paradigm of Information Warfare" in *Turning Point: The Gulf War and U.S. Military Strategy*, ed. L. Benjamin Ederington and Michael J. Mazarr (Boulder, Colo.: Westview Press, 1995), p. 162.

5. Henry Bartlett, G. Paul Holman, and Timothy Stone, "The Art of Strategy and Force Planning," *Naval War College Review*, Spring 1995: p. 121.

6. Hirsh Goodman and W. Seth Carus, *The Future Battlefield and the Arab–Israeli Conflict*, (London: Transaction Publishers, 1990), 167.

7. Joseph E. Goldberg, "Strategic Success" in *Essays on Strategy IV* (Washington, D.C.: National Defense University, 1987), 7.

8. Forrest C. Pogue, *George C. Marshall: Education of a General* (New York: The Viking Press, 1963), 323.

9. William T. Pendley, "Mortgaging the Future to the Present in Defense Policy: A Commentary on the Bottom-Up Review," *Strategic Review* (Spring 1994): p. 39.

10. "The Navy–Marine Corps Battleground," *Navy Times*, 23 January 1995, p. 7.

11. James S. Corum, *The Roots of Blitzkrieg: Hans von Seeckt and German Military Reform* (Lawrence, Kans.: University Press of Kansas, 1992), 205.

12. Michael J. Mazarr, *The Revolution in Military Affairs: A Framework for Defense Planning*, (Carlise, Penn.: U.S. Army War College Strategic Studies Institute Fifth Annual Conference on Strategy, April 1994), 3.

13. Amy McAuliffe, "Technology: Changing the Way the Army Does Business," *Military & Aerospace Electronics* (February 1996): p. 24.

14. Thomas L. Friedman, "The No-Dead War," *The New York Times*, 23 August 1995, p. 21.

15. William G. Stewart, "Interaction of Firepower, Mobility, and Dispersion," *Military Review* (March 1960): 25–33.

16. Jonathan Rauch, *Demosclerosis: The Silent Killer of American Government* (New York: Times Books-Random House, 1994), 229.

17. See Stephen Rosen's work, *Winning the Next War: Innovation and the Modern Military* (Ithaca, N.Y.: Cornell University Press, 1991).

18. Karl H. Lowe, "U.S. Armed Forces in the New Europe" in *European Security Policy After the Revolutions of 1989*, ed. Jeffrey Simon (Washington, D.C.: Defense University Press, 1991), 129.

19. David A. Fulghum, "Two-War Strategy May Be Abandoned," *Aviation Week & Space Technology*, 29 January, 1996, p. 40.

20. Tim Weiner, "Smart Weapons Were Overrated, Study Concludes," *New York Times*, 9 July 1996, pp. A1, A14.

21. Frank E. Jordan, "Maritime–Continental Debate: A Strategic Approach," in *Essays on Strategy V* (Washington, D.C.: National Defense University Press, 1988), 210.

22. Sidney Blumenthal, "The Return of the Repressed: Anti-Internationalism and the American Right," *World Policy Journal* (Fall 1995): p. 7.

23. Secretary of Defense William Perry stated on 16 February 1995 that a consitutional amendment to balance the federal budget by 2002 would result in a 20 to 30 percent reduction in defense spending.

24. Paul K. Davis and Donald Blumenthal, "The Base of Sand Problem: A White Paper on the State of Military Combat Modeling," *A RAND Note*, N-3148-OSD/DARPA (Santa Monica, Calif.: RAND Corporation, 1991), 1–22.

25. M. S. Watson, *Chief of Staff: Prewar Plans and Preparations, United States Army in World War II* (Washington, D.C.: The War Department, Office of the Chief of Military History, Department of the Army, 1950), 35. Quoted by General Paul F. Gorman in "The Secret of Future Victories," *IDA Paper P-2653* (Alexandria, Va.: Institute for Defense Analysis, 1992), I–7.

26. Lawrence Korb, quoted by Bradley Graham in "Pentagon Faces Familiar Crunch on Procurement," *Washington Post*, 10 March 1996, p. 6.

27. Jeff Erlich and Theresa Hitchens, "Counterproliferation Efforts Await Requirement Review," *Defense News*, 6–12 November 1995, p. 6.

28. Ariel Levite, *Offense and Defense in Israeli Military Doctrine* (Boulder, Colo.: Westview Press, 1990), 144–45.

2

Landpower and Strategic Dominance

- On the morning of 21 October 1805, the French and British fleets collided, just off the coast of Spain's Cape Trafalgar. When the day closed, eighteen French and Spanish ships had struck their colors. The most spectacular sea victory of the age had been won in 4 hours and the Royal Navy's greatest Admiral, Horatio Nelson, had achieved immortality. Six weeks later on 2 December 1805, the French Army met and defeated the combined armies of Austria and Russia near a small town named Austerlitz in Central Europe. It was a French strategic victory so complete and so overwhelming that French dominance of the European continent would not be successfully challenged again for 8 years. It would take 10 years and the combined efforts of several allied European armies to roll back French political dominance.

- In 1846, after difficult negotiations, Texas was formally annexed to the United States, despite Mexico's threat that this would mean war. Mexico, a second-rate military power without a navy, fought the United States for 2 years. Until a U.S. Army landed unopposed near Vera Cruz and fought its way into Mexico City, the Mexican government could not be induced to accept peace on American terms.[1]

- The Royal Navy subdued the German High Seas Fleet and dominated the world's oceans throughout World War I. But until America entered the war and American ground forces joined the British and French armies on the Western Front, the British and French faced an unbeatable enemy and the prospect of probable defeat.[2]

- Few challenges to Europe's stability have been as serious as the NATO governments' decision to deploy the American intermediate range nuclear force (INF) on German soil in the 1980s. Concerted efforts of the German antinuclear movement and the Soviet state nearly succeeded in disrupting the INF deployment and splitting the Atlantic alliance. Western observers wondered why NATO's leadership insisted on deploying the Pershing II missile in Central Germany when a comparable missile system could be launched from U.S. and British submarines in the North Sea. The former German Chancellor, Helmut Schmidt, reminded the German public that the deployment had to be visible to have the desired political impact.[3]

- Forty days of near-constant air and missile attack during January and February 1991 neither dislodged the Iraqi Army from Kuwait nor destroyed Iraq's nuclear facilities and mobile missile launchers.[4] It was the ground offensive that compelled the Iraqis to submit unconditionally to the American-led coalition forces.[5]

These accounts illustrate the centrality of landpower to the achievement of America's strategic objectives in war and peace. Why, then, given this record of experience, is there remarkably little appreciation in contemporary America for the strategic role of landpower? Part of the answer can be traced to America's reluctance to commit ground forces before conflict erupts to achieve important political objectives.

To understand the political forces that influence this thinking, it is essential to appreciate the beguiling notion that the United States is unassailable because it is protected by the Atlantic and Pacific oceans.[6] For about a century after 1815 American society enjoyed, and was conscious of enjoying, a remarkable freedom from external military threat.[7] One consequence of this experience is an isolationist impulse in American foreign policy which is founded on the idea of a fortress America rendered impregnable to attack. This impulse is further reinforced by the continuing absence of serious military threats on America's continental borders and the early American cultural disinclination to maintain standing armies.[8]

The concept is still seductive because it seems to promise less spending for defense and foreign aid. Although the United States acquired the geographic, demographic, industrial, and technological resources of a global power in the 20th century, the influence of America's early strategic immunity continues to be felt long after the technology of warfare eliminated it. To this must be added another observation: America has repeatedly fallen victim to the illusion of political influence without the commitment of American landpower.[9] The American willingness to apply the decisive strategic influence of landpower in wartime is seldom matched by an understanding of landpower's strategic value in peacetime.

What the isolationist impulse obscures is the larger question of how best to maintain an international political and economic order that is consistent with the requirements of American national security. Had America's government sought an answer to this question instead of asserting international claims that could not be secured without landpower, America could have decisively influenced the circumstances which resulted in a series of 20th century conflicts.[10]

PAST AS PROLOGUE

Woodrow Wilson (like Jefferson a century earlier) embraced grand objectives in the world but overlooked the need for an American Army to achieve them. Wilson perceived no connection between the prevention of aggression in Europe or Asia through the selective and skillful use of American landpower and the preservation of American security. The notion that threats to regional security could be closely linked to threats to global economic prosperity was understood by Wilson only insofar as these threats related to commerce. Since the world's oceans were the medium of transport for American commerce, this only justified the maintenance of American seapower.[11]

The possibility that a defensible bridgehead would be required, a continental ally who could provide a base from which effective landpower could be exercised, does not seem to have occurred to Wilson or his predecessors.[12] Underlying this outlook was always the noble conviction that military force in international relations constituted a form of logic that was ultimately inimical to liberty.[13] Of course, this attitude did not prevent the U.S. Congress from appropriating significant sums of money for a large fleet of warships which Wilson used at Vera Cruz to support the prewar American Army's expeditionary force in Mexico. But it left America without the essential feature of national political influence in Europe—a capable, modern Army.

If unpreparedness for war is one pattern in 20th century American politics, another is the swift return to an isolationist military posture immediately after conflict.[14] This is based on the belief that military power has no relevance to the task of establishing new political institutions in the aftermath of war. After World War I, America's political leaders avoided the political and military commitments to achieve international stability along liberal capitalist lines—the conquest and occupation of strategic territory to secure the peace. Sensing the incompleteness of the allied victory over Germany in 1918, General Pershing, President Wilson's Army Commander in Europe, advised a longer and more thorough occupation of Germany. In urging the President to occupy Germany with U.S. and Allied troops, General Pershing may have recalled any number of examples suggesting that occupation was necessary to secure the peace. America's war with Mexico provided one.[15]

Wilson rejected Pershing's recommendation. For domestic political reasons, Wilson could not ignore the public's demands for dismantling of the U.S. Army's Expeditionary Force once the Versailles Treaty was signed. Without a powerful American Army (which had been the real basis for America's negotiating strength during the conference) on the Continent responsive to the commands of the President, it is understandable that most of President Wilson's later proposals for collective security drew little more than curiosity from the British and the French. Unfortunately, while this truth escaped notice in Washington, it was not missed in Berlin, Rome, Moscow, and Tokyo.

President Wilson's Republican successors continued the same course and opted for a large U.S. Navy and a small, impotent American Army. They did not grasp the point that despite their impressive absolute and relative size, America's naval forces held a distinctly defensive posture[16] and could not deter aggression on land.[17] It was a peculiar marriage of Wilsonian idealism and Republican complacency that guided American policy in the thirties. Although the Republicans sincerely wanted to foster stability in postwar Europe, reassure the French, allay German grievances, and contain the spread of communism, they ignored the fact that successful strategy is a result of the organization and application of power.[18] Without a modern Army to apply power in Europe and Asia after 1920, no serious strategy could be devised to influence the events of the interwar years.

Curiously, America's elected leaders in the 1920s continued to express confidence in the survival of an international order that was quickly passing. Technological, economic, and political changes were steadily eliminating the circumstances of America's geographic isolation. Dramatic advances in aircraft, automotive, and communications technologies coincided with the onset of the depression and the rise of antidemocratic states in Germany, Russia, Italy, and Japan. Yet these developments did not yield an increase in funds for the modernization or enlargement of the U.S. Army. When Army Chief of Staff General Douglas MacArthur urged Congress to appropriate money in 1934 for the modernization and modest expansion of the U.S. Army to cope with the interwar revolution in military affairs, President

Roosevelt's Republican friend and confidante, Senator Gerald Nye called the Army Chief of Staff a "warmonger." Republicans in Congress were uninterested in the Army and rejected most of MacArthur's appeals to stockpile strategic materials as well as his plans for industrial mobilization—recommendations they would all remember five years later.[19]

However, some of MacArthur's warnings were heeded. MacArthur's insistence, in his final report as Chief of Staff, that a future war would be one of movement and maneuver in which "command of the air over attacking ground forces would confer a decisive advantage on the side that achieved it" was taken seriously.[20] In 1936, five years before the attack on Pearl Harbor, the President asked Congress to fund an increase in the number of aircraft in the Army's inventory. The number of aircraft purchased rose each year, with the result that 4,429 aircraft were purchased in FY1941, which ended in June 1941.[21] Funding for the ground forces, however, continued to fall, with the result that the U.S. Army in the 1930s was largely moribund.[22]

Instead of supporting measures for the modernization and expansion of the U.S. Army to deter Japanese and German aggression, until 1940 President Roosevelt limited his requests for military expenditures to a program for American naval construction to compete with Japan's increased production of warships. Like his predecessors in both parties, President Roosevelt privately hoped that the United States' participation in any future war with Germany or Japan could be restricted to the use of American naval power and airpower. Until the fall of France, Roosevelt continued to express the view that 10,000 American aircraft and an armada of battleships would suffice to aid America's allies in their fight on the Eurasian landmass.[23] For Roosevelt the prospect of building an American Army that would fight beyond America's borders raised the spectre of casualties on the scale of World War I. If America could exploit the armies of allied states for landpower while American military technology dominated the air and sea, Roosevelt thought, American casualties could be kept to a minimum.[24]

President Roosevelt's strategy to exert political influence through exclusive reliance on seapower and, later, airpower, did nothing to dissuade Germany, Japan, Italy, and Soviet Russia from aggressive action between 1938 and 1942.[25] In part, this view was due to a growing faith in both sea-based and land-based aviation as a new silver bullet in military affairs. In the interwar period, the public fascination with airpower in Britain and America prompted officials in both countries to urge reliance on airpower at the expense of modernized ground forces.[26] The British Air Ministry went so far as to state that defensive measures to defeat strategic bombers were futile. "To defend against aircraft with ground-based anti-aircraft weapons was useless; fighter planes were no match for the bomber."[27] The effect of such predictions, however, did not improve Britain's defense posture. The unintended consequence of Britain's overreliance on airpower and reluctance to construct and maintain a modern army in peacetime was a weak and inadequately prepared British Army that no amount of British airpower could rescue from defeat in May 1940.[28]

After the fall of France and the subsequent Battle of Britain in 1940, the substance of the debate inside the Roosevelt administration about what forces the United States would need to confront Germany and Japan began to change. While Britain's defeat of Germany's air offensive temporarily removed the threat of invasion, it also demonstrated the impotence of a security policy based primarily on airpower. President Roosevelt realized that American involvement in another world war would require the use of American ground forces. When the President turned to General Marshall for strategic advice, Marshall provided him with a memorandum, "Program for Victory," which had been prepared by recently promoted Lt. Col. Albert C. Wedemeyer in the Department of the Army's War Plans Division. Wedemeyer's memorandum, dated 21 September 1941, determined more than how and where the United States Army would fight World War II. Its conception and delivery were among the decisive acts of the war.[29]

Wedemeyer reasoned that the technology of the 20th century—railways, automotive and aviation technology—placed insular America at a disadvantage unless she could seize a foothold on the "world island" and one as close as possible to the heartland—European Russia. He persuaded Roosevelt that while air and sea forces would make vital contributions, effective and adequate ground forces would be needed "to close with and destroy the enemy inside his citadel." In order to take the strategic offensive, the United States would require an army capable of defeating the Germans. Though a citizen of the richest nation on earth, Wedemeyer was sensitive to the need for economy. He pointed out that a large-scale invasion of Europe with the use of allied bases and staging areas would be less expensive than building of amphibious forces for operations along the periphery of the world island. Eventually, his argument in favor of economy persuaded the President. The result was a plan to field a ground force consisting of eighty-nine Army divisions and six Marine divisions.[30]

The military posture of America's Army after World War II bore a striking resemblance to its posture after World War I. In 1945, Congress could not be convinced of the need to preserve the striking power of the Army while no imminent danger could be found to justify it. This is not evidence for neglect of the danger of unpreparedness for war. The codification of World War II experience in the National Security Act of 1947 provided explicitly for a mobilization planning and preparedness capability in the form of the National Security Council, the Joint Chiefs of Staff, and the National Security Resources Board.[31] With World War II behind them, and supposedly a long period of peace ahead, the Truman administration simply saw no reason to maintain a large and powerful Army.

By 1948, however, the strategic situation began to change. President Truman's Secretary of State negotiated the North Atlantic Treaty, which granted military assistance and endorsed strategic collaboration. In fundamental terms, the American policy of containment was conceived as the global strategy of an insular power to defend the Eurasian periphery against postwar Soviet Russia's formidable outward pressure from the Eurasian heartland.[32] Thus, in the years immediately following World War II, the Army still bore the brunt of defense cuts. Though instrumental in the effort to defeat and transform Germany and Japan into modern democratic nations with close political and economic ties to the United States, the U.S. Army was, in the words of General Ridgway, "skeletonized."[33] Part of the blame for the Army's poor state of readiness for war in 1950 must also be shared by the Army's senior leaders, who were unable to articulate the need for an American Army in an environment shaped by a postwar strategy of one-sided nuclear attack.[34] The result was a large Navy, an expanding Air Force, and an American Army that was not prepared to fight in Korea.[35] Many years later, General Bradley, on assuming the office of Army Chief of Staff, described the state of the U.S. Army:

> The Army had almost no combat effectiveness. Ike had left me an administration rather than a military force. Half of the 552,000 officers and men were overseas on occupation duty, serving as policemen or clerks. The other half were in the states performing various administrative chores. Actually the Army of 1948 could not fight its way out of a paper bag.[36]

Thanks to the sacrifice of thousands of American and Korean lives to achieve battlefield success in Korea, Congress provided a temporary increase in the Army's budget.[37] Concurrently, however, President Eisenhower decided to base American national security policy toward a new nuclear-capable Soviet Russia on massive retaliation with nuclear weapons, and this turn of events called into question the entire role of land combat. The strategic bombing doctrine of the U.S. Air Force fit well with the Eisenhower administration's policy of massive retaliation, itself driven more by economic than by military considerations.[38] A new generation of civilian and military analysts (predominantly Air Force and Navy officers) argued that the influence of airpower in World War II substantially reduced the military importance of territory, population, and industrial resources.[39]

In the complex and shifting strategy of air attack during World War II, American political leaders discovered the weapon they hoped would permanently neutralize the effects of geography, culture, religion, and race. Aircraft (and later missiles) obliterated the dividing line that had always separated war on land from war at sea. Carrier-based aircraft could strike targets on land, and land-based aircraft became the fleet's most dangerous enemy.[40] As mentioned earlier, President Roosevelt had hoped to destroy the German and Japanese industrial capacities to wage war with American airpower in order to break the morale of their respective populations. Although the German scientific–industrial complex produced more warfighting material in April 1945 than it did before America's bombing offensive began in 1943, the inability of the Anglo–American air campaign to achieve its own stated strategic goals in Europe did not seem to matter after the war ended.[41] Where military and political observers identified airpower's shortcomings, the airmen pointed to inadequate resources and support. When the same observers pointed to American airpower's successes against enemy surface ships, transportation nets, and unprotected enemy ground forces, the airmen showed little interest. After Hiroshima, however, these points seemed moot. Not only did the wholesale destruction of Japanese and German cities liberate the U.S. Air Force from the unattractive close air support mission,[42] American airpower now also held the promise of a new independent air arm that could prevail in virtually any situation.[43]

When the Joint Chiefs of Staff (JCS) met in January 1965 to advise the Secretary of Defense and the President concerning American military courses of action in Southeast Asia, the strategic utility of "airpower alone" dominated the discussion. Despite the misgivings of the Army Chief of Staff and the Chief of Naval Operations that bombing Vietnam would do little to rescue the South Vietnamese from defeat in 1965, General Wheeler, Chairman of the Joint Chiefs (CJCS), persuaded the JCS to submit a paper to the Secretary of Defense expressing unanimous support for the use of strategic airpower.[44] There was probably no point in dissenting from a course of action that Secretary McNamara had already embraced. On the basis of his calculations of anticipated bomb damage, McNamara was quite certain that airpower could prevail on its own.

After the bombing offensive failed to achieve the desired results, the JCS told the President that if the United States wanted to save Vietnam, it was going to have to commit ground forces to do it. The rest of the story is well known. American aircraft dropped 8 million tons of bombs (over twice the tonnage dropped by the Allies during World War II) on Vietnam, Laos, and Cambodia between 1962 and 1973—the U.S. Air Force accounting for 80 percent of the tonnage. Total aircraft losses, fixed wing and helicopter, came to 8,588. The Air Force lost 2,257 aircraft and 2,700 airmen while hundreds more endured torture in captivity. For all the expenditure of treasure, firepower, and lives, American airpower, while occasionally pivotal, was never decisive in the Vietnam War.[45] One of the reasons why so little was purchased at such great cost is that American airpower was not part of a broader offensive strategy that included American landpower. Again and again, fighter-bombers would clear away surface-to-air missiles and fortifications and lose planes and pilots doing so. But no American ground forces would move through the breach. As a result, in a few weeks, the enemy would rebuild the defenses and more American aircraft would be lost in the process of attacking them all over again.[46] Without the decisive use of American landpower, short of massive nuclear bombardment, no amount of American airpower was strategically decisive. Strategic ambiguity in national policy created conditions conducive to attrition warfare—the very outcome which modern military technology had been created to overcome. America's tenuous, ill-defined, and limited strategic goals impaired the conduct of the war and ultimately demoralized the Army.[47]

By 1967, even McNamara recognized that the United States would not achieve its original purpose in Vietnam and persuaded the President to establish a ceiling on U.S. troop strength in South Vietnam.[48] McNamara recalled years later: "We failed then—as we have since—to recognize the limits of modern high-technology military equipment, forces and doctrine."[49] All of this suggests that air superiority over a theater of conflict does not make up for the deficiency of the rest of one's forces on the ground. Airpower cannot counterbalance the advantages which the enemy gains by retaining the initiative, nor does it compensate for deficiencies in an overall strategy.[50]

Tragically, Vietnam left the Army in ruins. The Johnson administration's failure to keep pace with the needs of modernization, research, and development consigned the Army to years of retrenchment and reconstruction. Empirically, American airpower could not win a war and in the minds of the American public only American landpower could lose one.[51]

THE GULF WAR

Western leaders had long been aware of Kuwait's strategic importance. Britain was the first to grasp the significance of its central strategic position on the Eurasian landmass and cultivated a close relationship with the region's ruling elites during the 18th century.[52] When Kuwait, Saudi Arabia, Iraq, and Iran began exporting oil to the West, Kuwait became a bridgehead from which the British Army defended Iraq's northern oil fields against the Turkish Army in the 1920s. During the Iran–Iraq War, Kuwait's neutrality was a source of frustration and opportunity for the great powers that struggled to preserve access to the region's oil resources. Iraq's invasion and occupation of Kuwait changed all that. The prominent concern in the West after Iraq's occupation was whether Iraq would move against or into Saudi Arabia and the other Persian Gulf states. Iraq could then gain control of one-fifth of the noncommunist world's oil production, two-thirds of proven world reserves.[53] It seemed that Iraq's potential to change the balance of power in a region of vital interest of the United States was once again reminding Americans that American strategic immunity from external threats is an illusion.

Why Iraq invaded Kuwait when it did will be the subject of debate for many years. One important reason was the absence of any capable ground force in the region that could mount an effective counterattack against the attacking Iraqi Army.[54] American strategic intelligence clearly failed. American intelligence analysts drew the wrong conclusions from circumstantial evidence—that Iraq would not attack Kuwait, that it would attack Saudi Arabia, that it would not attack Israel, and that the Soviet Union was on America's side, to mention just a few.[55] Having no Army expeditionary force that could quickly attack to reverse Iraq's strategic gains, the United States reverted to the time-honored practice of embargo while light airborne and marine elements deployed along the coast to establish a tripwire defense of Saudi Arabia. While these forces deployed along Saudi Arabia's border with Kuwait, the Bush administration worked to build the international coalition and domestic American political consensus required for decisive military action against Iraq.[56] Against a more competent enemy, a lapse of strategic intelligence on the scale of Iraq's surprise attack is potentially fatal. In the case of the Gulf War, it was not.

The decision to use force was a bold one since reductions in the Army were under way before the war with Iraq and indeed continued immediately after the war ended. One reason the President was able to opt for the use of force was the level of public support for action in the Gulf. This sent a signal to Congress that the President deserved support to fight a regional conflict in defense of unambiguous U.S. and allied security interests.[57] The high level of public approval prompted Congress to support the President's request for permission to use U.S. troops in January 1991 with a supplemental defense budget for Desert Storm.

Fortunately, Iraq's armed forces remained idle for months while American and coalition armies assembled for an attack that national leaders on every side sought desperately to avoid. While the ground forces concentrated for a decisive blow against Iraq, the coalition air forces struck. Even though airpower could not compel the Iraqi Army to withdraw from Kuwait, the U.S. Air Force turned in a brilliant performance, whose impact was heightened by the acute vulnerability of Iraq and its air defenses to the technological superiority of American airpower.[58] Most important, the medium of television provided the airpower enthusiasts with the tool to demonstrate selectively the value of airpower to the American people. In contrast, the Army's leaders hedged against the possibility of failure by excluding the media until the outcome of the ground offensive could no longer be doubted.[59]

In truth, the results of the air campaign were mixed. The claim by the U.S. Air Force that airpower alone defeated the Iraqi Army, made in the first flush of victory, has not withstood even brief examination.[60] Airpower failed to destroy 50 percent of Iraq's armor as advertised,[61] and Iraq never ran out of armor. Like body counts in Vietnam, destroyed tanks and artillery pieces became an irrelevant measure of military effectiveness. Many bridges and roads were destroyed, but many were also bypassed or repaired so quickly that Iraqi lines of communication were never broken from the air. Hundreds of aircraft linked to the best intelligence surveillance equipment in the world were unable to find or destroy Iraq's mobile Scud missiles. The bulwark of the Iraqi force—the Republican Guard Corps—sustained modest damage during the air campaign and Baghdad's command and control of Iraqi forces in Kuwait were never paralyzed.[62]

Still, great claims were made regarding how effective the coalition aerial onslaught had been on the Iraqi Army. General Merrill McPeak, the USAF Chief of Staff, insisted that this was the first time in history that a field army had been defeated by airpower. He clearly had his own definition of defeat. In the war with Iraq, defeat meant the removal of Iraqi ground forces from Kuwait, something that required coalition ground forces to attack and liberate Kuwait. It was true that Iraqi military morale in Kuwait was largely destroyed by 40 days' exposure to coalition bombing, but this may be attributed in part to the poor quality of Iraqi troops. Recent history is full of examples of good-quality soldiers withstanding devastating bombardments and then fighting back against ground attack with considerable success.[63] A more accurate summation of the role of airpower in this and other conflicts may be found in the words of an Air Force Colonel who actually flew in the Gulf War: "Airpower can only do so much; the Army must go in on the ground to defeat the enemy's ground forces to finally win the battle."[64]

Although airpower did not produce the paralysis it had hoped for, it protected the assembling armies from air attack. And American airpower also demonstrated that, for the moment, at altitudes above 10,000 to 15,000 feet it had gained a decisive edge in its struggle with land-based counter-measures for air supremacy. At altitudes below 10,000 feet, coalition aircraft were always engaged and sometimes destroyed. When the Gulf War ended, however, roughly half of Iraq's Republican Guard Corps had man-aged to evade contact with U.S. Air and Ground Forces and escaped to Central Iraq. Today, other than on depriving Iraq of the means to build up yet more powerful forces, there is widespread disagreement on the quality and meaning of the coalition's victory over Iraq.[65] Iraq was not occupied. No line was drawn along Iraq's border with Iran behind which modern democractic institutions could take root and flourish inside Iraq.

The more important military event that largely escaped public detection was the U.S. Navy's role during the Gulf War. Without American control of the sea lanes, American ground forces would not have been able to reach the Arabian Peninsula in great strength for many months. American domi-nance at sea made the strategic offensive to liberate Kuwait possible. Nearly 90 percent of the Army's equipment and ammunition was moved by sealift from the United States and Europe to the Arabian Peninsula.[66]

Little that occurred ashore or at sea supported many of the assumptions and implications of the nation's maritime strategy. No opposing naval forces tried to challenge U.S. Naval Forces for control of the seas. Waves of enemy aircraft never attempted to attack the carriers. There was no submarine threat to the flow of men and materiel across the oceans. Forced entry from the sea was unnecessary.[67] American Marines arrived on the Eurasian landmass through allied airports and seaports in exactly the same way Army troops did—by commercial air.[68] And the Marines were utilized to augment the Army's ground forces as they were in World War I, Korea, and Vietnam. Thus, while sea control was vital to American military success in the Gulf War, as Admiral Owens noted afterward, control of events on land was not decisively influenced by American naval power.[69]

Desert Storm offers many lessons; the most important are the following: Bombardment from a distance can enable landpower to win, but stand-off weapons in the air and at sea cannot achieve victory without landpower. Without landpower, airpower and seapower cannot be strategically decisive. And, only American landpower can impose strategic conditions on the former adversary through occupation that will result in political change that benefits both the former enemy and the United States.

Iraq's behavior since 1991 has supported this opinion. Iraq's threatening moves in October 1994 precipitated a large deployment of Army heavy forces to Kuwait and, later, U.S. Marines to Jordan. Airpower enthusiasts in the Pentagon insisted that this deployment was unnecessary. However, as a Kuwaiti officer made clear to an American member of the United Nations headquarters in Kuwait: "If the U.S. Army comes, we will stay and fight the Iraqis. Otherwise we will retreat to Saudi Arabia."[70] Nevertheless, the notion persists that another peace dividend lies hidden somewhere in the budget of an active Army whose strength has fallen from 760,000 to 495,000 in less than 4 years.

THE FUTURE OF LANDPOWER IN NATIONAL MILITARY STRATEGY

As the preceding sections illustrate, U.S. national security interests and needs do not completely determine the structure of the American national military establishment. An American cultural disinclination to international engagement and popular misinterpretations of 20th century conflict are at least as powerful as defined national interests. Assumptions that have changed very little over the last 70 years continue to yield consequences in the present that are distressingly similar to the past. Perceptions of U.S. interests and defense needs today are reminiscent of the postwar perceptions that deprived the United States of a capable, ready Army when it was needed in the past. The following comments made in the aftermath of the Gulf War reflect conventional wisdom and are all too familiar to those who have not lost sight of the historical record:[71]

- Peace between the major European and Asian powers themselves will be quite robust well into the distant future.

- The possibility of war between smaller European states, though a serious concern, is more a political problem for European and other multilateral security institutions than a taxing military contingency for U.S. forces.

- U.S. interests in the Third World are neither vital nor significant; rather they are vague and ambiguous.

- U.S. forces will not become involved in the vast majority of Third World conflicts.

- But the subtler tools of power projection—security assistance, airpower, and naval forward presence in the context of crisis response—will have frequent use.
- Simultaneous contingencies affecting U.S. interests could occur, but it is extremely unlikely that more than one would require substantial levels of U.S. combat power.

A continuity with the past runs through these words at a deeper level, based on the intellectual underpinnings of an understandable American reluctance to engage in war as well as the assumptions concerning the dynamic international forces that link American strategic interests with American military power. These assumptions ignore the fact that wealth and power, or economic and military strength, are always relative. Since all societies are subject to change, the international balance of forces is neither still nor permanent.[72] These predictions also reflect a return to the American optimism that sprang up after World War I, the wishful thinking of the Roosevelt administration before World War II, and the guidelines by which a succession of administrations have determined what and how much American landpower is enough since 1945. They also discount the value of landpower to a nation that cannot withdraw from world affairs. These predictions constitute a wish to have an effective foreign and security policy while escaping the realities of international politics.

Although the Soviet threat has vanished, new threats are emerging. In 1995 and 1996, China launched ballistic missiles from bases on the Chinese mainland into the sea 84 miles north of Taiwan.[73] China and India may both have military ambitions contrary to American interests over the longer term. Russia's passion for preserving its control of Central Asia is breathing new life into a Russian military establishment whose performance to date has been mixed. Provided Russian military power is not directed at Central Europe, the Middle East, Japan, or Korea, there is little reason for concern. But if NATO's planned expansion extends America's defensive periphery to eastern Poland, this situation could change abruptly.[74] As the Army's leaders frequently note, however, the "911 calls" continue to come in while the active Army's budget heads south. Events in Somalia, Haiti, Bosnia, Rwanda, Algeria, Russia, and Iraq have revealed how erroneous many rosy predictions about a new world order were. If the previous description of the future world order is inaccurate, what lies ahead that will require the use of American landpower? Consider the following points:

- Only seven countries in the world today have enjoyed a form of representative democracy for more than 100 years and five of them speak

English: Great Britain, the United States, Australia, Canada, New Zealand, Switzerland, and France. Democracy is still strongest in those insular regions of the world where security has been strongest.

• Stable democracies do not suddenly appear. They develop. Creation of the social and institutional infrastructure requires time.[75] Moreover, the pattern of development inevitably reflects the distribution of wealth and resources in the society. The wealthy and the educated have better organizational skills and, therefore, political groups tend to emerge first among a small circle of elites. Thus, democracy begins with the rule of a narrow, enlightened elite and a limited participatory franchise. Over time, if the franchise widens and if constitutional rules limit political power, as in the United States after the American Revolution, democracy takes root and flourishes.[76] What evidence is there that the democratic gains of the last decade will be preserved in the years ahead? Reactionary forces in Russia, Eastern Europe, the Islamic world, Latin America, and China provide plenty of evidence of antidemocratic trends in current affairs. History teaches that civilization is fragile and that no improvement in human affairs is irreversible. Like invasion by the Roman Legions, the arrival of American landpower is synonymous with order, stability, and democratic civilization. The consequences for U.S. security interests of a broader antidemocratic roll-back in regions where American landpower is absent should not be underestimated.

• American interests can only be inferred from visible ties America has to other states. Regional crises with the greatest chance for misperceptions of U.S. resolve will be ones in which U.S. interests are ambiguous. In this connection, sea-based systems and virtually present aircraft do not constitute visible ties. As America's experience in every major conflict and more recently in Kuwait, Haiti, and Bosnia demonstrates, "boots on the ground" is the only visible tie that deters aggression, defends U.S. and allied interests, and promises to defeat America's adversaries. It is no accident that, as of this writing, 40 percent of the U.S. Army's Patriot batteries are deployed overseas and that two of the Army's heavy task forces are defending Kuwait while an additional two heavy brigades are operating in Bosnia.

• America's security interests are not limited to the continental United States. Vulnerable to Soviet missile attack for many years, North America is now vulnerable to attack from many states.[77] In some cases, the defense of North America will entail strikes by highly mobile ground forces to points deep inside enemy territory to destroy enemy weapons of mass destruction. In others, the requirement to invade and occupy strategic territory in the effort to neutralize these emerging capabilities will be indispensable to the United States. Stand-off weapon systems and nuclear retaliation are unlikely to deter antidemocratic regimes whose survival cannot be threatened by these systems.[78]

- The United States must continue to buttress the stability of key states around the world, working to prevent calamity rather than reacting to it.[79] The presence of Army combat troops on allied territory is an unambiguous definition of U.S. interests and a fact that no opponent can ignore. Ground forces ashore on permanent or temporary station are far less expensive and more easily deployed and protected than an armada of ships which are both remote from the scene of the action and acutely vulnerable to a host of new relatively inexpensive weapon systems.[80]

- U.S. regional deterrence strategy will continue to rely on conventional military threats to deny a future adversary's war aims promptly. American landpower is an impressive threat to any regime whose hold on power will not be undermined by "high-tech" military threats to the economic infrastructure. Army overseas presence is a key element in a preventive defense strategy that seeks to prevent potential dangers to U.S. security from becoming full-blown threats.[81] Though this will not apply in every case, the threat of defeat on the ground clearly applies to North Korea, Iran, Iraq, and many other states.

- Finally, the United States must consider the possibility that a new, high-technology military superpower could emerge. Today, this possibility seems remote. If, however, the American strategic alliance with traditional allies is allowed to lapse and the international environment becomes more and more unstable, other states may feel compelled to develop substantial military power to protect their interests.[82] Unless contained within an alliance framework, this could revive a strategic rivalry with their neighbors with grave consequences for regional and world peace.

Avoidance of war has been the foundation of American defense policy since the end of World War I. The desire to avoid war will continue to animate American thinking about security well into the 21st century. Americans also understand that security is the real basis for economic growth; not the other way around. Money flows into secure areas and out of flashpoint areas. Economic growth is the wellspring of democratic institutions.

American landpower has the capacity to enable states and peoples to develop political and economic structures that secure domestic prosperity and international peace. Japan's war with its neighbors and America did not end in 1945. It ended with the implementation of a new constitution and Japan's incorporation in a broader alliance of democratic states. Germany's war with Europe and the United States ended with its entry into NATO and the European Economic Community. These transformations were not simply the by-product of American military victory in World War II. America contributed to victory in World War I and no such change occurred. This is because the transformation of Japan and Germany into modern democratic states was achieved behind a defensive line drawn on the ground by American landpower.

But the evidence suggests that there are challenges requiring the commitment of American landpower which the United States may face sooner than it thinks. Some of these challenges will involve containing the spread of weapons of mass destruction through a readiness to strike preemptively with special operations forces the production facilities that provide these weapons. Other challenges will involve intervention in regions where instability in one state threatens an entire region with disintegration. Recent events in Bosnia, Rwanda, and Southwest Asia provide a glimpse of what may lie ahead in China, India, Pakistan, and North Korea. America's ground forces will have to be prepared to perform the tasks Caesar assigned to his Legions—win wars, restore order, and preserve a stable and prosperous peace wherever direct American influence is required.

Landpower alone cannot possibly solve all of the nation's future security problems in a world seething with disaffection and change. But without the application of landpower to areas of strategic importance to American and allied security international political order will deteriorate. Today's international security order is an order with the United States at its center, but an order built without ground forces is an order whose foundation rests on sand. Ships, planes, bombs, and missiles cannot do the job alone.[83] American strategic dominance will erode quickly without an Army organized, trained, and ready to operate in a new strategic environment where traditional service distinctions are increasingly meaningless.[84] Thus, the question is not whether American landpower is essential to American strategic dominance. The question is how landpower should be organized to operate *jointly with airpower and seapower* to preserve America's strategic dominance in the next century.

NOTES

1. Eugene Rostow, *A Breakfast for Bonaparte: U.S. National Security Interests from the Heights of Abraham to the Nuclear Age* (Washington, D.C.: National Defense University Press, 1993), 161–62.

2. Jeffrey Record, *Revising U.S. Military Strategy: Tailoring Means to Ends* (Washington, D.C.: Pergamon-Brassey's, 1984), 52–55.

3. Jeff McCausland, "Dual Track or Double Paralysis? The Politics of INF," *Armed Forces and Society*, 12, no. 3 (Spring 1986): 431–52.

4. Y. V. Lebedev, I. S. Lyutov, and V. A. Nazarenko, "The War in the Persian Gulf: Lessons and Conclusions," *Military Thought*, no. 11–12 (November–December 1991): 109–17. After the war, United Nations inspectors concluded that coalition air strikes had only inconvenienced Iraqi plans to build a nuclear bomb.

5. Rick Atkinson, *Crusade: The Untold Story of the Persian Gulf War* (Boston: Houghton Mifflin, 1993), 496.

6. Eugene V. Rostow, *Breakfast for Bonaparte*, 325.

7. John Shy, *A People Numerous and Armed: Reflections on the Military Struggle for American Independence* (New York: Oxford University Press, 1976), 233.

8. Robert Osgood, *Ideals and Self-Interest in American Foreign Relations: The Great Transformation of the Twentieth Century* (Chicago: University of Chicago Press, 1953), 17.

9. Selig Adler, *The Isolationist Impulse: Its Twentieth Century Reaction* (New York: Free Press, 1957), 29. Selig makes the point that Germany's challenge to British supremacy and Japan's victory over the Russians marked the turning point. He contrasts President Theodore Roosevelt's policies vis-à-vis Europe and Japan before the outbreak of World War I with Wilson's subsequent policies.

10. John Lewis Gaddis, "Risks, Costs and Strategies of Containment," in *Centerstage: American Diplomacy Since World War II*, ed. Carl Brown (New York: Holmes & Meier, 1990), 43–44.

11. David McCullough, *The Path Between the Seas: The Creation of the Panama Canal 1870–1914* (New York: Simon & Schuster, 1977), 251.

12. Nicholas John Spykman, *The Geography of the Peace* (New York: Harcourt, Brace & World, 1944), 57.

13. Robert W. Tucker and David C. Hendrickson, *The Imperial Temptation: The New World Order and America's Purpose* (New York: Council on Foreign Relations Press, 1992), 169.

14. Christopher C. Harmon, "On Strategic Thinking: Patterns in Modern History," in *Statecraft and Power: Essays in Honor of Harold W. Wood*, ed. Christopher Harmon and David Tucker (New York: University Press of America, 1994), 77.

15. Christopher Harmon, "On Strategic Thinking," 79.

16. Eric Nordlinger, *Isolationism Reconfigured: American Foreign Policy for a New Century* (Princeton, N.J.: Princeton University Press, 1995), 47.

17. Winston Churchill used this argument to reassure the Germans before World War I that the Royal Navy "could not endanger a single continental hamlet." See Sir Winston Churchill's *The World Crisis, 1911–1918*, vol. 1 (London: Odhams Press, 1938), 76.

18. Melvyn P. Leffler, "Was 1947 a Turning Point?" in *Centerstage: American Diplomacy Since World War II*, ed. (New York: Holmes & Meier, 1990), 27.

19. The National Industrial Recovery Act for 1934 provided for the construction of thirty-two ships including two aircraft carriers, but added none of the tanks,

artillery, and aircraft, which MacArthur had recommended. See *US Naval Admini-stration in World War II*, vol. 1, pt. 1: *Background During Peace* (Washington, D.C.: Bureau of Ships, 1947).

20. William Manchester, *American Caesar: Douglas MacArthur, 1880–1964* (New York: Bantam Doubleday Dell Publishing Group, 1983), 167.

21. John Brinkerhoff, "The American Strategy of Unpreparedness," in *Strategic Review* (Winter 1994): 36.

22. Martin Blumenson, *The Patton Papers 1885–1940* (Boston: Houghton Mifflin, 1972), 715.

23. Forrest C. Pogue, *George C. Marshall: Education of a General* (New York: The Viking Press, 1963), 323.

24. Eric Nordlinger, *Isolationism Reconfigured*, 58. Nordlinger holds that Roosevelt's logic was right and that the United States could have avoided direct participation in the European theater of World War II. Forrest C. Pogue mentions Marshall's difficulties with the issue several times: *George C. Marshall*, 323, 337, 455. Also, Irwin F. Gellman alludes to this in *Secret Affairs: Franklin Roosevelt, Cordell Hull and Sumner Welles* (Baltimore: Johns Hopkins University Press, 1995), 221–28.

25. Irwin F. Gellman, *Secret Affairs*, 90.

26. James F. Dunnigan and Albert A. Nofi, *Shooting Blanks: War Making That Doesn't Work* (New York: William Morrow, 1991), 34.

27. Patrick Glynn, *Closing Pandora's Box: Arms Races, Arms Control, and the History of The Cold War* (New York: A New Republic Book, 1989), 75.

28. Britain's defeat in 1940 was not enough to persuade General Eisenhower 4 years later that airpower was not a substitute for effective ground combat forces. Confident in 1944 that saturation bombing by massed American and British bombers in front of Caen would open the way for advancing British and Canadian troops to seize Paris, Eisenhower was surprised and shocked when German ground forces recovered and threw back the British attacks with heavy losses. According to many accounts, General Eisenhower was furious with both Field Marshal Montgomery and the American and British air forces. Eisenhower shouted: "With 7,000 tons of bombs dropped in the most elaborate bombing of enemy frontline positions ever accomplished, only seven miles were gained—can we afford a thousand tons of bombs per mile?" Norman Gelb, *Ike and Monty: Generals at War* (New York: William Morrow, 1994), 333.

29. John Keegan, *Six Armies in Normandy* (New York: Penguin Books, 1994), 33.

30. Ibid., 34.

31. John Brinkerhoff, "The American Strategy of Unpreparedness," *Strategic Review* (Winter 1994): 36.

32. Christopher Flannery, "Geography and Politics," in *Statecraft and Power, 10*.

33. Gen. Matthew Ridgway, *Soldier: The Memoirs of Matthew B. Ridgway* (Westport, Conn.: Greenwood Press, 1974), 286.

34. Harry G. Summers, Jr., "Mid-Intensity Conflict: The Korean War Paradigm," in *The United States Army: Challenges and Missions for the 1990s*, ed. Robert L. Pfaltzgraff, Jr., and Richard H. Shultz, Jr. (Lexington, Mass: Lexington Books, 1991), 44.

35. T. R. Fehrenbach, *This Kind of War: The Classic Korean War History* (London: Brassey's, 1988), 454–55. This is one of the reasons U.S. Marines were employed ashore in the same way Army combat troops were. There simply were not enough U.S. and allied ground combat troops.

36. Quoted from General Bradley's book *A Soldier's Life* by Colonel William J. Davies, ARNG, in "Task Force Smith, Leadership Failure?" *USAWC Military Studies Program Paper*, Carlisle Barracks, Penn. (15 April 1992).

37. Armored forces profited from the example of North Korean tanks in 1950 and the Army increased its armored strength from one combat command to four armored divisions between 1948 and 1956.

38. Earl Tilford, *Crosswinds: The Air Force's Set-up in Vietnam* (Maxwell Air Force Base, Ala.: Air University Press, 1993), 184.

39. Eric Nordlinger, *Isolationism Reconfigured: American Foreign Policy for a New Century* (Princeton, N.J.: Princeton University Press, 1995), 81.

40. Jan S. Breemer, "The End of Naval Strategy: Revolutionary Change and the Future of American Naval Power," *Strategic Review* (Spring 1994), 42.

41. Michael Sherry, *The Rise of American Airpower: The Creation of Armageddon* (New Haven, Conn.: Yale University Press, 1987), 164, 309.

42. Ibid., 309.

43. Robert S. McNamara, *In Retrospect* (New York: Random House, 1995), 172.

44. General Bruce Palmer's comments are taken from *Second Indochina War Symposium: Papers and Commentary*, ed. John Schlacht (Washington, D.C.: Center for Military History, U.S. Army, 1984), 154–55.

45. Earl H. Tilford, Jr., *SETUP: What the Air Force Did in Vietnam and Why* (Maxwell Air Force Base, Ala.: Air University Press, 1991), xviii.

46. Paul Seabury and Angelo Codevilla, *War: Ends and Means* (New York: Basic Books, 1991), 139.

47. Jeffrey P. Kimball, "The Stab-in-the-Back Legend and the Vietnam War," *Armed Forces and Society*, 14, no. 3 (Spring 1988): 433–58. Kimball makes a good case for why airpower was ineffective regardless what the strategic goals were.

48. John Schlacht, ed., *Second Indochina War Symposium*, 156.

49. Robert S. McNamara, *In Retrospect*, 322.

50. Seabury and Codevilla, *War: Ends and Means*, 140.

51. Ronald H. Spector, "The Vietnam War and the Army's Self-Image," *Second Indochina War Symposium*, 169–82.

52. Albert Hourani, *A History of the Arab Peoples* (New York: Time Warner Books, 1992), 280–81.

53. Eric Nordlinger, *Isolationism Reconfigured*, 77.

54. Norman Friedman, *Desert Victory: The War for Kuwait* (Annapolis, Md.: Naval Insitute Press, 1991), 32–33.

55. Paul Seabury and Codevilla, *War: Ends and Means*, p. xxvii.

56. Patrick Garrity, "Preparing for the Gathering Storm," in *Statecraft and Power*, 260–61.

57. L. R. Jones, "Management of Budgetary Decline in the Department of Defense in Response to the End of the Cold War," *Armed Forces and Society*, 19, no. 4 (Summer 1993): 480.

58. Jeffrey Record, "Air Force's Future Bright After Stellar Gulf Showing," *Air Force Times*, 11 March 1991, p. 25.

59. John J. Fialka, *Hotel Warriors: Covering the Gulf War* (Washington, D.C.: The Woodrow Wilson Center Press, 1991), 7–8.

60. John Pimlott and Stephen Badsey, *The Gulf War Assessed* (London: Arms and Armour, 1992), 272. Also see the U.S. General Accounting office report entitled *Operation Desert Storm: Evaluation of the Air War* (Washington, D.C.: Government Printing Office, July 1996), 4–5.

61. Stephen T. Hosmer, *Effects of the Coalition Air Campaign Against Iraqi Ground Forces in the Gulf War*, MR-305-AF (Santa Monica, Calif.: RAND Corporation, 1994), 58. According to Stephen T. Hosmer, a RAND Corporation analyst, the three Republican Guard Divisions in the Kuwait Theater of Operations as of 1 March 1991 left behind in their prewar deployment areas 166 tanks, 203 armored personnel carriers (APCs), and 99 artillery pieces. As percentages of prewar deployment totals, these amounted to losses of 21 percent tanks ($n = 786$), 28 percent APCs (736), and 32 percent artillery (308).

62. Barton Gellman, "Study on Gulf War Points Out Limits of Air Power," *The Washington Post*, 13 May 1993, p. A6.

63. John Pimlott and Stephen Badsey, *The Gulf War Assessed*, 122–23.

64. *The Gulf War Assessed*, 123. Forty-three Coalition aircraft were lost at altitudes below 15,000 feet.

65. Chris Hedges, "Bosnia and Iraq: The West Repeats Itself," *New York Times*, 3 March 1996, p. E5.

66. "The Navy-Marine Corps Battleground," *Navy Times*, 23 January 1995, p 7.

67. Inchon appears more and more to have been the last operation entailing forced entry from the sea. Subsequent attempts to repeat Inchon during the Korean conflict had to be called off because the North Koreans mined the approaches from the sea. See David Wood in "Navy Tries to Handle Mines," *The Plain Dealer*, 23 September 1995, p. B-11.

68. E. H. Simmons, "Getting Marines to the Gulf," *U.S. Naval Institute Proceedings* (May 1991): 51–54.

69. Vice Admiral William Owens, USN, "The Quest for Consensus," *Proceedings* (May 1994): p. 68. Also see Michael Langley's *Inchon Landing: MacArthur's Last Triumph* (New York: Times Books, 1979), 148–49. Also, General Almond explains the unique and fleeting nature of the Inchon landing in his report

to the United Nations given during a conference on United Nations military operations in Korea, 29 June 1950–31 December 1951, 5, 10–11.

70. This information was provided to the author through Army channels during Vigilant Warrior by Cpt. Steven Pinette, U.S. Army, who was serving with the UN Forces in Kuwait.

71. See Michael E. O'Hanlon, *The Art of War in the Age of Peace: U.S. Military Posture for the Post–Cold War World* (Westport, Conn.: Praeger Publishers, 1992), 5. The author selected O'Hanlon not because he disagrees with everything O'Hanlon suggests, but because O'Hanlon's suggestions are not unlike many of those recommendations made by defense planners after World War I.

72. Donald Kagan, *On the Origins of War and the Preservation of Peace* (New York: Anchor Books-Doubleday, 1995), 568.

73. James Hackett, "Missile Menace Lurking in China," *The Washington Times*, 14 January 1996, p. B4.

74. Alan Philips, "Dr. Strangelove Puts Peace in Doubt: Russia Sees NATO as Potential Enemy," *Daily Telegraph*, 13 February 1996, p. 18.

75. William E. Odom and S. John Tsagronis, *Peru: Prospects for Political Stability* (Washington, D.C.: Hudson Institute, February 1992), 56.

76. Mancur Olson, *The Rise and Decline of Nations* (New Haven, Conn.: Yale University Press, 1983), 17–35.

77. Bill Gertz, "N. Korean Missile Could Reach US, Intelligence Warns," *Washington Times*, 29 September 1995, p. 3.

78. Dean Wilkening and Kenneth Watman, *Nuclear Deterrence in a Regional Conflict* (Santa Monica, Calif.: Rand Corporation, 1995), 15, 37.

79. Robert S. Chase, Emily B. Hill, and Paul Kennedy, "Pivotal States and U.S. Strategy," *Foreign Affairs* (January–February 1996): 49.

80. See *Navy Carrier Battle Groups: The Structure and the Affordability of the Future Force*, U.S. General Accounting Office Report to Congress, February 1993, pp. 5, 33, and 94.

81. Secretary of Defense William J. Perry, testimony before the Senate Armed Services Committee, 5 March 1996, p. 2. Secretary "outlines preventive defense" in what appears to be a departure from the previous enlargement and engagement policy.

82. Patrick Garrity, "Preparing for the Gathering Storm," in *Statecraft and Power*, 261.

83. T. R. Fehrenbach, *This Kind of War*, 454–55.

84. Merril A. McPeak, *Selected Works 1990–1994* (Maxwell Air Force Base, Ala.: Air University Press, 1995), 310.

3

Meeting the Demands of Revolutionary Change in Warfare

On reflection, the history of military affairs can be seen as a continuous quest for victory, and evolution is simply the term given to that process by which the structures of military organizations change over time in pursuit of battlefield success. How modern armies meet the demands of war helps to explain why the factors of science, technology, social change, organizational culture, and economic strength all interact to shape warfighting organizations and repeated revolutions in military affairs (RMA). In this sense it is important to distinguish between evolutionary and revolutionary change. In evolutionary change, progress is made by improving the last generation of military equipment and organizations, but continuity still exists between the old and new generations. In periods of revolutionary change, almost no continuity exists between generations—we are looking at something entirely new.[1]

This chapter argues that RMAs are not necessarily driven by huge and obvious advances in technology. The longbow, which certainly revolutionized warfare, was a relatively small technological advance over the "short bow"—a simple question of materials technology and manufacturing technique. Likewise, the change necessary to allow bullets to fit snugly into gun barrels, thus making possible first rifles, then fully automatic weapons, was a metallurgical change which is minor when compared with the enormous changes in microcircuitry which have occurred over the last 15 years.

Rather, RMAs come about not because technology has improved, but because armed forces devise new ways to incorporate new technology by changing their organization, their tactics, and, sometimes, their whole concept of war.[2] In view of these observations, this chapter attempts to isolate and analyze the more obvious regularities and patterns associated with changes in how armies periodically reorganize and reequip to produce revolutionary change. While the conception of organizational change presented in this chapter is not predictive, it may assist efforts to identify the evolutionary trends within which future warfighting organizations for land combat should be developed.

The need for understanding the nature of organizational change in military affairs is particularly acute today. Most arguments for or against change in the contemporary U.S. Armed Forces reflect a large measure of vested interest. Military leaders with strong allegiance and nostalgia for the arms to which they have devoted their lives do not relish the idea of change.[3] To the degree that any military establishment allows doctrinal organization and training methods to ossify or tries to centralize control over ideas for change, it risks obsolescence, whatever its current technical prowess might be.

Because the development of modern military organizations has often been characterized by problems and processes of strategy and structure analogous to those experienced by corporate business, this chapter begins with a brief discussion of how America's private sector is coping with the information age. A distinguishing feature of the modern world has been that superior economic competitiveness and superior military power have tended to accompany one another.[4]

OBSERVATIONS FROM THE PRIVATE SECTOR

General Krulak, Marine Corps Commandant, had sound reasons for sending his senior officers to the New York Stock Exchange in December 1995. Wall Street traders are among the world's fastest decision makers. What better way to determine whether there are methods already in use that would enable military leaders to change the way they organize forces and think about combat in order to act more quickly and effectively?[5] Business leaders are concerned about the uncertainties of change in the marketplace, where billions of dollars are at stake in the same way that the professional military is concerned about the impact of change in many areas on warfare. The difference between the professional peacetime military establishment and the private sector corporation lies in the unforgiving nature of the marketplace. Whereas military defeats in war are frequently necessary to induce change in the way the professional military organizes, trains, and equips to fight,[6] the marketplace teaches every day that a failure to anticipate change and to adapt accordingly always results in a financial debacle!

Military leaders are not alone in their desire to see the universe as stable, orderly, and predictable. America's industrial age corporate leaders were comfortable with their methods of operation, production, marketing, and managerial techniques until they discovered in the 1980s that they were ill suited to the new marketplace. Why? Mass production assembly lines inhibit necessary change and if change occurs at all, it is carefully controlled through fixed processes and structures. This approach was no longer practical in the environment of the 1980s, where the factor of knowledge had begun to displace capital and labor as the primary building block of information age power. In the last decade, when the rapidly changing relationships between cause and effect in the new information age business environment began to defy corporate management's best efforts at control, it became clear to business leaders that incremental improvements would not work.

Rather than trying to perfect flawed, inefficient systems, the most successful corporations opted for fundamental change. This is because tinkering around the edges through incrementalism could not produce the needed improvements in performance when the demand for success in an extremely competitive global market required profound change. Traditional adaptive organizational paradigms impose an overly mechanistic and orderly vision of change on organizations that are already full of complexity, change, and disorder.[7]

Recognizing there was a gap between business theory and the realities of a fundamentally new, information age marketplace, corporations set out in the early 1980s to restructure, reorganize, and reequip for a new kind of private sector warfare. As in war, there were winners and losers. What follows are observations about the winners:

- Highly successful companies did not simply proclaim a set of core values or ideology; they immersed their managerial elite as well as their employees in a performance ideology to a degree that was obsessive.

- At the same time, successful companies which were unwavering in their core ideology and values were still willing, even eager, to overthrow everything else: strategies, structures, procedures, measurements, and incentives. They understood the difference between "what we stand for" and "how we do things."

- Successful companies maintained ideological control but promoted operational autonomy. In the last decade, their story in business can be characterized as the triumph of distributed brains over centralized brawn.[8]

- What looks in retrospect like brilliant foresight and planning is more often the result of "Let's just try a lot of stuff and keep what works."[9] Ironically, these companies are frequently referred to as "visionary."

Bill Gates's Microsoft is among the best known, so-called visionary corporations. Microsoft's first operating principle is simple: radical autonomy. From the beginning, members of the Windows NT group organized themselves into small units with their own rules, styles, and ways of working. With the ideological goals and values of Microsoft for orientation, these groups struck out in whatever direction seemed promising.

The organizational process, however, is referred to as "flattening the organization." Organizations flatten their structures by eliminating the need for intermediate management by exception. In the private sector, a structure such as the insurance pricing bulletin board reduces the need for supervision of agents by raising the level of authority of the individual agent. Electronic posting of the limits of the authority affords centralized transmission of standards and immediate processing of requests by subordinates for exceptions to policy only.[10] In terms that General Patton would have understood, this means organizing the arms of combat at increasingly lower levels in the form of combat commands or regimental combat teams and relying on a subordinate battalion commander's understanding of the division commander's operational intent.

The second principle was minimal top-down coordination.[11] Recent studies of Microsoft offer a strong argument for reducing the number of administrative layers in organizations and for placing decisions closer to the action. In this connection, Microsoft concentrated on building an organization that shared information effectively rather than on hitting a market "just right" with a visionary product. Companies that concentrated primarily on hitting the market with a visionary product idea and attempted to ride the growth curve of an attractive product life cycle failed. In this sense, visionary products are the private sector equivalents of high-technology silver bullets in military affairs.

Microsoft's success in the private sector further demonstrates that the ideal horizontal structure produces the least disorder in information flow.[12] This observation suggests that there is probably room to eliminate some of the current Army echelons of command and control with their origins in the age of Napoleon in a new information age warfighting paradigm.

Microsoft's transformation into a visionary corporation was also premised on dramatically improving the corporation's performance to achieve extraordinary results. This transformation required changing the organization's culture, work-force management methods, and information management. Under Gates's leadership, top management imposed a new vision of high performance to be achieved through increased commitment to exploit new technology, along with performance measurement systems, to assess attainment of the organization's goals. In the Army, where performance evaluation of units and commanders is thoroughly subjective, this may mean developing objective criteria in peacetime training to determine who is and who is not competent to command in combat before the shooting starts! Attempts to develop these in the past have been resisted on the grounds that such criteria are too hard to identify.[13]

However, this attitude may be changing. Major General Fred Gorden, former director of military personnel management, identified versatility as a key attribute of leadership that should figure prominently in the selection and advancement of officers. He noted, "Versatility translates into creativity in leadership, not only in our commissioned and noncommissioned officers, but also in our new soldiers."[14] The important point is that the military may be on the verge of understanding what the private sector already knows. Accounting for individual differences in knowledge, skill, and proficiency encompasses a range of performance indicators.[15] It is a mistake to assume that there is one best model (the Officer Evaluation Report, OER) for thinking about performance in the context of officer selection for advancement.

Of course, whenever emphasis is placed on performance data and more efficient utilization of manpower, management creates a new organizational culture focused on its performance, productivity, and goals. This produces success and success, in turn, breeds more success. Accomplishments become linked to new methods and new attitudes.[16] This makes further change possible. Along the way, however, other corporations invested billions in new technology and still failed to achieve results in the marketplace.

Frustrated with rising labor costs in the sixties and seventies, especially of skilled labor, in the early eighties auto industry executives searched for information age technology that would provide them with full visibility on production and reduce the need for skilled labor. Their best engineers built detailed models of decision processes, input, and objective functions and designed an impressive production control system. Still, the system was too rigid and too dependent on centralized authority and control to keep pace with changing market conditions. One analyst observed that "the American auto industry had perfected the methods of fighting the last war and, this time, the Japanese beat the pants off them!" Why?

Auto industry executives failed to recognize the dynamic nature of their production processes. They became fixated on winning wage battles with organized labor and limited the goal of their system to cost reduction. In doing so they consolidated control and limited the ability of subordinates to adapt and modify the process. By imposing these restrictions on a process requiring continuous adaptation they firmly entrenched the organization and set the conditions for failure. The failure precipitated wholesale changes in leadership and organizational structure. It took the new team ten years to reengineer the organization around a productivity enhancement system.[17]

In the end, efforts to minimize the cost–benefit ratio through the carefully coordinated action of thousands of little cogs, all to be interconnected and fine-tuned to the performance of their special tasks in the hands of a supreme management team, did not work. Like many large institutions, the auto industry was well adapted to periods of incremental change, but could not manage transforming change. For the industry, the information age business environment proved to be an unstable one, filled with fluctuation, uncertainty, and unwelcome change. The industry's leaders attempted to impose order through the use of technologically sophisticated, information age decision-making aids on the fluid information age market and failed.

In retrospect, it seems clear that only organizational strategies which link the work activities of organizations at every level by treating chaos and instability as sources of creative renewal will succeed in producing organizations that can effectively exploit information age technology. Innovation, that is, the application of knowledge to produce new knowledge, is not, however, a product of simple inspiration, best done by loners in their garages. It requires systematic effort, decentralization and diversity, that is, the opposite of central planning and centralization.[18]

Unfortunately, without the violence of war to impart the inspiration for change through the need for survival, very few military establishments turn out to be capable of maintaining a degree of order in peacetime which makes change possible.[19] Yet, when professional military establishments think about future conflict and embrace change in peacetime, the results in war are frequently "revolutionary" in character.

CONCEPTS OF CHANGE IN WARFARE: DOMINATING MANEUVER

Knowing whether or not there is a new revolution in military affairs requires some basis for judging the extent to which contemporary warfare is actually changing into a new form which diverges dramatically from previous experience.[20] Thomas Kuhn's research in the physical sciences is one useful analytical tool for understanding change in many areas. Kuhn describes a paradigm or model as the common set of beliefs shared by scientists in any field.[21] When a dominant set of beliefs is challenged by a newer, more useful set, a "paradigm shift" or revolutionary change occurs. Alvin Toffler and Heidi Toffler employ the concept of "paradigm shift" by depicting revolutionary change in contemporary society's social, political, and economic structures in the form of waves; the "third wave" is the most recent and profound source of change in human affairs. However, Tofflerian waves are based on economic production modes set at the supercivilization level. As a result, they tend to be too abstract to account for many details in past changes in the patterns of Western warfare and the close interrelationship of these changes with the evolution of modern society. For these reasons, the Tofflers provide a future third wave vision that, from a military perspective, is not always supported by the historical record.[22]

Because a detailed account of the evolution of modern warfare is beyond the scope of this work, this chapter will attempt instead to explain revolutionary change in modern warfare by focusing on the conduct of dominating maneuver. The reader will recall that in *maneuver warfare*, the objective is to gain a positional advantage in time and space that places the enemy at such a disadvantage that he is compelled to surrender or be destroyed. This is in sharp contrast to *attrition warfare* in which the objective is to inflict more casualties and physical damage on the enemy than the enemy can afford to sustain.

In the execution of dominating maneuver, however, an attacking force conducts decisive operations incorporating some or all of the features of an RMA. Armed forces execute dominating maneuver when they successfully exploit technology, organization, training, and leadership to attain qualitatively superior fighting power as well as dramatic positional advantages in time and space which the enemy's countermeasures cannot defeat. Such operations result in a paralyzing blow against an opposing force with near- simultaneous effects on every level of war—strategic, operational, and tactical.

An important precondition for the conduct of dominating maneuver is battlespace dominance by the attacking force. Battlespace dominance implies a superior knowledge of and influence over events within a defined space or area of operations for a specific period. For a conceptual understanding, it is necessary to examine the evidence provided by three examples of revolutionary change in modern military history in which dominating maneuver was featured: Napoleon's Ulm campaign in 1805, the German attack on France in 1940, and Operation Desert Storm in 1991.[23]

Ulm 1805

Of Napoleon's campaigns, none is more important to an understanding of dominating maneuver than the Ulm campaign of September–October 1805. Alerted by French intelligence agents in Germany to Austrian and Russian military mobilization, Napoleon moved his 200,000 troops 300 miles from their encampment in Boulogne in a wide envelopment along multiple axes across Western Europe to converge on the Austrian rear in Ulm. Thanks to careful French diplomacy, strict security measures, and the elimination of the French Army's dependence on fixed supply points, the operation was completed in only 7 weeks!

Separate corps-size elements (25,000–30,000 troops) were given independent missions with mutually supporting objectives. Occupied with a 30,000–man French cavalry screen in the Black Forest region, the Austrians unwisely discounted the possibility that the main body of the French Army would advance on a broad concentric front over difficult terrain. Moreover, the Austrians thought, French forces would have to concentrate before attempting any significant attack, and this French military buildup would provide the Austrians with adequate time to concentrate their own forces for a counterstrike. Surprised and isolated by the crushing rapidity of the French advance and by the presence of the French Army far behind their front, the Austrian forces at Ulm were compelled to surrender. Yet the Ulm campaign was not only an overwhelming victory for the French, it also decisively set the terms for Napoleon's subsequent battle with the combined Austrian and Russian armies at Austerlitz in December—a titanic action which ended with the virtual destruction of those armies.[24]

How did these dramatic victories occur?

Napoleon brought about a revolution in military affairs by assimilating the weapons technology of the age into a consistent pattern of military theory, organization, and leadership. This congruence of French weapons, tactics, organization, and thinking about war reflected Napoleon's understanding of how to use existing technology to the limit and at the same time make its very limitations work to French advantage.[25]

First, prior to Ulm armies were generally small—30,000–70,000 troops—and the battlefield rather than the theater of war was the commander's arena. Social and industrial revolution in France radically changed this condition and created both mass armies and the means to mass-produce standardized weapons and supplies. To an extent not thought possible in an age without radio communications, this facilitated decentralized control of forces moving simultaneously on multiple axes of advance. Standarized artillery, improved artillery munitions, glass jars for preserving food, and rifled muskets were all part of the industrial age RMA. Napoleon's appreciation of these new battlefield dynamics enabled the French to wage a war of greater spatial scope and duration.

Second, Napoleon organized his forces into today's familiar system of battalions, brigades, divisions, and corps. In fact, put aside the weapons and vehicles modern technology has provided and there is really little difference between Napoleonic organizations and those of today. But, in their time, these organizational innovations had a revolutionary impact![26] What the campaign of 1805 revealed to a startled world was a 200,000 man Grande Armée organized into six army corps of roughly 25,000–30,000 troops, each containing units of "all arms" and each provided with a uniformly structured staff to direct its operations.[27] Napoleon's corps were, in fact, miniarmies that could sustain independent operations for long periods. Although Napoleon added manpower to enlarge his maneuver force, he also more than quadrupled the number of operational maneuver units at his disposal. This increased the French potential for brilliant and unusual maneuvers.

Third, the Ulm and Austerlitz campaigns of 1805 were the first test of the new Napoleonic cavalry system and the first of its triumphs.[28] To win, Napoleon needed a well-developed communications system to convey to him timely, accurate information. All the advantages of the corps system were of no value if the information to guide the movement of the separate corps to the enemy's weak points was unavailable. He also needed the means to deny information to his enemy. If the enemy could find his forces, French positional advantages would be at risk. In Napoleon's day, reliable information arrived on horseback. For this reason, except for the numbers of light cavalry necessary for the security of each corps, all mounted units were concentrated in the Grande Armée's Cavalry Reserve.[29]

In 1805 during the opening advance across Germany, the light cavalry of each corps formed an advancing screen, shifting rapidly forward by every possible route with detachments of light infantry in close support, preventing enemy observation, seizing towns and enemy supply depots for follow-on forces and dispatching information hourly to Imperial headquarters. Once the Grande Armée began decisive operations to close with the enemy's main body, the Cavalry Reserve's light cavalry and dragoons moved forward to thicken and expand the screen. In this way, critical information could be passed and acted upon in the space of a few hours across extended distances. With each succeeding campaign, Napoleon added more and more light cavalry to the Grande Armée. Until the irreplaceable losses of his most experienced cavalry during the Russian campaign, no field commander in Europe knew more about the area of operations and the enemy's place in it than Napoleon.[30]

Fourth, no examination of Napoleon's contribution to the RMA of his day can be even partially complete without a reference to his leadership and that of his subordinates. It has been said that no leader was ever better served by his subordinates. Though Napoleon never committed his thoughts to writing, the record suggests that, thanks to his force of personality and vivid imagination, he could convey an understanding to his subordinate commanders of what the operation's overarching goals were. The Prussians later termed this understanding of the higher commander's purpose "operational intent." When his junior commanders exercised initiative and made bold decisions based on minimal, time-sensitive information as they did on the approach march to Vienna in 1805 and at Auerstaedt in 1806, the French won decisively. When they waited passively for his orders, as they did at Leipzig in 1813 and Waterloo in 1815, the French were defeated.

On reflection, Napoleon's willingness during the Ulm campaign to delegate command, to accelerate the tempo of operations, to risk dispersion on the approach march, and to concentrate large, independent bodies of troops at critical points on the battlefield produced a relatively inexpensive victory in terms of French human and materiel resources as well as a new conception of time and space. Of course, for full effect, Napoleon had to ensure that the points in time and space which were selected for attack had a strategic impact. Napoleon's superior knowledge of the area of operations, his acute sense of timing, and the depth of his operational focus guaranteed that the effect of the whole French campaign was greater than the sum of its individual parts—single engagements, actions, and battles. In this environment of French battlespace dominance, the Austrians imploded and their will to resist collapsed under the weight of Napoleon's theaterwide offensive. Strategically focused, sequential operations and engagements culminated in a dominating maneuver to destroy the enemy's armed might.

France 1940

Napoleon's demonstration of dominating maneuver became the organizing imperative of the great offensive campaigns of the late 19th and 20th centuries. Analyses of subsequent Prussian–German campaign strategy in 1866, 1870, 1914, and 1940, for example, revealed that the intent of the

Prussian and German opening operations was to repeat Napoleon's achievement in the campaign of 1805. They sought to bring on a battle of annihilation through dominating maneuver by inflicting a strategic defeat on the enemy which his tactical measures could not remedy. Later Soviet–Russian concepts of theaterwide offensive operations extended the Napoleonic emphasis on speed and decisiveness to argue that multiple successive operations and strikes against the enemy's center of gravity would be necessary to achieve dominating maneuver on an even larger scale.[31]

It was, however, not until the innovative application of automotive, aviation, and communications technology to military use in the context of the 1940 German Blitzkrieg that the operational dimensions of time and space along with the organization, training, leadership, and equipment of the armed forces were again subject to radical change. The details of the German plan to execute an armored sweep through the Ardennes to the French coast and split the Allied armies in two are too well known to recount here. But it is worth noting that the failure of the German 1918 offensives to achieve similar aims fostered a compulsion for self-examination that led to a keen appreciation in the German officer corps for the potential impact of new technology on organization, leadership, and training.[32]

When war came, the interwar deliberations on the potential impact of changing battlefield dynamics enabled the Germans to exploit radio communications, aircraft, and armored vehicle technology in order to change plans minute by minute in the face of enemy opposition in order to confound, confuse, and eventually defeat numerically superior enemy forces. For the first time real-time communications allowed operational-level commanders to coordinate directly with their tactical leaders on the battlefield.

This accelerated response time between tactical and operational leaders, as accentuated by quicker movement of maneuver and support elements, lent new and critical significance to the place in the enemy's front where the least resistance was encountered. Once armed reconnaissance revealed a weak spot in the enemy's horizontally organized front, German armored columns could shift to that point quickly, attacking on a narrow front to cut lines of communication, overrun enemy command and control nodes, and immobilize the enemy defense system. Predictably, this new war of movement that spontaneously set up objectives, bypassed resistance, and reinforced success depended heavily on a flexible structure for (1) the collection, transmission, and analysis of time-sensitive information and (2) the capacity for quick, independent thought and decisive action among subordinate battlefield commanders in order to exploit information.

Clearly, these points reveal differences in the methods of command, in the ways new technology is exploited, and in the preparation of forces for combat, all of which endowed the 1940 Blitzkrieg with an advantage in the *observation–decision–action cycle*. Whereas British, American, and French armies[33] of the period calculated the speed of any combined arms unit as that of the slowest element, German generals like Guderian, Kleist, and Rommel measured it by that of the fastest—the tank—and insisted that their divisions move as rapidly as possible. In contrast to the Germans, the British, French, and American commanders were accustomed to a training environment characterized by set-piece battles in which speed of movement, improvised attacks, and tactical innovation were not encouraged. Seldom were British and French generals asked to think quickly.[34] This would not change in the U.S. Army until General Marshal had retired or relieved 500 General Officers and Colonels from the Regular Army in order to elevate a new generation of officers with a different view of warfare.[35]

Worst of all, whereas the Germans had organized their armored forces into 14,000 man "Panzer Divisions" of all arms, the British and French division structures were still organized on the model of the large 20,000–25,000 man infantry divisions of the First World War. As a result, they lacked sufficient transport, self-propelled artillery, tanks, and ground and air reconnaissance assets. For example, in contrast to Germany's World War I divisions, whose reconnaissance capability was limited to one squadron of cavalry, Germany's World War II divisions began the 1940 campaign with a 500 man reconnaissance battalion, two cavalry squadrons, a bicycle company, a detachment of four armored cars, and a mobile signals detachment.[36] Before the Polish campaign, the German Air Force assigned 288 aircraft to direct army control for reconnaissance, a proportion of one squadron for each division.[37] In the third year of World War II, the size and quantity of elements in the German "Panzer" division devoted to reconnaissance more than doubled! These observations reveal a great deal about the way in which the German Army had been organized and trained before the war to use tactical intelligence and to avoid centers of enemy resistance, rather than deliberately attack them.

In the air war, differences in the perception of how airpower could be employed also influenced events. Although the British and French military establishments understood that aviation allowed for the deep attack of many targets beyond the visual range of attacking ground forces, they also believed that opposing air forces would spend most of their effort attacking each other. Thus, while the Allies envisioned aerial bombing to incapacitate the enemy's strategic resources by destroying critical warfighting and industrial facilities, the British and French did not anticipate the use of airpower in close coordination with ground attack. Predictably, the timely arrival of German airpower over the battlefield to impart momentum to a stalled German attack came as a complete surprise to the British and the French. The thought that air power might supplant artillery as the principal means of fire support for attacking ground forces in order to sustain the momentum of the armored thrusts had not occurred to those in command of the Allied Forces.

Thus, in 1940, a radically new German concept of warfare—Blitzkrieg—that compressed timelines for operations and expanded battlespace was put into action. Unlike Napoleon's aim of physically destroying the enemy through a battle of annihilation, Blitzkrieg had the goal of paralyzing the enemy through the revolutionary use of armored, motorized, and air forces. It combined human potential with innovative technology to stretch the battlefield farther and to create a warfighting environment which was critically unbalanced in favor of the attacking German armies. Thanks to the "near-right" mix of technology, organization, prewar training, and leadership, the Germans achieved battlespace dominance in the first hours of the conflict and maintained it throughout the campaign. In fact, the conduct of dominating maneuver on the scale of the 1940 Blitzkrieg was more than ever before a function of Germany's capacity to dominate the battlespace.

These points notwithstanding, the German offensive failed to deprive Britain of the means with which to carry on the war. Nearly 365,000 Allied troops (nearly a third French and Belgian) escaped to England from Dunkirk and other channel ports while the German Army consolidated its position for a final, set-piece assault on the coastal cities. The reason for this failure is simple. It arose out of the unanimous lack of appreciation among Germany's national leadership for the potential of Germany's new combined arms force.[38]

Had Guderian and his commanders been released from the strict control imposed on them from above; had they been allowed to pursue the advance as they saw fit, and not been shackled to the mass of the Army group; had the liberating idea of "organized velocity" predominated over the paralyzing fear of exposed flanks, then the fate of the Anglo–French troops in northern France might well have been sealed, and an operational triumph through dominating maneuver transformed into a strategic victory on the scale of Austerlitz. In the end, Guderian achieved *victory* without superior military technology. In fact, the Germans owed their success to their practice of compensating for insufficient numbers of advanced aircraft, self-propelled artillery, and tanks through means of superior organization, training, and leadership. Guderian wrote on the eve of World War II: "The tight concentration of our limited forces in large units, and the organization of those units as a panzer corps would, we hoped, make up for German numerical inferiority."[39]

In the long run, however, superior German fighting power could not compensate for the chronic lack of adequate modern military equipment in Germany's armed forces. The deadly combination of Hitler's insistence on a positional war of attrition in the east along with Russia's vast open spaces and inexhaustible supply of manpower combined to eliminate the German capability for dominating maneuver by January 1944. The German experience does demonstrate, however, that without the right organization for combat within a coherent doctrinal framework, technology alone does not bring about an RMA.[40]

Desert Storm 1991

Much like Napoleon's Ulm campaign and the German Blitzkrieg of France, the campaign to liberate Kuwait was not a true military contest. Contrary to what many predicted before the war began, it was a strategic victory so complete and so overwhelming that the issue was never seriously in doubt.[41] Coalition casualties were negligible and not one American tank was destroyed by enemy fire. Desert Storm bears a superficial resemblance to the 1940 Blitzkrieg. The enemy whose terrritory was to be attacked provided an area of operations offering the space to execute brilliant and unexpected maneuvers. The victorious ground troops were commanded by leaders whose thinking relative to their opponents was unconstrained. Most important, the leaders commanded troops who were better trained and better equipped than their opponents. These points are worth considering in the context of all future American military operations.

What changed in 1991 was the sudden availability of precise deep strike delivery systems on land and aboard ships and aircraft, combined with a vast inventory of lethal conventional munitions and long-range aircraft which could be guided by target acquisition instruments to enemy targets under near-constant surveillance. Equally important for the outcome were the decisive American overmatch in the direct-fire battle and the integration of tactical and strategic systems to support the tactical fight. There is also no doubt that the Iraqi Air Force was no match for the coalition Air Forces deployed against it. Soviet Major General Nikolai Kutsenko stated at the time of the coalition's war with Iraq, "Iraq's armament, including that which is Soviet made, was primarily developed in the 1960s–1970s and lags at least one-to-two generations behind the armament of the multinational forces."[42] Thus, the poor quality of most Iraqi forces in the air and on the ground is at least as important to an analysis of the Gulf War as any assessment of American military superiority.

To a much greater extent than ever before, the coalition theater commander was technologically positioned to influence action on the battlefield by directing global military resources to the points in time and space he regarded as critical to the campaign's success. For the Iraqi enemy, whose air defenses (ranging from highly sophisticated to antiquated) failed and whose intelligence-collection capability was either destroyed or deceived, the deep, close, and rear battles were compressed into one seamless continuous fight. From the vantage point of the Iraqi command structure, the categories of American capabilities and weapon systems directed against Iraqi forces in terms of their strategic, operational, or tactical points of origin were indistinguishable. In effect, Iraq was attacked by U.S. forces from various points around the world and subjected to a new form of multidimensional envelopment.

Of decisive importance was not a single factor, but rather a combination of factors. On the one hand, the doctrine the Iraqi Armed Forces assimilated as a result of the decade-long conflict with Iran militated against Iraq's use of decentralized, mobile warfare. Although these attrition tactics—which incorporated many advanced forms of military technology, including Exocet missiles, Scud missiles, and remotely piloted vehicles—eventually wore down the Iranians, they were ineffective against the American-led coalition, which differed dramatically from the Iranian forces. Being steeped in this ponderous doctrine prevented the Iraqis from adopting a different form of warfare consistent with Iraq's new political–military objectives, strategic situation in 1990–1991, and opponents. Clearly, similar technology in different hands can be used in different ways and with different degrees of success. From all indications, the Iraqis anticipated that their defensive posture would result over time in a stalemate. In terms of the rapid retirement of U.S. Marine forces from Lebanon in 1982 after the bombing of a Marine installation in Beirut, this may have been a reasonable expectation. However, Kuwait lies at the heart of vital U.S. and allied strategic interests, Lebanon does not. Iraq seems to have missed this salient point.

If the problem of projecting military power is viewed in a historical context, it is not hard to understand the Iraqi perception of time. In the months preceding the Allied landings in Normandy during June 1944, 2,500 heavy bombers dropped thousands of tons of explosives while 7,000 fighters and fighter-bombers pulverized German forces in northern France. Nearly two years were required to assemble the naval transport and ground forces to support the invasion. What once took months, even years, was accomplished during Desert Shield and Desert Storm in weeks or even days by fewer but more specialized forces. By quickly establishing qualitative and quantitative superiority in the pre–ground attack period, strike forces were enabled to secure the initiative, accelerate the pace of events, increase the intensity of the total coalition attack, and reduce the time needed to prepare the Iraqi enemy for ground assault. Before the ground campaign began, large numbers of demoralized Iraqi troops began deserting or surrendering.

In this connection, American concepts of time and space were clearly different from Iraqi concepts. American air–land battle doctrine predisposed the American armed forces to deploy specialized combat formations to exploit Iraqi weaknesses throughout the depths of the Iraqi defense system. New intelligence and target-acquisition sources substantially reduced the climate of uncertainty which had plagued the senior leadership of earlier operations. Knowing precisely where to direct the main attack against the Iraqi defense was not a hit-or-miss proposition. Combined with real-time communications, these surveillance capabilities created the opportunity to direct redundant warfighting systems against Iraqi targets throughout the Southwest Asian theater of operations during all phases of Desert Storm.

Redundant strike systems such as the Army Tactical Missile System (ATCMS) and sea-launched cruise missiles (SLCMS) hastened the collapse of the Iraqi will to resist—a condition which had characterized the campaigns in 1805 and 1940. Since nominally strategic, operational, and tactical capabilities could now be integrated for employment at any level of war simultaneously, Iraqi forces throughout the theater were compelled to operate as though they were all within visual range of American forces. Global positioning systems (GPS) guided the smallest American combined arms units into action with clinical accuracy as to location, even in hours of total darkness. Thanks to GPS, the U.S. VII Corps was enabled to attack from a direction and at a time for which the Iraqi leadership was least prepared. In response, the Iraqi Armed Forces (like their ill-fated predecessors, the Austrians and the French) simply lost coherency and fled the field or succumbed to destruction.

However, not every undertaking was an unqualified success. The hunt for Iraq's mobile Scud missiles was a miserable failure. Between 17 January and 2 February 1991, Iraq launched fifty-seven missiles, twenty-nine against Saudi Arabia. As during the Iran–Iraq War, the missiles were employed as strategic weapons and were targeted primarily against cities:

Tel Aviv (nineteen), Haifa (nine), Riyadh (thirteen), Dahran (fourteen), and Hafr al Batin (one). Of these fifty-six, there is evidence that the Patriot missile system intercepted thirty-six. Although Iraq launched nine missiles on one day, on average, Iraq launched between three and four missiles a day. In most cases, the missiles were launched either during the hours of darkness or under heavy cloud conditions.[43]

Despite their ability to roam freely above 15,000 feet over a flat Iraqi landscape and to fly 1,500 sorties against Iraq's ballistic missile infrastructure and resources, the U.S. Air Force was unable to find more than a handful of mobile missile launchers. It attacked those it could find, but the evidence is clear that the Air Force often attacked decoys and that it never actually destroyed a single mobile missile launcher.[44] It also seems likely that U.S. forces began the ground campaign with an exaggerated sense of the destructiveness of their aerial weapons. An example of this was the praise heaped on the F-117A "stealth fighter" by the media and the Air Force. Reports of the F-117A's invisibility were overstated, particularly as all coalition aircraft were effectively stealthy once Iraqi air defenses had been blinded in the first few hours of the air war. In addition, it soon became clear that F-117As did not operate independently of radar-suppression assets, enjoying the benefit of some clever radar-jamming devices.[45]

Much of the bomb damage assessment made during the war amounted to little more than careful viewing of strike videos. When U.S. Ground Forces overran Iraqi Republican Guard positions on 26 February, for example, the U.S. troops discovered that the Republican Guard formations were well supplied, were at full strength, and had sustained relatively minor damage during the air campaign.[46] Over time, units in the Republican Guard Corps—Iraq's only capable military organization, though small in number—learned to cope with air attack, suggesting that an air campaign's greatest impact on defending forces is achieved in its first hours and days. These observations should not be considered evidence for what the air campaign did not accomplish, but, rather, yet another in a long line of demonstrations that what looks quite badly damaged or hurt may, in fact, be intact[47]—in effect, simply more evidence for the persistence of the *fog of war*.

Although senior military leaders stressed that the air and ground campaigns against Iraq were joint operations, naval forces clearly played a subordinate role. Part of the reason is that no other nation in the world has a navy that can challenge the U.S. Navy for control of the seas. Another reason was that carrier-based aviation, especially those naval fighters launched from the U.S.S. *Saratoga* and the U.S.S. *John F. Kennedy* in the

Red Sea, were heavily dependent on the U.S. Air Force in-flight refueling capability in order to reach Iraqi targets. Moreover, naval fighter aircraft carried fewer bombs and missiles than their USAF counterparts and were able to fly far fewer sorties against the enemy. During the conflict, a planned amphibious assault on Iraqi forces in Kuwait was cancelled after two Navy combatant ships struck mines and it was determined that the Iraqis had heavily mined the sea approaches to the Kuwaiti coast.[48]

Up to a certain point, Desert Storm is as much the operational masterpiece of the late 20th century as Ulm was of the early 18th. But splendid triumph though it was, like the battle of Chancellorsville in 1863, "it bore no abiding fruits"[49] in political or military terms and the reason seems clear. Voices that might have urged more rapid and decisive action at the time were silent. Human factors like these are difficult to evaluate, but it seems clear that the thinking of the national command authorities was dominated by intelligence estimates which were focused on measurable objective issues, not on subjective ones: on how many tanks Iraq had rather than on the quality and motivation of their crews.[50] Despite having achieved battlespace dominance, the attacking coalition forces were unable to capitalize on their information age advantage to the extent they should have.[51] Instead, approximately two divisions of the Iraqi Republican Guard Corps, 500–700 tanks, and a fleet of helicopters escaped destruction.[52]

Had the U.S. Army's attacking ground forces been released from the strict control imposed on them from above,[53] had they been directed to exploit the enemy's blindness, to advance as rapidly as they could without being reminded constantly of the near-paralyzing fear of casualties, the fate of the Republican Guard Corps and Iraq's reactionary regime might well have been sealed and a strategic victory through dominating maneuver transformed into an Austerlitz. Since this did not occur, Desert Storm offers at best a glimpse of what dominate maneuver in the future may resemble, but not much more.[54]

VISIONS OF FUTURE WAR

The foregoing historical discussion points to the possibility of dramatic change in the American concept and practice of warfare. New equipment and weapon systems, employed in great numbers at critical points in time and space, now offer the potential for continuous offensive operations. They permit the retention of intitiative and the exploitation of opportunities for the annihilation of the enemy's forces in a high-speed, integrated campaign. Lethal, precision-guided munitions are launched at still greater ranges, for the most part well beyond the visual range of the enemy. Smaller combined arms combat formations with advanced indirect- and direct-fire weapon systems dominate larger areas than in the past. Aided by enhanced surveillance capabilities in the form of unmanned aerial vehicles, airborne radars, and satellites, fewer armored and air-mobile ground forces can now concentrate the effects of combat power against the enemy. Rather than move to contact, "all arms" units electronically search and then destroy the enemy on the battlefield.

All of this suggests that in the future the tactical, operational, and strategic levels of war as separate and distinct loci of command and functional responsibilities will be spaced and timed out of existence. This form of warfare (which we shall call information age warfare) enlists the tactics of fire and movement directly in behalf of the strategic goal. This does not mean, however, that there is no longer a requirement for commanders to think about tactical goals, their coordination and combination into operational goals, and the translation of the attainment of operational goals into strategic results. This simply suggests that the merging of the levels of war takes place in the area of execution while the conceptual framework of operations remains in place. What follows is one short example of what land warfare may look like in the near future.

In the early phases of future war, precision-guided missiles will play a decisive role in the effort to gain and retain the initiative. Carefully timed mass strikes will paralyze large ground and air forces in the theater of war that are dependent on fixed installations for frequent refueling and resupply. The vulnerability of static ground forces to mass strikes creates the incentive for military leaders to conduct high-speed ground offensives to strike deep into the enemy's territory, where that enemy is less likely to employ weapons of mass destruction. Modern air defense systems will drive jet-driven aircraft to higher and higher altitudes with the result that stealthy, rotor-driven aircraft along with unmanned strike aircraft will gradually supplant traditional airframes in the close air support role. Unmanned aircraft will operate day and night over the field of operations collecting information and targeting enemy forces. In sum, the effects on U.S. forces will be to extend the depth of warfare further, forcing all elements of American JTFs to operate as if within visual range of the enemy, tending to compress rear, close, and deep combat operations into one continuous fight.

Recognizing that the development of American military tactics, doctrine, and warfighting organizations for future conflict has been rendered more difficult because the character of the threat is no longer specified, it is not surprising that the Army's Force XXI program has not resulted in any significant change in the warfighting structure of Army forces since Desert Storm.[55] Perhaps it is also because the most significant trends in the evolution of warfighting structures over time are so self-evident that the professional military rarely discuss them. Because these trends have survived the test of time, strategy, and technology, they merit attention before proceeding to a discussion of Army warfighting organizations for the future.[56]

- First, the technology of war creates a steady rise in the lethality of weapons and munitions, greater mobility, and the endless requirement for dispersion. These influences, in turn, compel armies to integrate more and more arms and services at progressively lower and lower levels of organization. As new technologies confer a greater warfighting potential on armies, this potential gradually finds its outlet within a fixed "all arms" framework. Only the need to adjust the proportion of arms to different tactical situations seems to limit the degree to which the various arms are grouped together permanently. Probably the most important corollary to this observation is the growing dependency of armies on their capability to conduct decentralized operations in an ever-expanding battlespace.

- Second, battlespace is continually expanding. Theaters of war are regions of temporary, concentrated armed effort within a global military framework. In this sense, American airpower and landpower are now global weapons.[57]

- Third, expanding battlespace increases the volume of information that is relevant to the commander's coherent view of the operational environment. When combined with the accelerated pace of operations resulting from technological change, the uncertainty and ambiguity of this environment add complexity to an already compressed decision–analysis cycle. Contrary to what many third wave thinkers suggest, supercomputers do not solve this problem because they generate information faster than they can analyze it! This is why the fog of war will persist into the future. And this is why greater autonomy at lower levels on the scale of Microsoft's radical autonomy is necessary to overcome the fog and friction of future war.

- Fourth, expanding battlespace dramatically increases the need for timely and accurate information because the dispersion of forces and the volume of information potentially degrade the coherency of battlefield perception. This condition results in a convulsive expansion in wartime of the formations and instruments of information collection and reconnaissance. In the language of Force XXI, this expansion is essential to dominant battlefield awareness and dominant battlefield knowledge. Awareness means knowing where the enemy is. Knowledge—the product of reconnaissance—

informs you about what the enemy is doing or is going to do. Both
conditions are essential features of future warfighting.

- Fifth, all arms and services on the ground develop a need for the same
mobility and nearly the same degree of protection as the warfighting
organizations they support. This is particularly true for logistics units that
accompany combat formations in order to sustain the fight. The Civil War,
World War I, World War II, and the Gulf War demonstrate that the side
capable of sustaining the rapid, safe delivery of the strongest and best-
equipped combat forces to the warfight is frequently more successful than
the side that pins its hopes for military success on a fleeting technological
advantage in weapons technology. Unsurprisingly, ways to streamline, to
economize, and to impart velocity to logistics become a means of increasing warfighting potential. Thanks to the absence of any significant threat
at sea, the new combination of prepositioned Army heavy equipment sets
ashore and fast sealift creates the capability to close more than 30,000
Army heavy combat troops in less than 30–40 days on the periphery of
the Eurasian landmass. This capability is unprecedented in American
history and dramatically improves the logistical picture for deploying
American forces.

- Sixth, after its introduction to warfare, the technology of aviation (manned
and unmanned) begins, on the one hand, to reinforce the effects of existing
trends, and, on the other, to assist military organizations to cope with the
aforementioned effects. When integrated with ground elements, aviation
provides ground forces with information, security, protection, "operational reach," and increased tactical efficiency. In 1945, the victorious
advance of the 14th British Army in Central Burma was made possible by
the combination of air and surface transportation. The combination of
air-landed infantry and armor achieved a tempo which the lightly
equipped, foot-mobile Japanese could not resist. General MacArthur
employed General George Kenney's Air Forces and General Eichelberger's Ground Forces in the Pacific in a similar fashion with equally
impressive results. To a large extent, the U.S. Army's reconnaissance and
attack helicopters have been developed to acquire permanently a close air
support capability that receives low priority in the U.S. Air Force.[58]

- Finally, as mentioned, the strategic environment matters. When international stability is at risk, strategic considerations dominate national policy
in democratic states. Because of the German threat in the 1930s to the
independence of Belgium, Luxembourg, and the Netherlands, the British
Army sought the capability to move four infantry divisions, one cavalry
division, two air defense brigades, and one tank brigade to the European
continent within 30 days.[59] Today's strategic environment with its emphasis on readiness for rapid deployment, joint operations, reduced man-

power, and leaner logistics creates important design parameters for Army forces. In addition, most hypothetical conflict scenarios for the future anticipate little, if any, time for mobilization and this, too, influences force design.

To the strategic environment may be added two of the US Army's most pressing needs: the need to emphasize qualitative improvements to compensate for reduced numbers of Army ground forces and the need for adaptable warfighting structures which can fulfill a wide range of mission requirements to include operations other than war (OOTW) more flexibly. The Army's ability to adapt its warfighting structure to these trends will, in large part, determine whether it will retain the capability to dominate maneuver within a joint strategic framework in the next century.

The implications of this analysis are many (Figure 3.1). Of these, the point that the technology of warfare rarely serves as the driving force behind doctrinal military innovation is by far the most important. Military history suggests that technological advantage is rather transitory in nature, readily copied, and countered. Truly large payoffs require changes in strategy, doctrine, and organization.[60] It should not be inferred from this statement that new technology has nothing to contribute to the operational capabilities of American ground forces. On the contrary, new information-age military technology in the offense or the defense offers means of attack that are accurate, lethal, and effective at short as well as long ranges, all at the same time.

In addition, there is the notion that to be strategically decisive, landpower and airpower must be employed together in pursuit of complementary goals. For instance, the ground and air campaigns against Germany were so interdependent that it is impossible to judge what either of them might have accomplished if either had gone unassisted by the other. If the Germans had been able to devote resources to aerial warfare without concern for the protection of France and Italy against atttack, they might have been able to mobilize enough fighter and antiaircraft strength to turn back the bomber offensive. Air and ground forces together achieved the goals of the American strategy to defeat Germany.[61] A similar case can be made for the conduct of the Gulf War. At the same time, while no serious American land campaign can be undertaken today without American control of the seas, America's future adversaries in areas of strategic importance are continental powers. As a result, they are not vulnerable to American seapower in the way that Japan was in World War II.[62]

Figure 3.1
"All Arms" Formation History

```
1750: THE ALL ARMS FORMATION IS THE FIELD ARMY
      (50,000 TROOPS)

   1805: THE ALL ARMS FORMATION IS THE NAPOLEONIC CORPS
         (30,000-50,000 TROOPS)

      1914: THE ALL ARMS FORMATION IS THE INFANTRY DIVISION
            (28,000 TROOPS)

         1940: THE ALL ARMS FORMATION IS THE PANZER DIVISION
               (14,000 TROOPS)

            1945: THE ALL ARMS FORMATION IS THE COMBAT
                  COMMAND (4000-5000 TROOPS)
```

THE HISTORICAL TREND IS TOWARD SMALLER, MORE MOBILE, INTEGRATED "ALL ARMS" COMBAT FORMATIONS

Finally, in order to realize the immense potential inherent in new information age technology, the U.S. Army must modify its existing organization for combat. Furthermore, today's technological menu is so rich in comparison to the buying power afforded by contemporary Army budgets that organizational change must of necessity outpace the procurement of promising new military technologies. It is against this background that an examination of the Army's options in its effort to assimilate the weapons technology of the current age into a consistent pattern of military theory, organization, and leadership must begin.

NOTES

1. Col. Richard Dunn III, "From Gettysburg to the Gulf and Beyond," *McNair Paper No. 13* (Washington D.C.: Institute for National Strategic Studies, 1991), 3.

2. Frederick Kagan in a letter to the author dated 12 December 1995. At this writing, Professor Kagan was assistant professor of military history in the Department of History at the United States Military Academy.

3. Harold Winton, *To Change an Army: General Sir John Burnett-Stuart and British Armored Doctrine, 1927–1938* (Lawrence, Kans.: University Press of Kansas, 1988). Also see, in Matthew Cooper, *The German Army, 1933–1945: Its Political and Military Failure* (Lanham, Md.: Scarborough House, 1978), the chapter "Strategic Revolution."

4. Robert Gilpin, *War and Change in World Politics* (London: Cambridge University Press, 1981), 139.

5. Gilbert Lewthwaite, "Top Marine Fights Old Mind-Sets," *Baltimore Sun,* 12 December 1995, p. 2.

6. Gordon W. Prange, *At Dawn We Slept: The Untold Story of Pearl Harbor* (New York: McGraw-Hill, 1981), 98–106. This author describes how the Japanese naval leadership moved the carrier from a supporting to a leading role in naval warfare and its impact on the United States Navy, which until Pearl Harbor had resisted this change.

7. Douglas Kiel, *Managing Chaos and Complexity in Government: A New Paradigm for Managing Change, Innovation and Organizational Renewal* (San Francisco: Jossey-Bass, 1994), 14.

8. William C. Taylor, "Control in an Age of Chaos," *Harvard Business Review* (November–December 1994): 65.

9. Ibid., 71.

10. Col. V. J. Warner, "Industry Lessons Learned in the Implementation of Decision Support Systems and Their Application to Army Training XXI." Unpublished essay prepared in the Army Chief of Staff's Office.

11. Taylor, "Control in an Age of Chaos," 74–75.

12. Kiel, *Managing Chaos and Complexity in Government,* 156.

13. Stefan T. Possony and Jerry E. Pournelle, *The Strategy of Technology: Winning the Decisive War* (Cambridge, Mass.: Dunellen, 1970), 80. Also see Eliot Cohen and John Gooch, *Military Misfortunes: The Anatomy of Failure in War* (New York: N.Y.: The Free Press, 1990), 215.

14. Michael G. Rumsey, Clinton B. Walker, and James H. Harris, eds., *Personnel Selection and Classification* (Hillsdale, N.J.: Lawrence Erlbaum Associates, 1994), foreword.

15. John P. Campbell, "Alternative Models of Job Performance and Their Implications for Selection and Classification," in *Personnel Selection and Classification,* 45.

16. Kiel, *Managing Chaos and Complexity in Government,* 42–43.

17. Warner, "Industry Lessons Learned in the Implementation of Decision Support Systems."

18. Peter F. Drucker, *Post-Capitalist Society* (New York: HarperCollins, 1993), 190.

19. Russel F. Weigley, *Eisenhower's Lieutenants: The Campaign of France and Germany, 1944–1945* (Bloomington: Indiana University Press, 1970), 730. Weigley asks why this cannot be made better after detailing the flawed decisions of Eisenhower, Bradley, and many other commanders during the war.

20. Daniel Gouré, "Is There a Military–Technical Revolution in America's Future?" *The Washington Quarterly* (Autumn 1993): 174–92.

21. Thomas S. Kuhn, *The Structure of Scientific Revolutions* (Chicago: University of Chicago Press, 1970), 10.

22. Robert J. Bunker, "The Tofflerian Paradox," *Military Review* (May–June 1995): 102.

23. Douglas A. Macgregor, "Future Battle: The Merging Levels of War," *Parameters* (Winter 1992–1993): 33–48.

24. Martin Van Crefeld, "Revolution in Strategy," in *Command in War* (Cambridge, Mass.: Harvard University Press, 1985).

25. Ibid., 59.

26. Col. John R. Elting, *Swords Around a Throne: Napoleon's Grande Armée* (New York: Macmillan Publishers, 1988), 57.

27. Van Creveld, Command in War, 60.

28. Ibid., 232.

29. Ibid., 233.

30. Ibid., 233–34.

31. John Depres, "The Timely Lessons of History: The Manchurian Model for Soviet Strategy," *RAND Report R-1825-NA* (Santa Monica, Calif.: RAND Corporation, 1976).

32. Gen. Heinz Guderian, *Guderian: Erinnerungen eines Soldaten*, 13th ed. (Stuttgart, Germany: Motorbuch Verlag, 1994), 38–39.

33. James S. Corum, *The Roots of Blitzkrieg: Hans von Seeckt and German Military Reform*, (Lawrence, Kans.: University Press of Kansas, 1992), 190. The interwar American Army was by far the worst in this sense.

34. Len Deighton, *Blitzkrieg: The Rise and Fall of Hitler to the Fall of Dunkirk* (New York: Ballantine Books, 1980), 155.

35. Martin Blumenson and James L. Stokesbury, *Masters of the Art of Command* (New York: Da Capo Paperback, 1975), 370–74.

36. Corum, *Roots of Blitzkrieg*, 45–46.

37. Deighton, *Blitzkrieg*, 162.

38. Matthew Cooper, *The German Army, 1933–1945: Its Political and Military Failure* (Lanham, Md.: Scarborough House, 1978), 237.

39. Guderian, *Guderian*, 79–80.

40. Corum, *Roots of Blitzkrieg*. This is really the message of Corum's entire work.

41. Jeffrey Record, *Hollow Victory: A Contrary View of the Gulf War* (New York: Brassey's, 1993), introduction and final chapter.

42. John Pimlott and Stephen Badsey, *The Gulf War Assessed* (London: Arms and Armour, 1992), 123.

43. Joseph S. Bermudez, Jr., "Iraqi Missile Operations During Desert Storm," *Janes Soviet Intelligence Review* (March 1991): 132–34.

44. Norman Friedman, *Desert Victory: The War for Kuwait* (Annapolis, Md.: Naval Institute Press, 1991), 253. It is difficult to avoid the conclusion that a better solution would have been to deploy the combination of recon–attack helicopters (like the Army's new RAH 66 Comanche) and air mobile infantry mounted in UH60 Blackhawks to hunt the mobile launchers in the Scud basing areas. This is what the SAS was able to accomplish in Northern Iraq.

45. Pimlott and Badsey, *Gulf War Assessed*, 122–23. Also see Tim Weiner, "Smart Weapons Were Overrated, Study Concludes," *New York Times*, 9 July 1996, pp. A1, A14.

46. This is from the author's personal observation and experience on 26 and 27 February 1991 in action against Republican Guard troops. Of thirty-nine tanks in one Iraqi combined arms task force, only three had been damaged during the air campaign. The remaining thirty-seven tanks along with nearly fifty other armored vehicles were destroyed by ten moving M1A1 tanks in 3 minutes during an attack on 26 February 1991.

47. Friedman, *Desert Victory*, 254.

48. David Wood, "Navy Tries to Handle Mines," *The Plain Dealer*, 23 September 1995, p. B-11.

49. Col. G.F.R. Henderson, *Stonewall Jackson and the American Civil War* (New York: Da Capo Press, 1988), 693.

50. Friedman, *Desert Victory*, 237.

51. Michael Evans, "Yes, It Really Was a Famous Victory: Michael Evans, in Kuwait, Argues That Tactical Brilliance, Not Just Force of Arms, Won the Gulf War," *The Times* (14 March 1991): 14. The Iraqis were not unaware of the VII U.S. Corps attack around their flank. British forces captured electronic intelligence equipment that showed the Iraqi command structure had traced the ground thrust across central Kuwait.

52. Peter Turnley, "Special Report: The Day We Stopped the War," *Newsweek*, 20 January 1992, p. 18. Some estimates of the numbers of escaping Iraqi troops are higher.

53. See Michael R. Gordon and Bernard E. Trainor, *The Generals' War* (Boston, Mass.: Little, Brown, 1993). The book is devoted to a discussion of these issues.

54. Joseph D. Douglass, Jr., "Critical Questions Loom in Assessing the Gulf War," *Armed Forces Journal International* (April 1991): 46–47.

55. TRADOC PAMPHLET 525-5, *Force XXI Operations: A Concept for the Evolution of Full-Dimensional Operations for the Strategic Army of the Early Twenty-First Century* (Fort Monroe, Va.: HQTRS TRADOC, August 1, 1994), 4–5. For reasons that are never given, this pamphlet reaffirms the need to organize around all of the existing command echelons.

56. Cpt. Jonathan M. House, *Toward Combined Arms Warfare: A Survey of 20th Century Tactics, Doctrine, and Organization* (Leavenworth, Kans.: Combat Studies Institute, 1984), 188. Also see Corum's *Roots of Blitzkrieg, 43–48*.

57. Paul F. Herman, Jr., "The Revolution in 'Military' Affairs," *Strategic Review* (Spring 1996): p. 28. Herman discusses what he calls a Desert Storm–plus capability and outlines the implications for the future structure of American airpower and landpower in this context. *Force XXI Operations*, p. 4–7. The manual says, "Improved intelligence and advanced information systems, along

with high-technology weapons, will greatly expand the battlespace of future maneuver formations."

58. Cpt. Jonathan M. House, *Toward Combined Arms Warfare, 189.*

59. Gaines Post, Jr., "Mad Dogs and Englishmen: British Rearmament, Deterrence, and Appeasement, 1934–35," *Armed Forces and Society*, 14, no. 3 (Spring 1988): 332.

60. Ariel Levite, *Offense and Defense in Israeli Military Doctrine*, JCSS Study No. 12 (Boulder, Colo.: Westview Press, 1990), 140.

61. Russell F. Weigley, *The American Way of War: A History of United States Military Strategy and Policy* (Bloomington: Indiana University Press, 1973), 358–59.

62. Michael Howard, *The Lessons of History* (New Haven, Conn.: Yale University Press, 1991), 91–93. These points are considered by Howard from a British vantage point in the context of deterring and fighting World War I.

4

Organizing within the RMA Trendlines

While military strategy concerns the use of military power to achieve strategic goals, how military power is actually organized to fight and win in combat is the concern of organizational or force design. The concrete results of these designs are expressed in different types of organizational structure, the ways in which military resources are allocated, and the lines of command authority and information flow.[1]

For example, General Leslie McNair's program to reorganize the U.S. Army's World War I combat divisions from a square configuration with four regiments to a triangular structure with three regiments was designed to meet the nation's strategic needs for a larger pool of mechanized Army divisions that could be moved overseas quickly. With these needs in mind, General McNair implemented organizational change to exploit new military technology in the effort to accommodate new strategic requirements. The results were enormous gains in the areas of *tactical mobility, firepower,* and *savings in manpower*.[2] Today's Army continues to reflect the distinguishing features of the industrial age forces that he helped develop during World War II. Proportionally, today's Army force structure is still composed of large industrial age combat forces capable of massing firepower (Figure 4.1).

During the last years of the 20th century, however, the U.S. Army has the opportunity to shape itself into a force prepared to face a fundamentally changed warfighting environment. The opportunity is unique because the

Figure 4.1
Current Army Force Structure

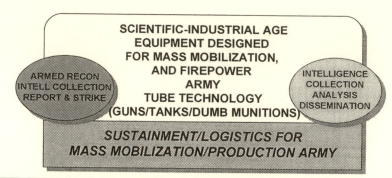

SCIENTIFIC-INDUSTRIAL AGE
EQUIPMENT DESIGNED
FOR MASS MOBILIZATION,
AND FIREPOWER
ARMY
TUBE TECHNOLOGY
(GUNS/TANKS/DUMB MUNITIONS)

ARMED RECON
INTELL COLLECTION
REPORT & STRIKE

INTELLIGENCE
COLLECTION
ANALYSIS
DISSEMINATION

SUSTAINMENT/LOGISTICS FOR
MASS MOBILIZATION/PRODUCTION ARMY

THE CURRENT ARMY'S TRAINING AND ORGANIZATION CONTINUES TO REFLECT THE DISTINGUISHING FEATURES OF THE INDUSTRIAL AGE FORCES THAT EMERGED FROM WORLD WAR II, KOREA, AND VIETNAM—MASS MOBILIZATION AND FIREPOWER. PROPORTIONALLY, THE ARMY WAS COMPOSED OF LARGE COMBAT FORCES CAPABLE OF MASSING FIREPOWER, A LARGE SUSTAINMENT BASE, AND LIMITED NUMBERS OF FORCES DEVOTED TO ARMED RECON, INTELLIGENCE COLLECTION, ANALYSIS, AND DISSEMINATION.

Army both has a temporary respite from major conflict and has taken the time to study the force design implications of information age warfare outlined in *Force XXI*. Embedded in the *Force XXI* vision are important implications for how the Army should organize to fight in the future. These implications point to future organizations for combat that can capitalize on information age technologies to confer greater warfighting capabilities on smaller combat formations. Among these implications is the recognition that success in future warfighting rests on the foundation of information dominance. Thus, *Force XXI* strongly emphasizes the importance of armed and manned reconnaissance along with surveillance assets in the context of future conflict. When these enhanced reconnaissance and surveillance systems are linked to deep strike weapons, their combat capability is multiplied.

In addition, *Force XXI* (Figure 4.2) envisions the capability to allow early entry ground forces to fight their way in from the air and to promote greater modularity in tactical logistics. Finally, *Force XXI* establishes the need for absolute unity of effort among all arms and services as the cornerstone of future success in warfighting.[3] This places emphasis on the creation of Army organizations that can support, integrate, and benefit from multi-service C4ISR.

But how should the U.S. Army's senior leaders organize the Army in peacetime to respond to these requirements in wartime? Or put a different way, can America's Army begin the process of organizing to fight within

Figure 4.2
Force XXI

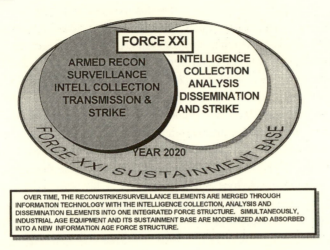

OVER TIME, THE RECON/STRIKE/SURVEILLANCE ELEMENTS ARE MERGED THROUGH INFORMATION TECHNOLOGY WITH THE INTELLIGENCE COLLECTION, ANALYSIS AND DISSEMINATION ELEMENTS INTO ONE INTEGRATED FORCE STRUCTURE. SIMULTANEOUSLY, INDUSTRIAL AGE EQUIPMENT AND ITS SUSTAINMENT BASE ARE MODERNIZED AND ABSORBED INTO A NEW INFORMATION AGE FORCE STRUCTURE.

the trendlines outlined earlier and still preserve its capacity to cope with contemporary threats? If the need arises, the Army must still be ready to deploy and fight with existing active forces and with some elements of the Reserve Component (RC).[4]

In the attempt to answer these questions, this chapter argues that the Army cannot transform itself into the Army envisioned in *Force XXI* between now and the end of the decade. However, it can move to an intermediate force design that will begin to bridge the gap which separates today's Army from that envisioned in *Force XXI*. With these points in mind, this chapter examines the centerpiece of the Army's contemporary warfighting paradigm—the division—and explores design options in the context of a new organization for combat. The chapter sets the stage for an example of how the Army could deploy and fight with a new organization for combat to conduct dominating maneuver within a joint operational framework.

OPTIONS FOR CHANGE WITHIN THE STATUS QUO

General John Shalikashvili, Chairman of the Joint Chiefs of Staff, has said that the "main purpose of the armed forces is to fight and win the nation's wars."[5] It is also clear that the armed forces will have new expanded and diverse missions in an unpredictable, rapidly changing world environment. Not every aspect of an organization for combat will fit well with the future environment. Still, it is the warfighting orientation which must shape organizational change, not operations other than war. In this connection, the question for the Army is whether the division structure is the appropriate combat formation to integrate, exploit, and effectively employ the multitude of emerging military capabilities in the future warfighting environment.

As mentioned earlier, Lieutenant General McNair was instrumental in the design of the division, which is still the basis for the Army's current structure for war on the tactical level. In contemporary Army thinking, the division is still the dominant U.S. Army organization that trains and fights as a team. Five types of divisions exist in the current force: armored, mechanized, infantry, airborne, and air assault.[6] The division is a self-sustaining force capable of independent operations for an extended period. It usually fights as part of a Corps containing three to five divisions and is commanded by a major general. As a result, the division combined arms team is still the centerpiece of the Army's warfighting structure and doctrine.

The Army's ten active component divisions are organized with varying numbers and types of combat, combat support, and combat service support units. However, the basic organizations are alike and generally include the following elements:

- Division headquarters with C2 for units assigned or attached to the division

- Three brigades of infantry, mechanized, and tank battalions to destroy the enemy and to seize and hold key terrain

- One brigade of artillery to provide fire support for maneuver brigade

- One aviation brigade to provide attack helicopter support and air transport capability

- One engineer brigade for combat engineer support

- One brigade-size division support command (DISCOM) to provide combat services support to all units assigned to the division

- Division troops: one cavalry squadron for reconnaissance and security; one signal battalion for communications; one military intelligence battalion for intelligence collection, analysis, dissemination, and deception; and one air defense battalion to protect the division from air attack

In retrospect, General McNair's understanding of the linkages between strategy, technology, and force design seems impressive. When McNair began developing the division structure, he wanted the Army division to have only the minimum essential forces that it needed to conduct offensive operations in fluid maneuver warfare against relatively limited resistance. On the basis of British and French experience during World War I, Army planners in 1917 were primarily concerned with the ability of the division organization to conduct sustained combat from prepared positions—trenches. Logistics and fire support were placed in depth behind the lines of entrenched infantry. In response to these conditions the division grew in strength to 28,000 troops. From the beginning, then, the limiting factors on a division's size were time, space, and the requirements of contemporary warfare.

Consequently, to maximize the proportion of forces available for combat and to reduce paperwork and related obstacles to rapid decision making, McNair insisted on small division staffs and restricted the number of wheeled vehicles in the division support units. The fewer vehicles that were organic to a division, McNair reasoned, the less shipping space would be necessary when the division was moved overseas. This meant that when the war began the standard division base consisted of the three infantry regiments, four artillery battalions, one ground reconnaissance troop, and an engineer battalion.

General McNair also eliminated specialized units from the infantry division structure that were required only for specific situations or missions. Eventually, he consigned antiaircraft artillery, nondivisional tank battalions, mechanized cavalry, and combat engineer battalions to the command of group headquarters under Corps command when not attached to divisions. Some group headquarters, notably those of mechanized cavalry, also acted as tactical control headquarters.[7]

When the U.S. Army employed these concepts overseas, the results in action were mixed.[8] Corps and field commanders who followed Army doctrine by shifting these nondivisional units from infantry division to infantry division according to the situation found that they could employ the fighting power of such elements only at the cost of much inefficiency. Increasingly, commanders found it expedient to leave the nondivisional units attached to the infantry divisions on a habitual basis. Thus, the triangular infantry division became much larger and more motorized than McNair had originally envisioned. These observations, however, mask the true manner in which the divisions were internally organized to fight.

Many of the nondivisional elements were permanently organized with the division's infantry regiments to form regimental combat teams (RCTs). The RCTs had their own artillery, engineers, tank destroyers, self-propelled antiaircraft guns, and medical and logistical support. In practice, the RCT evolved into a small division in itself. As the Second World War in Europe progressed, the division headquarters provided support to the RCTs, which actually fought the tactical battles.[9]

In the same period, the U.S. Army's armored division underwent even more profound changes than the infantry division. When Major General

Jacob Devers became Chief of the Armored Force in August 1941, he sought to establish a more flexible and functional organization. His reorganization reversed the ratio of medium to light tanks, leaving the armored division with two armored regiments consisting of two medium and one light tank battalion. While this new structure retained six armor battalions, it reduced the number of armored infantry battalions to three. This reflected the Army's long-term goal of establishing armored corps comprising two armored and one motorized infantry division.

By early 1943, however, British experience against the Germans and American intelligence evaluations of German performance against the British and Russian armies reinforced McNair's earlier insistence on a less cumbersome division structure. For that matter, the one U.S. Army armored division employed in the closing months of the North African campaign never operated as a coherent division.[10] In fact, the division's dispersal into three or four subgroups simply demonstrated the difficulties of controlling such a large formation. As a result, the Army established a new armored division structure for combat in September 1943 (Figure 4.3). This structure eliminated the armor brigade headquarters from the division and created two combat commands, A and B. These headquarters might control any mixture of subordinate battalions given to them for a particular mission. A third combat command R, to control the formations not assigned to either combat command A or combat command B, was also added.

The new armored division also included three battalions each of tanks, armored infantry, and armored artillery. Again, in practice, the armored division's forces were further subdivided and organized to fight as combat commands under Brigadier Generals. The actual task organizations of these commands varied, but a typical combat command included elements from all the arms of combat and service.

Though doubtless inspired by the German concept of the combined arms battlegroup, the combat command was a distinctly American solution to the problem of incorporating and exploiting new technology.[11] It also became an object of envy and admiration among the opposing German troops who were compelled to fight against it. The historian Chris Gabel explains why, in the following description of what it was like for a German defender to confront a combat command from Major General Wood's 4th Armored Division:

A German defender unfortunate enough to find himself in the path of the 4th Armored Division in August 1944 first had to deal with the fighter-bombers of the XIX Tactical Air Command (TAC), which maintained constant patrols in advance of Wood's armored columns. Army Air Force liaison officers riding in the lead tanks provided targets to the fighter bombers and kept the ground troops informed as to what lay ahead of the column. . . . Behind the fighter bombers came the division's light liaison aircraft, from which the combat commanders guided their columns around obstacles because experience had shown that the medium tanks could generally cut through any resistance encountered. Self-propelled artillery placed well forward in the column and ready to fire engaged any defenders too strongly emplaced for the medium tanks to dislodge. Engineers also accompanied the lead elements to remove obstacles. . . . Wood also took medical and maintenance detachments out of the division trains and added them to the combat trains so these services were immediately available to the leading elements.[12]

If this organization for combat was so effective in combining and employing all the arms of combat, then why was it abandoned after the war? There are many reasons. One may have been the unresolved conflict between the protagonists of the "Patton school" of armored warfare, founded on the use of armored, mechanized, and air forces engaged in deep penetration attacks, and adherents of the traditional strategy, based on mass infantry armies with lots of artillery. Another reason was certainly the postwar conviction that large-scale conventional warfare was a thing of the past. What had just happened in the European theater seemed unimportant to a future in which the Japanese experience in Hiroshima nullified the art of war. In the face of what appeared to be a permanent alteration in national

Figure 4.3
1944 Combat Command Organization

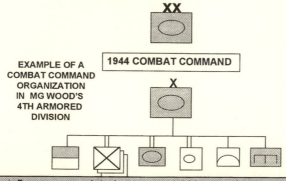

* As the war in Europe progressed, the Army's armored divisions organized into combat commands for close combat. The combat command was similar to the "all arms" German battlegroup. It contained elements from many subordinate regiments and battalions and was frequently commanded by a Brigadier General.
* The Combat Command became the model for the brigades in the postwar heavy division.

military policy after the Korean War ended, the Army's senior leaders were preoccupied with how best to secure a role for the Army in a national military strategy dominated by nuclear weapons.[13]

In the strategic environment of uncertainty after the Korean War, the Army's affirmation of the prevailing triangular division-centered force design actually resulted from the absence of any consensus among senior Army leaders concerning the requirements for future warfare.[14] For the Army's postwar senior leaders, the incorporation of nuclear firepower and its effects into Army organization and doctrine through the pentomic division was really secondary to the more pressing need for an austere and economical force design with the division organization as its foundation. Army tactics and organizations were to be subjected to slight modification with a view to coping with the weapons of mass destruction, but analysis really did not extend to the first-order questions of the limitations imposed on Army organizations for combat by two-sided nuclear warfare.[15]

The Reorganization Objective Army Division (ROAD) program of the mid-1960s actually restored most of McNair's triangular structure to the division, with the exception that the brigade level of command was now designed to replace the World War II combat command headquarters with multibattalion organizations that could be tailored to the tactical situation. The ROAD organization called for a division base consisting of a headquarters element; three brigade headquarters; a military police company; aviation reconnaissance, engineer, and signal battalions; division artillery brigade; a support brigade; and a mix of infantry and tank battalions. Like combat commands in the World War II armored divisions, the brigade headquarters had no permanently assigned units but operationally controlled from two to five maneuver elements and support units as the tactical situation required. Using this concept, the Army reorganized various types of divisions to meet opponents on real and potential battlefields.[16] During the Vietnam period when division commanders and their units were given responsibility for large chunks of territory, the ROAD division structure seemed eminently suitable to the environment.

At the moment, the Army's senior leaders are considering options for a new division structure ranging from retaining today's basic structure while inserting new technologies to adopting a flexible, brigade-based division structure that could be tailored for specific missions.[17] Imparting flexibility to the structure is important. In many respects, the current division structure limits the value of new warfighting arrangments. Air and ground formations seldom train together, if at all. Brigades are still organized around branches—pure units—armor, infantry, artillery, and so forth. Along with the practice of temporarily cross-attaching ground forces to create ad hoc combined arms formations on multiple levels, all the echelons of command and control are preserved. Moreover, the division's size—11,000 to 18,000—seems at variance with warfare's evolutionary trends.

On a political level, it is difficult to anticipate what will happen next in Congress, but further cuts in the Army's size would mean the disestablishment of at least one or two divisions. For a global power like the United States which is constantly in search of strategic alternatives, the elimination of a large warfighting formation like a division could significantly constrain contingency planning and response options.[18] Simply making the current U.S. division organization smaller (as the French have with their rapid deployment forces) may not remedy this situation. In fact, increasing the ratio of command, control, and support to fighting forces without creating any more combat power or flexibility at the level where it is most needed—on the battlefield—violates the last ten years' experience in the private sector. The contemporary ten division force consists of roughly 810 combat platoons, which, at an approximate strength of between 20 and 40 men, translates in war to 30,000 combat soldiers in direct fire contact with the enemy. What the Army needs is a warfighting organization with a form that parallels the shift of warfighting functions and activities to progressively lower levels.

One way to modify the division organization without dramatically changing the existing warfighting structure is to disestablish divisions as standing organizations and to convert the current brigade task force into what amounts to a regimental combat team. This is similar to the brigade-based division option discussed previously. Brigade task forces would continue to wear division patches and would maintain their traditional links to parent divisions. But division headquarters would assume a role analogous to that of the combat commands of the Second World War's armored divisions. In this setting, division commanders would assume command and control of whatever type and number of independent brigade task forces were needed for the specific mission. This approach is appealing for several reasons.

First, because of basing constraints, seven of the Army's ten active divisions have brigades which are based separately from their parent division organizations. Structuring these brigades to operate more or less independently will be necessary to ensure their deployability in most cases. Second, it would not be difficult for the Army permanently to assign brigades those elements—artillery, engineer, air defense, signal, military intelligence, and combat service support—which are routinely cross-attached to brigades for deployment to combat or training. Brigade commanders often complain that these elements are too infrequently task organized with their units in training to ensure their smooth cooperation in war. Thus, converting ten divisions to thirty standing brigade task forces would add cohesion and continuity to the Army at a level where it is most critical to success in combat. It also creates more deployable maneuver forces that will influence the national command authorities as they decide what course of action to take in a crisis. Third, the various branches and services of the Army are less likely to obstruct a change which does not fundamentally alter current professional and career development paths.

This arrangement could also result in more than ten division headquarters once these are no longer tied to a large fixed base. As an example, Active Component divisional headquarters could be established that are specifically designed to command, control, and train the fifteen Army National Guard Enhanced Brigades or to conduct deep operations such as Mobile Strike Forces with Corps Aviation Brigades, Armored Cavalry Regiments, and Rocket Artillery (MLRS) Brigades. In addition, one or more divisional headquarters could be oriented on contingency operations that entail peacekeeping or humanitarian relief duties.[19] This would also preserve the corps headquarters as the Army's largest deployable echelon that normally commands and controls Army ground forces as part of a JTF.

Actual reorganization of the Army along the lines discussed is one way to cope with the near-term need for change within the trendlines. In the long run, however, the disadvantages of this approach may outweigh its obvious near-term advantages. This option fails to flatten the Army's warfighting organization genuinely by eliminating redundant echelons of command and control that simply slow the observation–decision–action cycle. Why preserve the existing industrial age command and control structure: company/battery/troop–battalion/squadron–brigade/regiment–division–corp–army? Although positioning the brigade task force at the center of Army warfighting doctrine shifts elements from one echelon to another lower echelon, it still involves infusing largely unchanged warfighting organizations with new technology; an approach that has failed before! This option still fails to move and shape combat formations in the directions that *Force XXI* suggests will be decisive in future war: surveillance/intelligence–collection–armed reconnaissance–analysis–dissemination and strike!

In the environment of future conflict, air- and space-based sensors will be linked to digitized information systems to identify key elements of the enemy's armed strength thoughout the depth of his deployment. Armed with this real-time information, future JTF commanders will be able to conduct precision guided missile and rocket artillery strikes from air, land, and sea to prepare the enemy for rapid exploitation by highly mobile air–ground forces through a combination of enveloping maneuver and paralyzing offensive action. Why can't advances in microcircuitry and weapons technology assist in eliminating one or more of the aforementioned echelons as well as in reshaping combat formations? Why can't new technology extend human potential in new, more economical and efficient ways that are within reach today? The answer, of course, is that it can.

MOVING TO AN INTERMEDIATE FORCE DESIGN

In contrast to industrial age warfare, information age operations are conducted in an environment where the possibilities for deception are endless, the weapons of mass destruction are ever-present, and the requirement to dominate the battlespace is paramount. In addition, the capability to dominate maneuver in the future described by *Force XXI* is critically dependent on the ability of an armed force to achieve information dominance, increasingly the essential precondition for battlespace dominance.

This observation implies a continuous fight for critical information both inside and outside the organization for combat. As illustrated in the context of Ulm, Blitzkrieg, and Desert Storm, for military operations to be coherent, in addition to seeing, deciding, and orchestrating the movement of forces, the commander must be able to conduct operations in predictable periods and be able to adjust quickly to changing circumstances.[20] Thus, for the wartime commander, the first objective of the lethal and nonlethal military actions in all operations is to achieve a condition of situational awareness which is superior to the opponent's, thus making possible the effective application of force at the decisive points.[21]

External to successful warfighting organizations, the fight for superior situational awareness of both enemy and friendly forces entails a range of actions to confound, mislead, blind, and disintegrate the enemy's command and control structure as well as his will to fight. In more modern parlance, these actions involve deception, disinformation, and decimating strikes to paralyze the enemy force. Internal to warfighting organizations, the fight for information frequently involves cutting through existing military information networks designed to produce accurate and timely information by any and every available means.[22] During Desert Storm, the American capacity to destroy an enemy's situational awareness clearly exceeded the

American capability to share and exploit information on a real-time basis.[23] General Buster Glosson, USAF, discusses his own experience with fighting for information: "An intelligence disaster during Desert Storm was precluded by one individual—Admiral Mike McConnell (then Chief of the Defense Intelligence Agency). He and I would talk as often as three times a day on secure telephone and secure faxes. We both have been criticized because we short-cut the system. That occurred because the intelligence process was broken."[24]

The point is that successful warfighting organizations are simply better organized and more adept than their opponents at sharing the critical information quickly and at knowing what information is critical at what echelon of command.[25] Reflecting on the impact of how armies organize to fight on the use of information in war, Martin Van Creveld, a noted author in military affairs, observes:

> The nature of the task to be performed is not the only determinant of the amount of information required for its performance; *equally important is the structure of the organization itself.* The more numerous and differentiated the departments into which an organization is divided, the larger the number of command echelons superimposed upon each other, the higher the decision thresholds, and the more specialized its individual members, then the greater the amount of information processing that has to go on inside the organization. *Uncertainty, in other words, is not dependent solely on the nature of the task to be performed; it may equally well be a function of a change in the organization itself.*[26]

Although these information-related activities—collection, transmission, processing, analysis, denial, dissemination and, exploitation—have always had a place in U.S. military operations, that place has generally been secondary.[27] Still, the importance of these activities to the success of the operations in 1805, 1940, and 1991 demonstrates their critical importance to victory in future war. At this point, the reader may ask, if successful warfighting structures cope with the fluidity and uncertainty of war by embedding the critical information processes into their organization for combat as well as their warfighting doctrine and concepts of command, how should the Army's organization for combat change to exploit information age technology more effectively to maximize combat power within a broader, joint military framework? As noted earlier, the technical ability of modern American military command and control systems in their various forms to make their influence felt at every level already exists.

Part of the answer lies in understanding at what echelon all the needed combat arms and components are united under the command of a single force commander. Depending on the circumstances, in the United States Army, this echelon is either the division or the corps. As mentioned in the preceding chapters, field armies normally consist of more than one corps. In the evolving structure of "joint" operations, this echelon is normally the Joint Task Force (JTF). Because this work assumes that future conflict will be a joint undertaking, it is important for the reader to understand how JTFs are constructed.

In most cases, JTFs are not built from scratch. The JTF for Atlantic Resolve was built around V U.S. Corps, the Haiti JTF around XVIII U.S. Corps, Somalia's relief and evacuation task forces around 1st Marine Expeditionary Force, and, more recently, NATO's peacekeeping force in Bosnia around the ACE Rapid Reaction Corps. More often than not, the Army Corps Commander becomes the JTF Commander who augments his existing staff from the other service components. The Deputy Corps Commander becomes the "Commander, U.S. Army Forces," and the other components of the JTF are treated in the same way with the result that the various service forces continue to operate independently. LTG Cushman, a retired Army General, has observed, "While this command structure suffices for administration such as personnel management, to fight using these component commanders as operational commanders of their forces alone simply will not work. For fighting, the forces must be mixed in a task organization that is designed for the mission."[28]

Still, mixing these forces is easier said than done. Contrary to popular belief, resistance to closer integration is not simply a function of parochial attitudes in the services. It is based to a much greater degree on the absence of a common operating environment created by flexible and robust joint command, control, communication, computer, and intelligence (C4I) systems embedded in the warfighting organizations of the services.[29] This is because force integration in the context of a JTF places far greater demands on C4I structures than service-pure organization does.

If the need for joint and integrated C4I can be seen as an effort to exploit existing capabilities across service lines in new ways, the best approach is to provide an Army organization at every level of command that can serve as a joint "clearinghouse" for information processes to which all services are connected. Because the Army Corps structure is frequently the nucleus around which JTFs are built, the Army should be in a position to furnish the backbone for joint C4I in the same way that it provides the foundation for logistical support in joint operations on land to the Air Force and Marine

Corps. In the new information warfare paradigm, this organization is called the *C4I battalion*.

In the C4I battalion organization shown in Figure 4.4, the structure has an internal and an external orientation. Internally, the command and control company includes the communications elements necessary to link the command group horizontally and vertically with other JTF components. This means communications consisting of ultra-high-frequency (UHF) and super-high-frequency (SHF) satellite communications; tropospheric scatter; and UHF, very-high-frequency (VHF), and high-frequency (HF) radio. Externally, the Information Warfare Company incorporates technical means for intelligence collection, transmission, and analysis that are essential to sharing information. Internally, digital systems can transmit this information to subordinate elements. This company also includes the electronic warfare capabilities to target, deceive, and disrupt the enemy's C4I.

The non-line-of-sight (NLOS) battery includes unmanned aerial vehicles and over-the-horizon attack systems that specifically support countersurveillance, operational security, as well as command and control warfare. The incorporation of tactical air and chemical defense systems into the C4I battalion establishes an instantaneous interface with the system of information dissemination and collection. When the C4I battalion is equipped with technology that is compatible with and linked to systems like the Air Force's joint surveillance target attack radar system (JSTARS) and airborne warning and control system (AWACS) or the Navy's program for Space and Electronic Warfare (SEW), it is easy to anticipate the utility of this organization to a JTF Ground Component Commander (GCC) who needs a

Figure 4.4
Example of a C4I Battalion Organization

•GROUP HEADQUARTERS COMPANY *(INCLUDES AG COMPONENT , MEDICAL AND*
                                    SUPPORTING MAINTENANCE ASSETS)

•NON-LINE-OF-SIGHT (NLOS) BATTERY. *(INCLUDES UAVS AND OVER THE*
                                    HORIZON ATTACK SYSTEMS)

•INFORMATION WARFARE COMPANY. *(INCLUDES INTELLIGENCE COLLECTION , JAMMING*
                                    ANALYSIS , CHEMICAL DETECTION CAPABILITY)

•AIR DEFENSE BATTERY. *(SHORT RANGE TACTICAL AIR DEFENSE SYSTEMS)*

•COMMAND AND CONTROL COMPANY. (COMMUNICATIONS *DESIGNED TO SUPPORT*
                                    DISPERSED, HIGHLY MOBILE COMBAT GROUP)

•CHEMICAL CO: INCLUDES CHEMICAL RECON AND LIMITED DECONTAMINATION
                                    CAPABILITY

•MILITARY POLICE SECURITY DETACHMENT. (INCLUDES SUFFICIENT MANPOWER AND
                                    FIREPOWER TO PROVIDE SECURITY FOR C2
                                    NODES AND SUSTAINMENT OPERATIONS.

standing C4I structure that can be quickly established in an austere theater of war. Without detailing all of the technologies and capabilities that could be included in this organization, it is important to remember that this organization (like most from now on) must be designed from the outset for adaptation to future demands, even though we cannot be sure today what those demands may be.

In wartime, the C4I battalion would operate in a fragmented organization designed to extend information processes over vast distances. Employing the deep/close/rear battlefield framework, it is possible to imagine component parts of the organization operating at distinct loci of command and control. There are those who will argue that the future compression of deep, close, and rear battles into one fight makes this framework irrelevant to the conduct of future operations. However, this artificial analytical construct continues to assist the Commander in the horizontal distribution of warfighting tasks and activities. C4I Groups at the corps-based JTF level and the theater level would of necessity be somewhat different in composition. The key aspect of this architecture, however, is that any part of this JTF-oriented C4I structure has the technological capability to access the information which any other part of the system possesses. When the multiple uses of digital computer technology are considered in the context of netting the thousands of communications, combat formations, radars, rocket artillery groups, tactical ballistic missile, and air defense systems together, the advantages of this nonlinear, multiservice approach to Army redesign are obvious (Figure 4.5).

Having established the need for a C4I organization at every echelon with Joint C4ISR plugs, the next question is, How many echelons does the information age Army need? Or where can the U.S. Army warfighting structure economize in a way that is consistent with the trendlines? In view of the merging of the traditional levels of war into a new structure characterized by simultaneous, multiservice operations and the demonstrated success of radical autonomy in the context of Mircosoft's commercial

Figure 4.5
Command and Control Scheme for Employment in Combat

GROUP TACTICAL OPERATIONS CP	GROUP MAIN CP	GROUP SUSTAINMENT OPERATIONS CP
C2 CO (-)	C2 CO. (-)	C2 CO. (-)
NLOS (-)	INFO WAR CO. (-)	MP SECURTY DET (-)
INFO WAR CO (-)	NLOS (-)	CHEMICAL CO (-)
CHEMICAL CO (-)	MP SECURITY DET (-)	ADA (-)
ADA (-)	ADA BATTERY (-)	

enterprise or Guderian's and Wood's battlefield opportunism, flattening the Army's warfighting organization between the corps nucleus of the JTF and the battalion battlegroup seems essential.

Keeping in mind the desirability of maintaining the JTF (corps/MEF level) Commander as the integrating mechanism for joint operations and the parameters depicted in the intermediate force design illustration, it is possible to determine the likely structure of the Army component(s) of a future JTF:

- A warfighting organization that is both smaller in size and more numerous in quantity than the existing division organizations: Some portion of these organizations are configured for delivery by air from bases in the continental United States.

- In its form, command structure, and composition, an organization for combat which reflects the shift of warfighting functions and activities to lower levels: While the composition of the organization will vary, depending on the specific mission orientation, all information age military organizations are modular in character insofar as they share a common architecture for C4I and logistics.

- An organization that has high operational and tactical mobility so that it can concentrate the effects of its weapons against the enemy and still evade destruction by the enemy's weapons of mass destruction: It can dominate much larger areas with new technology than is now possible by sensing and engaging the enemy at long ranges while simultaneously maneuvering at high speed to exploit the enemy's weaknesses in close combat.[30]

- An organization that can sustain itself within the JTF multiservice framework for extended periods: Its equipment is capable of supporting near-continuous operations without extensive maintenance.

In broad outline, the information age organization should incorporate the force design directions indicated by the RMA trendlines. For simplicity, this information age warfighting organization is called a "Combat Group." The building blocks of the Combat Group are drawn directly from the implied *Force XXI* design parameters illustrated by the intermediate force design. The C4I structure has been addressed. It is enough to reinforce the point that the C4I architecture will permeate the organization. In a similar vein, to be self-sustaining, the Group must incorporate a support formation that provides all of the transportation, maintenance, supply, and repair needs for the Group to operate independently for longer than a few days.

Continuous advances in technology have reinforced the need for a mobile and highly trained reconnaissance element that can mobilize combat power out of proportion to its actual size while rapidly reporting critical information to the wartime commander. However, none of the technological advances to date has invalidated the need for the trained soldier in this special capacity. To assess enemy strength, resistance, location, and movement over wide areas; to communicate with and coordinate over great distances; to position forces accurately; and to acquire targets and guide ground and air forces to those targets beyond the normal visual range require technology that extends the human potential of air and ground reconnaissance forces.[31] The integrative potential for the merging of these information processes into a unified effort resides in three areas: the C4I Bn, the Indirect Fire Bn, and the Recon Squadron. At the heart of this organizational structure, however, are the elements which add the critical mass still required in close combat.

Figure 4.6
Organic C4I Structure

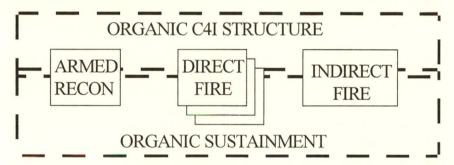

In Figure 4.6 the components of the design parameters are converted to combat organizations which integrate all of the combat arms at a lower level than is the case today. All of the organizations examined here comprise a soldier strength of roughly 4,000 to 5,000 troops. In Figures 4.7, 4.8, 4.9, and 4.10, four possible types of Combat Groups are depicted. Considered in succession, all of the Combat Group structures organize existing capabilities in ways that are calculated to confer a degree of combat power that is proportionally greater than the size of the actual unit. Take for instance the Heavy Combat Group (Figure 4.7).

Heavy Combat Group. **Mission Profile:** Conduct Decisive Maneuver Operations (Offensive and Defensive). **Equipment Includes:** (132) M1A1/2 Tanks, (132) M2/3A2 AFVs (includes [27] 120mm Mortars), (24) 155 SP Paladin Howitzers, (9) MLRS, (7) RAH66, (3) UH60 + engineer mobility equipment, light armored and wheeled vehicles.

Figure 4.7
Structure of Heavy Combat Group

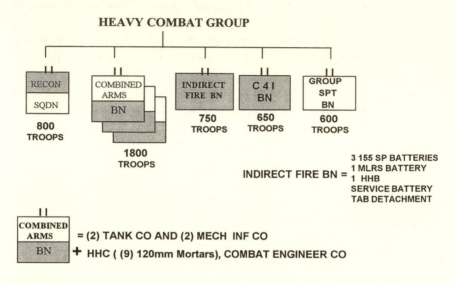

The 4,600 man Heavy Combat Group consists of a recon squadron, three balanced combined arms battalions, a hybrid indirect fire battalion, a C4I battalion, and a support battalion. As balanced task organizations, the combined arms battalions require no further internal modification or cross-attachment to be effective. With organic engineer mobility assets, these units can execute deliberate or hasty obstacle breaching operations as necessary. In addition, the group has an armed recon capability and an indirect fire capability that facilitate independent combat operations over great distances. Modernized rotor-driven aircraft augmented by UAVs create the capability to quickly orchestrate MLRS (ATACM capable) and 155 millimeter artillery fire in support of a wide range of offensive and defensive combat operations. Until RAH66 Comanche aircraft[32] are added to the Army's inventory, (twelve) Kiowa Warrior aircraft[33] would operate in place of the proposed (seven) RAH66s. Although OOTW is not listed as a primary mission, there is nothing to prevent a Heavy Combat Group from executing these types of missions. Armored forces do not take heavy casualties and the experience in Bosnia, Haiti, and Somalia indicates that armored forces play a decisive role in the establishment and preservation of civil order.[34]

An organic support battalion draws its sustainment supplies directly from a JTF General Support Group and this removes the requirement for intervening division support echelons to distribute supplies and ammunition to the fighting units. The C4I battalion links the commander and his subordinates to the information and other joint warfighting resources that are essential to a uniform and coherent understanding of operations in progress.

Airborne-Air Assault Group. **Mission Profile:** Designed to be delivered by air in order to conduct Forced Entry Operations, close and deep Economy of Force Operations in support of decisive operations; Contingency Operations and OOTW as needed. **Equipment Includes:** (24) Towed 155mm Howitzers, (9) RAH66s, (15) AH64s,[35] (93) UH60s + small arms and wheeled vehicles.

The 4,150 man Airborne-Air Assault Group (Figure 4.8) confers the tactical mobility and firepower on the Army's elite light infantry formations which its airborne infantry currently lack. Mobility on the future battlefield is essential to the survival of the Army's light infantry. Strategically, airborne forces have always had the advantage of reaching the scene of the action quickly. However, without modern aviation and information resources, this strategic advantage is quickly transformed into a tactical liability on the future battlefield. In the wars of the future, there is simply no point in deploying highly trained light infantry without mobility and protection. In this organization, the airborne infantry can be delivered by parachute and link up with their air mobility assets later or this formation can potentially self-deploy over short distances (Sicily to North Africa/Italy to Croatia) with its own aircraft.

Figure 4.8
Structure of Airborne-Air Assault Group

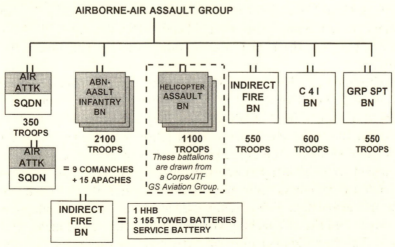

In the active Army, there are ten UH60–equipped lift battalions consisting of 300 UH60s (Blackhawk medium lift helicopters) configured for the assault mission. These ten battalions are scheduled to increase in number and can be organized with the roughly 182 CH47 Chinook heavy lift helicopters into 4 General Aviation Support Groups to support the air assault operations of the 7 Airborne-Air Assault Groups. Like the Light Recon–Strike Group, this Group can be entirely transported by either military air transport or a mix of military and commercial air transport (Army overseas presence in USEUCOM could be structured to include both an Aviation Support Group and an Airborne-Air Assault Group).

The advanced aviation warfighting systems in the organization provide reconnaissance, protection, and firepower to attacking infantry formations whether they are moving in the air or on the ground. These systems are also critical links in the system that integrates air and naval power with the maneuver of attacking ground elements. Aviation elements whose vision is often obstructed by undulating or densely forested terrain benefit from the infantryman who directs their fire, and, they, in turn, help to shape the airborne infantry's encounter with the enemy on terms that are favorable to the infantry. As in Combat Group formations, indirect fire support is an integral part of the organization for combat. Towed artillery is the mainstay of airborne and air assault infantry formations. When and if high mobility artillery rocket systems (HIMARS: truck mounted MLRS) become available, a HIMARS battery would become part of this battalion-size element.

Heavy Recon-Strike Group. **Mission Profile:** Conduct Close and Deep Economy-of-Force Maneuver Operations (Guard, Screen, Cover) in support of JTF mission, Security Operations to protect JTF. **Equipment Includes:** (126) M1A1/2 Tanks, 153 M2/3A2 AFVs (includes [27] 120mm Mortars), (24) 155mm self-propelled Paladin Howitzers, (9) MLRS, (30) RAH66, (15) AH64s, (15) UH60s + other wheeled and light armored vehicles.

With somewhat different purposes in mind, the 5,000 man Heavy Recon-Strike Group (Figure 4.9) is equipped with the aviation and ground assets to reach far ahead of advancing Heavy Combat Groups to develop the situation and to facilitate close cooperation with Air Force and Army deep battle systems. The significant infusion of advanced manned and unmanned aviation warfighting systems enables this formation to overcome the landforms that mask vision in close combat, orient the JTF Commander to the true disposition of the enemy, and harmonize as well as integrate the movement and fire of attacking ground forces with air and naval striking power. This formation is particularly effective against the moving enemy

Figure 4.9
Structure of Heavy Recon-Strike Group

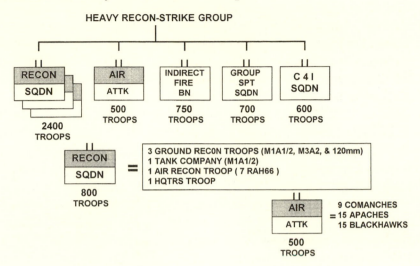

that seeks to avoid detection and destruction by outpacing electronic surveillance. More than any other formation, this one is equipped to both
discover and destroy the enemy.

The Heavy Recon-Strike Group is designed to protect and secure the JTF
while it assembles or deploys for decisive operations. Such a force is critical
in the task of disrupting the enemy formations throughout the entire depth
of its deployment and preventing if from responding coherently to the
deployment/attack of the main JTF forces. The enemy's disruptive actions
will use long-range tactical ballistic missile, air strikes, and even diversion-
ary or spoiling ground attacks. This force also assists in the Joint Force
Commander's effort to deceive the enemy as to the timing and location of
the main attack.

Light Recon-Strike Group. **Mission Profile:** Versatile, Economy-of-
Force Battlegroup designed to be delivered by air in order to conduct Close
and Deep Maneuver Operations, Support Forced Entry Operations, Contingency Operations and OOTW as needed. **Equipment Includes:** (126) AGS,
(160) LAV(PI) (include [27] 120mm Mortars), (9) MLRS, (30) RAH66, 25
(UH60) + engineer mobility equipment and wheeled vehicles.

Strategic mobility requires a mix of capabilities that will allow early entry
ground forces to fight their way in or, soon after arrival, expand their
battlespace to quickly establish control or win the conflict.[36] The 4,850 man
Light Recon-Strike Group (Figure 4.10) is equipped with the Armored Gun

Figure 4.10
Structure of Light Recon-Strike Group

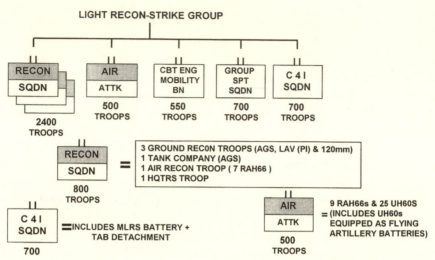

System (AGS)[37] and a version of the Light Armored Vehicle (LAV). While the Department of the Army decided in January 1996 to halt acquisition of the AGS for reasons of economy, the importance of the AGS in the context of this study cannot be overestimated. It is light enough to be airlifted by current and future air transport systems and can supply the mobile, antiarmor firepower needed in close combat.[38] Its top-attack and kinetic energy munitions are useful for more than antitank warfare. At the same time, the AGS preserves the intimidating character of the tank that experience in Somalia, Haiti, and Bosnia indicates is still of enormous value. The LAV produced by General Motors of Canada for the Marine Corps is modified for use in this formation by adding thermal imagery sights, an improved fire control system, reactive armor, and digital burst communications for secure operations over long distances. However, other light armored vehicles can be used as well. Still, the LAV (block III) does offer advantages in terms of interoperability with the USMC in future crisis response operations.

With MLRS and (fifteen) UH60s fitted with rocket pods and Hellfire missile mounts, this organization can fight and survive across the spectrum of conflict. Since the organization is designed to operate in an austere logistical environment, this Group has only two types of armored chassis—AGS and LAV (PI)—and two types of airframes—UH60 and RAH66. Again, until the RAH66 comes on line, a larger number of Kiowa Warrior aircraft will be needed. As always, the MLRS is ATACM-capable. Not shown are the numbers of hand-held and vehicle-mounted laser designating elements.

With the exception of very few items of equipment,[39] all of these Group organizations can be constituted from existing Army assets today. In the current ten division active Army structure, there are roughly 2,000+ M1A1/A2 tanks, 2,000+ M2/3A2 Bradley AFVs, 500 SP 155 millimeter M109 Howitzers, 40+ MLRS batteries (9 launchers each), 800+ AH64s, 300+UH60s, 130+ AH58s,[40] 182 CH47 heavy lift helicopters, and other armored vehicles. Reorganizing these assets into combat groups like the ones outlined here could be accomplished in stages over a 2 to 3 year period in order to preserve the readiness of the existing force to fight. In the corporate experience in the 1980s, reorganizing and consolidating increased organizational efficiency and saved money. The potential for savings here is real as well.[41]

More important than the details of the Groups' composition is the larger aspect of orchestrating the actions of a Combat Group comprising 4,000 to 5,000 troops. Given the self-contained character of the formation and the degree of tactical autonomy which the *information warfare paradigm* will confer on this organization, a Brigadier General with a robust, experienced staff will be needed to command a Combat Group. A deputy commander not shown in this scheme may also be appropriate. How this command and staff structure could be organized is shown in Figure 4.11.

In line with the requirement for closer integration of warfighting activities to maximize the combat value of new technologies, the traditional G1, G2, G3, G4, and G5 staff structure is modified in favor of one that more closely aligns mission-essential functions with mission-oriented activities.[42] Operations and intelligence are integrated into one structure. The mission of the Strike Coordination officer is to synthesize and orchestrate the various long-range precision strike capabilities that exist in all of the services within the maneuver framework of land warfare. He is an essential

Figure 4.11
Staff Structure of a Combat Group

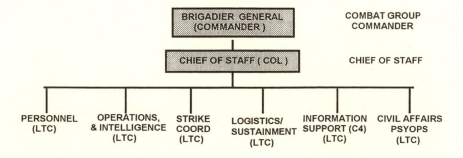

feature of the growing intelligence, surveillance, and reconnaissance complex. The Information Support officer assists the commander with the orchestration and utilization of the information aspects of command, control, communication and computer assets. The Psychological Operations–Civil Affairs officer is both an integral part of the modern warfighting process and the permanent link to the interagency process in the context of OOTW. The staff will have the required depth of military experience and education to be effective if former battalion commanders are assigned to key positions in the Group staff.

With this kind of "C4I overhead," battalion-size elements not normally assigned to a particular Combat Group could be "plugged into" or "unplugged from" the group as necessary. Seen in the context of the close/deep/rear battle framework, this approach can be applied at the corps-based JTF level with the result that a corps-based JTF could be made much more robust in C4I to embrace a larger span of command and control than is currently possible in Army-pure divisions or corps.[43] Of course, within the corps-based JTF structure, additional groups will be needed both to augment and to support the warfighting activities of the combat groups. These Groups would provide the capability to wage war on the operational level. An Army corps–based JTF may include some or all of the following Groups depending on the mission:

- *General Support Groups:* A Corps Support Command (COSCOM) includes nearly 22,000 troops in supply, medical, transportation, police, and so on. This approach assumes that the robust sustainment at the Group level facilitates some economy at the JTF level. To achieve the desired level of modularity outlined in *Force XXI*, this will entail converting the COSCOM to (three) 4,000 to 5,000 man Ground Component Support Groups. The current structure of the COSCOM is shown in appendix B.
- Engineer Support Group (combat and construction engineer battalions).
- Rocket Artillery Group (MLRS/ATACM Battalions as deep strike assets) (see Figure 4.12).
- Theater High Altitude Air Defense (THAAD) Group (antitactical ballistic missile assets) (see Figure 4.12).
- Air Defense Group (tactical air defense for ground forces).
- Aviation Strike Group (AH64 attack helicopter battalions).
- Aviation Support Group (logistical and helicopter lift assets).
- C4I Group (could include elements from corps signal brigade, military intelligence brigade, military police brigade, psychological operations, and civil affairs brigade).

Figure 4.12
Structure of Corps Rocket Artillery Group and
Theater High Altitude Area Defense Group

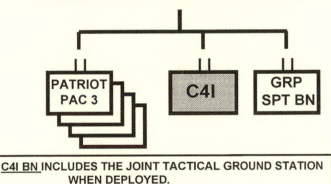

CORPS ROCKET ARTILLERY GROUP

MLRS BN

C4I

GRP SPT BN

THEATER HIGH ALTITUDE AREA DEFENSE GROUP

PATRIOT PAC 3

C4I

GRP SPT BN

C4I BN INCLUDES THE JOINT TACTICAL GROUND STATION WHEN DEPLOYED.

THESE BNS CONTAIN FOUR FIRING BATTERIES OF THE PATRIOT ADVANCED CAPABILITY LEVEL 3 (PAC 3) SYSTEM..
THEATER HIGH ALTITUDE AREA DEFENSE (THAAD) SYSTEM WILL BE FIELDED AFTER THE YEAR 2,000.

Again, each group is organized with the forces, organic sustainment, and C4I capability appropriate to the operational level of war. For instance, a Rocket Artillery Group could have four MLRS battalions capable of firing several different types of rocket propelled munitions to include ATACMs. An Air Defense Group could consist of some mix of Patriot and other air defense battalions. An Aviation Support Group would include a mix of assault and heavy lift helicopters. An Aviation Strike Group could have four AH64 battalions. A C4I Group would consolidate intelligence and signal formations. Current corps-level combat service support elements could be reorganized into Support Groups that sustain multiservice operations ashore.

Groups like the one illustrated in Figure 4.13 will be subordinated to one of the three corps-based JTF command posts (CPs): Sustainment Operations CP, Deep Operations CP, or Close Combat Battle CP. Clearly, any of these Group structures can be plugged into a MEF, subordinated for specific missions to the theater-level Joint Forces Air Component Commander (JFACC), or integrated with the theater missile defense force as well.

While the Group organization for combat supplants the brigade and division maneuver echelons, the augmented Corps Command structure orchestrates the operational activities of the JTF. In this way, the JTF is actually greater than the sum of its parts. Thus, the echelonment of forces changes from brigade, division, corps, army (Joint Forces Land Component Commander [JFLCC]; currently 3rd U.S. Army), theater/strategic, or warfighting CINC to Group, JTF, and Joint Land Force with the warfighting CINC or theater commander potentially "double hatting" as the Joint Forces Land Component Commander.[44]

Because this modular organizational structure accommodates the need for multiservice force integration at increasingly lower levels than is now possible, determining how many and what types of "Groups" should be deployed to join a JTF becomes a function of the mission. A peacekeeping

Figure 4.13

Example of a Corps Headquarters Structured to Operate in a JTF-Based Army

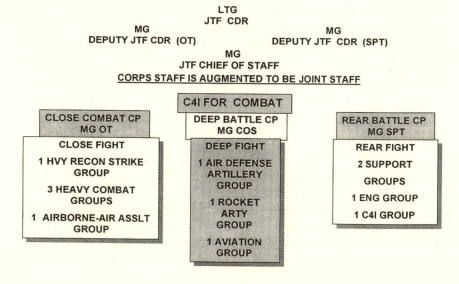

role has emerged for the U.S. Army. If a future peacekeeping mission involves a long deployment, in Haiti or in Bosnia, Groups can be rotated in and out of the theater of operations as necessary. One type of Group can be employed for the initial period of operations and replaced with different Groups later. Or a Group command structure can remain in place while battalion-size elements are rotated through the area of operations.

Currently, the requirement to deploy forces quickly and for unspecified periods (Haiti, Somalia, Bosnia) compels the Army to remove key elements from division organizations in order to create smaller, more deployable ad hoc formations. This renders the division vitually unusable for any other operation. Within the framework of the Group-based force, this would no longer be necessary. Instead of stripping out the command, control, and support elements of a division in order to reinforce brigade task forces for deployment to contingencies, the Army can deploy a Group structure with robust C4I and support elements under the command of a General Officer with a complete staff.

In a JTF based on flexible Groups, structural uniformity in terms of C4I, logistics, and reconnaissance throughout the Army's combat, combat support, and combat service support formations creates tremendous organizational flexibility. Any Combat Group organization may be directed to conduct joint operations across the spectrum of conflict (see Figure 4.14). In response to a set of mission-specific conditions, battalion-size elements can be plugged into or unplugged from a Group structure and Groups can be added to or subtracted from a JTF as necessary. As self-contained and self-sustaining organizations, Combat Groups also retain the capability for independent operations while providing whatever mix of forces the mission demands. Thus, the presumed advantages of cross-attaching units within the division structure are not sacrificed.

When viewed in the context of the current Army missions, the "Group" structure suggests new ways to organize Army Forces to operate as corps-based JTFs. By eliminating division headquarters and embedding deployable corps headquarters in standing JTFs the Army, in conjunction with resources from other services, could provide standing JTF headquarters for the regional unified commands. In the current environment of "no-notice" conflict and crisis, Army forces must be able to reach a potential conflict area quickly with sufficient combat power to influence the situation. A mix of forces linked to the APA and prepositioned equipment sets ashore could be kept ready for deployment to JTF commands on a rotating basis. At home, the Active Component (AC) could also begin the process of integrating portions of the Army National Guard within an AC C4I structure. Additional

Figure 4.14
**Example of an Airborne-Air Assault Group Tailored
for a MOOTW Mission**

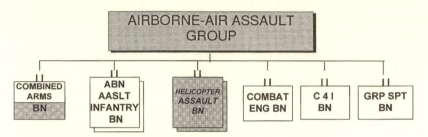

Because of the requirement in this MOOTW mission for a mix of heavy and light forces
on the ground, one of the airborne-air assault battalions was replaced with a combined
arms battalion. At the same time, combat engineers were deployed instead of the
artillery battalion.

However, the essential building block features of the group in terms of command,
control, communications, intelligence, and logistical support were retained.

Corps/JTF structures could be maintained to command, control, train, and
prepare Army forces overseas and in CONUS to include the Army National
Guard (more about this later). A willingness to eliminate unnecessary
echelons of command and control could lead to the emergence of new joint
warfighting headquarters capable of controlling a mix of Army Heavy and
Airborne-Air Assault Combat Groups.

CONCLUSIONS

Since the end of the Gulf War, the U.S. Army has considered how it could
reorganize and still field a force capable of fighting decisively at all levels
of conflict. Technological improvements in the lethality and accuracy of
weapons, information systems, and human potential point to the kind of
organizational change outlined here. Of course, this is not the only way to
organize. The four basic combat structures and the Group organizations at
echelons above the Combat Groups incorporate the processes of flattening
and consolidation that have been implemented to produce revolutionary
results in many fields of human activity.[45] And it is also not a revolutionary
proposal. These structures are simply designed to produce change at the
beginning of a new RMA.

More important, the Group approach organizes Army Ground Forces in
peacetime for the way they are likely to fight in war without imparting
rigidity to a structure that will require flexibility.[46] The Group structure is

one way to develop a well-balanced, powerful, mobile fighting unit for information age conflict. Improved C4I systems, as well as a broadening of the concept of combined arms to include "all arms," are prominent features of this design. For surprise, shock, mobility, flexibility, and information collection, all Group structures include modernized rotary-wing aviation as a component part of the formation. All of the organizational changes are designed to make fire support (air and artillery) more responsive to the tactical and operational commanders.

For equally important reasons, this information age structure emphasizes the requirement for armed manned reconnaissance in war. This is based on the recognition that while surveillance provides information, reconnaissance provides knowledge (see Figure 4.15). Armed reconnaissance allows the friendly force to probe and test where remote, unarmed sensors can only display. These points allude to the difference between *dominant battlespace awareness* (DBA) and *dominant battlespace knowledge* (DBK). The difference between the two is that DBA simply alerts friendly forces to where enemy forces are operating. On the other hand, DBK tells the friendly force what the enemy is likely to do. DBK allows the friendly force to fight more

Figure 4.15
Intermediate Force Design

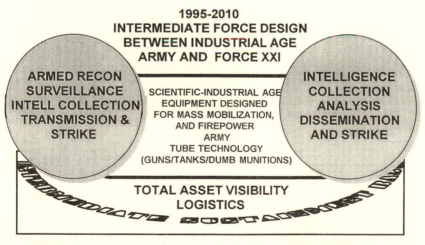

CURRENT TECHNOLOGICAL ADVANCES IN MICROCIRCUITRY, DIRECTED ENERGY, AND BIOCHEMICAL ENGINEERING ARE ALTERING THE RELATIVE BALANCE OF FORCES IN FAVOR OF ELEMENTS TRADITIONALLY ASSOCIATED WITH RECON, STRIKE, SURVEILLANCE, AND INFORMATION ANALYSIS. IN ADDITION, THE CAPABILITY TO ACHIEVE TOTAL ASSET VISIBILITY CREATES NEW OPPORTUNITIES TO RESHAPE THE SUSTAINMENT BASE TO SUPPORT A NEW KIND OF ARMED FORCE.

efficiently and effectively. Armed reconnaissance is the difference. The information age Army provides the basis for this capacity in land warfare, which is further enhanced through integrated multiservice C4I by the constellation of JSTARS, UAVs, U2, Guardrail, and many other systems.

The overreliance on technology to gather intelligence has been cited by many as the single shortage that hit the coalition forces hardest in the Gulf conflict.[47] General Bradley's decisions in July and August 1945 to halt the advance of American forces close to the Falaise Pocket and, later, at the Seine River allowed the bulk of the German Army in France to escape to Belgium, where it subsequently launched an offensive during December that inflicted over 120,000 U.S. casualties. One of Bradley's reasons for this decision was uncertainty about the enemy's disposition and strength, even though he had access to the famous Ultra intelligence intercepts that theoretically provided an accurate, real-time picture of German forces.[48] The reasons for related decisions in the Gulf War were similar in character. Fighting in every war has demonstrated the ambiguity inherent in reconnaissance operations and the interdependence of security and reconnaissance. Recent experience with efforts to track dismounted and rotary wing aircraft with JSTARS reinforces this interdependence.[49] Without air and ground manned reconnaissance in contemporary and future conflict, force protection is an illusion.

Using technology to compensate for an increased span of control at the corps/JTF level increases coordination of tactical units, speeds the intelligence–analysis–decision–action loop, and enhances coordination of tactical missions with operational objectives. If, however, the tactical commander does not have the initiative, authority, and doctrine along with the information to make decisions based on his understanding of the operational goals and situation, no amount of technology will result in winning decisions. At the very least, flattening the Army's warfighting structure will necessitate a radical revision of current programs for educating and training leaders at every level, especially the operational level. Ideally, immersing tactical commanders in operational doctrine will enable them to cope more effectively with the information overload that will inevitably result no matter what C4I structure is developed.

In moving past a global strategy focused on containment to one of rapid response to regional crisis, tactical logistics must not be allowed to obstruct change in the Army. Meaningful information to improve asset visibility will help, but modularity in the structure and delivery of supplies and equipment is vital. No amount of infrastructure renewal will suffice to compensate for dependence on fuel, water, food, and ammunition if the Army continues to operate from a framework of abundance.[50] Fuel efficient engines and equipment reliability must receive priority in the context of equipment modernization. Cohesive, task-organized fighting forces and logistics packages are inseparable from this process.

What is also clear from developments in international military affairs since the end of the Gulf War is that the United States' closest NATO allies are moving in force design directions that are consistent with the Group approach. The British have long regarded the division structure as an echelon of command and control rather than as a fixed formation. Today, the combination of reductions in numbers of units and troops has driven the British Army to orient contingency planning along lines of reinforced brigade structures commanded by Brigadiers. Contemporary German Army doctrine organizes warfighting around large mobile brigades. Within the constraints of economy and technological change, none of America's traditional military partners can avoid moving to a fixed all-arms structure smaller than the current division.[51] The French government's decision to end conscription and to reduce the size of its army in 1997 will have a similar impact on French military thinking. This creates enormous strategic opportunities for the United States in the context of military cooperation. The Group structure not only is adaptive to allied formations, but can become a model that allied forces may be willing to adopt. This could provide the foundation for a commonality of equipment and doctrine that could lead to a future situation in which portions or entire sets of equipment belonging to the U.S. Army could also be used by an allied army.[52]

Having devised this new Army warfighting structure for joint operations, the key questions are How does this organization assist in the process of observation–orientation–decision–action in the context of warfighting operations? And how do these organizations interact with one another as well as across service lines in the warfighting environment of the future? In order to provide some possible answers to these questions, the next chapter will examine this proposed structure from a variety of perspectives so that an operational image of these organizations can emerge.

NOTES

1. Christopher Dandeker, "Bureaucracy Planning and War: The Royal Navy, 1880 to 1918," *Armed Forces and Society* 11, no. 1 (Fall 1984): 130.

2. Martin Blumenson, *The Patton Papers 1885–1940* (Boston: Houghton Mifflin, 1972), 943.

3. *Force XXI Operations: A Concept for the Evolution of Full-Dimensional Operations for the Strategic Army of the Early Twenty-First Century* (Washington, D.C.: U.S. Government Printing Office, 1994).

4. James Berry Motley, *Beyond the Soviet Threat: The U.S. Army in a Post–Cold War Environment* (Lexington, Mass.: Lexington Books, 1991), 121.

5. Quoted by Col. Harry Summers, USA (ret.), in his essay "The Mission to Bosnia Has Been Handled Well," *Air Force Times*, 18 March 1996, p. 70. The Chairman added, "We need to be very careful that peacekeeping does not become a way of life."

6. Some would argue that the structure of the 2nd ID (Mech) in Korea constitutes a sixth type. For planning purposes, however, it is considered a mechanized division by the Joint Staff and the Services.

7. The observations that follow are drawn from the TRADOC publication *Toward Combined Arms Warfare: A Survey of 20th Century Tactics, Doctrine, and Organization*, 106–10.

8. Martin Blumenson, *Kasserine Pass: An Epic Saga of Desert War* (Berkeley, Calif.: Berkeley Publishing, 1983), 11–59, 101–211.

9. Ibid., 109.

10. Ibid., 111. Also, Martin Blumenson mentions this in passing during his discussion of Major General Jack Wood's operations in northwestern France after the breakout from Normandy. See his work *The Battle of the Generals: The Untold Story of the Falaise Pocket—the Campaign That Should Have Won World War II* (New York: William Morrow, 1993), 158–69.

11. Martin Blumenson, *The Patton Papers: 1885-1940* (Boston: Houghton Mifflin, 1972), 943.

12. Dr. Christopher Gabel, *The 4th Armored Division in the Encirclement of Nancy* (Leavenworth, Kans.: Combat Studies Institute, 1986), 5.

13. Dr. John J. Midgley, Jr., *Deadly Illusions: Army Policy for the Nuclear Battlefield*, (Boulder, Colo.: Westview Press, 1986), 33.

14. Ibid., 69. The author writes: "Within a month after approving the Pentomic division structure as an organizational concept, General Taylor directed Continental Army Command to prepare advance plans for the reorganization of the infantry and armored divisions. The designs of the revised divisions and the tactical doctrine they were to apply, reflected compromises among the Pentomic Concept and the desires of the service schools. As the new divisions took shape it was clear that *the overriding consideration in their design was austerity, rather than nuclear operations*."

15. Ibid., 36.

16. John B. Wilson, "Influences on Divisional Organization," *Information Paper* provided to the Office of the Army Chief of Staff, 28 December 1995, p. 7.

17. Amy McAuliffe, "Technology: Changing the Way the Army Does Business," *Military & Aerospace Electronics* (February 1996): 25.

18. Sheila Foote, "Coats Adds Voice to Call for New Defense Strategy," *Defense Daily*, 25 April 1996, p. 150.

19. Col. John A. Bonin, "Brigades: Building Blocks for FORCE XXI," *USAWC Research Project* (Academic Year 1994–95), 52–53.

20. Jeffrey R. Cooper, "Implementing Coherent Operations: An Action Plan for the Deputy Chief of Staff, Operations and Plans, U.S. Army," paper prepared under contract to the Department of the Army by *SRS Technologies*, June 1994, p. 79.

21. Clarence Robinson, "Information Dominance Edges Toward New Conflict Frontier," *Signal* 48, no.12 (1994): 37–40.

22. Martin Van Creveld, *Command in War* (Cambridge, Mass.: Harvard University Press, 1985), 259. Military observers often refer to these means as the commander's *directed telescope*.

23. Jeffrey Record, *Hollow Victory: A Contrary View of the Gulf War* (New York: Brassey's, 1993), 121.

24. Quoted by David A. Fulghum from "Glosson: U.S. Gulf War Shortfalls Linger," *Aviation Week & Space Technology*, 29 January 1996, p. 59.

25. Directions for Defense, Report of the Commission on Roles and Missions of the Armed Forces (24 May 24 1995): 2–29. This point is discussed in connection with the USMC and the U.S. Army.

26. Van Creveld, *Command in War*, 269.

27. C. Kenneth Allard, "Turning Point: The Gulf War and U.S. Military Strategy," in *The Future of Command and Control: Toward a Paradigm of Information Warfare*, ed. by L. Benjamin Ederington and Michael J. Mazarr (Boulder, Colo.: Westview Press, 1995), 179.

28. LTG John H. Cushman, USA (ret), "Make It Joint Force XXI," unpublished manuscript, p. 17.

29. *Directions for Defense*, 2–5, 2–8.

30. John C. F. Tillson, "Force Planning for the 21st Century," *IDA Paper PP-2640* (Alexandria, Va.: Institute for Defense Analysis, 1992), 10–13.

31. *Force XXI Operations*, pp. 4–8.

32. The RAH66 Comanche is the first helicopter designed specifically for the role of armed reconnaissance. It is smaller and lighter than the AH64. It is 43 feet long and weighs 7,700 pounds. Its exceptionally sophisticated detection and navigation systems allow it to operate at night and in severe weather. Its composite airframe incorporates stealth technology to assist in evading detection. It fits easily into transport aircraft or onto ship transport. With its remarkable range—1,260 nautical miles—it can self-deploy as needed to most locations. The Army plans to buy 1,300 RAH66s, with the first arriving in the force during 2004. In this scenario, the arrival date has been advanced to 2003. *An Analysis of U.S. Army Helicopter Programs* (Washington, D.C.: Congressional Budget Office, December 1995), 18.

33. The Kiowa Warrior is an upgraded version of a Vietnam era airframe. The helicopter has a gross weight of 4,500 pounds, a top speed of 120 knots, and a cruising range of 215 miles. It is equipped with air-to-air stinger missiles, Hellfire antitank missiles, a machine gun, or 2.75 inch rockets. Ibid., 10.

34. See report by Jennifer Taw and Bruce Hoffman, *The Urbanization of Insurgency: The Potential Challenge to U.S. Army Operations* (Santa Monica, Calif.: RAND Corporation, 1994).

35. AH64 is the primary attack helicopter of the Army. It is a dual-engine aircraft equipped with Hellfire antitank missiles, a 30 millimeter chain gun, and rockets. Its target acquisition designator sight and pilot night vision sensor allow it to fly and operate at night and in poor weather. It weighs 17,650 pounds and has a top speed of 155 knots. *Analysis of U.S. Army Helicopter Programs*, 12.

36. *Force XXI Operations*, 3–9, 3–17.

37. Like many experienced armor officers, the author would prefer a fourth crew member to the automatic loader. The automatic loader adds considerable weight to the vehicle—almost 1,000 pounds—and cannot compete with the speed and reliability of a human being. In addition, the reduction of the crew to three actually degrades combat operations in the field, where the loader frequently dismounts and contributes enormously to the security of the vehicle and crew.

38. The AGS is ideally suited for the C-17 because the C-17 can land on shorter runways than either the C141 Starlifter or the C-5 Galaxy. If all the C-17s flew, the most M1A1s that the USAF could deliver in a 24 hour period would be 120 tanks. This would not include any of the regiment's additional equipment. At the same time, none of these points addresses the fuel and repair part issue for the M1A1. In contrast, the Institute for Defense Analysis estimates that a Light Recon-Strike Group could be delivered in fifty-five C-5 sorties in less than 24 hours. The C5A upgrades and C-17 probably reduce this overall number. See "Force Planning for the 21st Century," *IDA Paper P-2640* (October 1992).

39. These items include the RAH66 Comanche and the new improved Paladin self-propelled 155 millimeter Howitzer or Crusader (advanced artillery system). Other items may include new unmanned aerial vehicles and over-the-horizon attack systems that are now in development.

40. This is the armed version of the OH58D helicopter, which was designed to fill the interim requirement for an armed recon helicopter until the much more advanced Comanche is available. This is, however, a Vietnam War vintage aircraft.

41. The fiscal analysis of this proposed forces structure is discussed in detail in the chapter "Streamlining Defense for Strategic Dominance."

42. Robert Holzer, "U.S. Navy to Study Efficiency of Staff Functions," *Defense News*, 12–18 February 1996, p. 12.

43. Gen. J. H. Binford Peay, III, "The Five Pillars of Peace in the Central Region," *Joint Force Quarterly* (Autumn 1995): 31–33. General Peay discusses his activities in connection with C4I upgrades and reorganizations that have

improved the JFACC's C2 of sea-based and land-based aviation platforms in war. Many of these initiatives are worthy of closer examination in the context of JTF C4I.

44. The warfighting CINC could do this by appointing the Army's deployable JFLCC as his deputy. This would preserve the C4I advantage of maintaining the Army's JFLCC.

45. Matthew Cooper, *The German Army: 1933–1945* (Lanham, Md.: Scarborough House, 1978), see the chapter "Strategic Revolution." According to Cooper, similar attempts in the 1930s to change warfighting structures were only partially successful; for this reason the German Army was ultimately unprepared for the kind of war it was compelled to fight between 1941 and 1945. The Germans improvised on the battlefield to compensate for organizational problems. This is the origin of the Kampfgruppe concept.

46. Robert F. Holz, Jack H. Hiller, and Howard H. McFann, *Determinants of Effective Unit Performance: Research on Measuring and Managing Unit Training Readiness* (Alexandria, Va.: U.S. Army Research Institute for Behavioral and Social Sciences, July 1994), 176. The authors of this Army study emphasize the importance of organizing as a combined arms and services team for performance at the National Training Center and in combat. They conclude that waiting until deployment to organize for combat undermines readiness.

47. David A. Fulghum, "Glosson: U.S. Gulf War Shortfalls Linger," 59.

48. Dr. Samuel Lewis, "Reconnaissance: Fighting on the Upper Seine River, August 1944," in *Combined Arms in Battle Since 1939*, ed. Roger J. Spiller (Fort Leavenworth, Kans.: U.S. Army Command and General Staff College, 1992), 213, 214, and 219.

49. David A. Fulghum, "Rough Balkan Terrain Forces Change in Joint STARS' Tactics," *Aviation Week & Space Technology*, p. 67.

50. Scott W. Conrad, "Moving the Force: Desert Storm and Beyond," *McNair Paper 32* (Washington, D.C.: National Defense University Press, 1993), 54.

51. Richard L. Kugler, *U.S. West European Cooperation in Out-of-Area Military Operations: Problems and Prospects* (Santa Monica, Calif.: RAND National Defense Research Institute, 1994), 121, 130–131.

52. Craig Whitney, "Chirac Reaps Glory, and Grumbling, on French Defense Cutbacks," *New York Times*, 24 February 1996, p. 3. Also, see comments concerning plans for reorganization of the NATO armies in *The Military Balance* (London: Brassey's, 1993–94), 34–35.

5

Fighting with the Information Age Army in the Year 2003

While exact totals are unknown, the services spend billions of dollars each year on simulation programs, initiatives, and demonstrations. Most of these activities are enormously helpful to defense planners. Yet, many civilian and military leaders are increasingly skeptical of the way in which many high-technology weapons are modeled and simulated. While serving as Commandant of the Marine Corps, General Carl Mundy warned against what he called the "Spielberg effect," in which the impact of simulation overwhelms and frequently misrepresents the genuine capabilities and limitations of new technology.[1] Experienced military leaders know that although simulations can greatly improve the military's understanding of what weapon systems may or may not work in the future, the most realistic computer simulation cannot replace actual fieldwork with ground troops and aircrews. This is because all computer simulations are by their very nature only mathematical approximations of wartime reality. Notwithstanding these limitations, the Department of Defense has implemented the Joint Warfare System (JWARS) initiative, which will consolidate all OSD, service, and Joint Staff analytical efforts under one theater-level modeling architecture.[2]

With very few exceptions, however, most of the current models and simulations are very limited in that they were originally designed to measure tank versus tank or aircraft versus aircraft engagements.[3] Consequently, the more esoteric, but equally important contributions of tactical and strategic intelligence, communications, information warfare, manned reconnaissance, and ground force maneuver are seldom adequately considered.[4] For similar reasons, the prosecution of modern land warfare with both new precision strike capabilities and tactically and strategically mobile ground forces demands significant change in the way quantitative models are used to simulate warfare. Of course, this is easier said than done. The capacities and complexities of modern ground forces are much more difficult to quantify than the presumed effects and accuracy of precision guided munitions and missiles.[5] Therefore, because their combat power derives from their maneuverability through enhanced battlespace awareness and the speed at which they can strike, information age ground forces like the ones described in the preceding chapter are devalued in virtually all current models and simulations.[6]

The primary focus of the scenario outlined in this chapter is the value of landpower in the context of joint warfighting. It is designed to be a tool for exploration, not an answer machine.[7] The rendering is not perfect. A fully joint appraisal would address the entire range of activities across the services and unified commands that must also be tracked and understood to appreciate the impact of modern space-based and sea-based intelligence, surveillance, and reconnaissance capabilities on the conduct of land warfare. However, the goal of this chapter is more modest. It is to begin to develop a concept for the potential employment of information age ground forces that will enhance the reader's understanding of landpower's contribution to joint operations in a new strategic environment in which dangerous and cunning enemies armed with information age technology can achieve surprising and often unanticipated outcomes in future conflict. War, in common with sport, has the characteristic that what worked well yesterday may not work well tomorrow, precisely because it worked yesterday. "History shows that the making of false assumptions about the enemy is a perennial problem."[8]

BACKGROUND

- It is the year 2003. Israel, Syria, and the United States have signed peace accords resulting in the placement of an Army Heavy Combat Group in the Golan Heights to demilitarize the area. This ends the Israeli–Syrian conflict, but the agreement also prevents both states from directly participating in any conflict between the United States and other regional actors. This does not prevent Israel from linking the sensors in its own antimissile defense system with deploying U.S. systems.[9]

- After sanctions against Iraq are lifted in late 1997, Iran and Iraq negotiate a secret Nonaggression Pact obligating both parties to cooperate militarily against the United States and its allies in the event of conflict. The two countries begin work on establishing a secure C4I network in the region. In the 3 years following the lifting of sanctions, Iraq's leader, Saddam Hussein, resolves the internal dispute with the Shi'a Arab population in the south and reestablishes control in the north. Under pressure from the Turkish military, the Kurds are forced to submit to Iraqi governmental control.

- Once sanctions are lifted, infusions of Russian, Chinese, and North Korean military aid assist Iraq in recovering most of its former military capability along with improved air defenses and modern theater ballistic missiles.[10] Iraq adds T-80s and MIG 29s to its inventory. With the help of private sector firms in Japan and Western Europe, modern cruise missile and air defense technology finds its way to Iran and Iraq.[11]

- Alarmed by the steady buildup of Iraqi and Iranian military strength, Kuwait and the United States decide in 1997 to station an Army Heavy Recon-Strike Group in Kuwait[12] to assist in the training of Kuwaiti and allied GCC (Gulf Cooperation Council) forces as well as to deter Iraqi or Iranian aggressive action in the region.

- Disappointed with its inability to gain membership in the European Economic Community (EC) in 1998, Turkey decides to renegotiate the terms of its membership in NATO and to opt for temporary neutrality until its demand for entry into the EC is met. A short war with Greece in 1999 adds to Turkey's problems in Europe and the United States. NATO pressure on Turkey to withdraw its victorious forces from Athens poisons Turkey's relations with the West. In its neutral status, Turkey becomes an overland conduit for the transport and sale of Iraqi oil to the world market.[13] In the same year, Bahrain's government is overthrown and replaced by a pro-Iranian Islamic revolutionary regime.

- Turkey's unwillingness to continue its participation in the NATO Alliance is balanced by the entry of the Polish, Hungarian, Czech, and Slovak republics into NATO in January 2000. On the one hand, this strengthens America's position in Europe and America's military alliance with Germany. On the other, Russia drops out of the partnership for peace program and seizes the opportunity to distance itself further from the United States and Western Europe.[14]

- In the fall of 2002, opposition to Saudi family rule becomes open revolt. Arabia's Eastern Shi'a province is paralyzed by discontent while religious opposition to the Saudi family in Mecca and Medina prevents the Saudi National Guard from protecting the regime.[15] At Saudi insistence, all U.S. military personnel are withdrawn from Saudi Arabia. Fearing internal unrest on the Arabian model, the remaining Gulf States decline to grant U.S. military access until there is irrefutable evidence for Iranian or Iraqi aggression.

- With assured access to world oil markets through Turkey and Russia, Iranian and Iraqi leaders meet in October 2002 to plan a joint attack to seize control of the oil fields on the Arabian peninsula.

- Events in the Arabian Peninsula and rumored Iraqi cooperation with its old enemy Iran prompt the government of Kuwait in December 2002 to ask for a cautionary deployment of U.S. ground and air forces to deter an Iraqi attack, despite Iranian and Iraqi warnings that American attempts to reinforce Kuwait will result in "catastrophic conseqences for Kuwait and the United States." The United States responds by deploying (1) III Corps Close Battle Command Post and an Army Heavy Combat Group that draws equipment from the Army's prepositioned set in Kuwait; (2) U.S. Air Forces consisting of three Wings with AWACS aircraft, fighters, bombers, tankers, and support elements to airfields in Egypt, Spain, and Italy[16]; (3) an Army Theater Air Defense Group to Egypt; and (4) three Carrier Battlegroups (CVBG) and a Marine Expeditionary Force (MEF) to the Indian Ocean. These deployments begin on 1 January 2003.

- Presidential Selective Reserve Call-Up is announced on 4 January. U.S. Military Airlift and fast sealift procurement programs as outlined in the latest *Mobility Requirements Study Bottom-Up Review Update*, 28 March 1995, sections I–IV, are executed on schedule.[17]

The Iraq–Iran Plan of Attack

Encouraged by events in the Arabian peninsula, Iranian and Iraqi leaders conclude that it is time to attack to seize the oil fields on the Arabian Peninsula and to strike back decisively against the West. When Iraqi and Iranian military leaders meet in early October 2002 to plan their offensive to capture the Arabian Peninsula, their thinking is dominated by the Gulf War experience. This thinking underpins a plan of attack that is focused in its early phases on the American military's traditional centers of gravity— ports, airfields, fuel, water, and prepositioned equipment sites.

Before the detailed planning begins, the Iraqi and Iranian military representatives agree to a set of guiding operational principles: First, Iraq will focus its military effort on the area north of Bahrain to include Kuwait, northern Saudi Arabia, and Jordan. Second, Iran will focus its military effort on the area from Bahrain to Muscat with the object of denying U.S. forces access from the sea to the Persian Gulf region. Third, how and when Mecca and Medina will be seized and occupied will be determined after the eastern half of the Arabian Peninsula is firmly in Iraqi and Iranian hands. This geographic focus eventually produces a three phase plan for Iranian and Iraqi forces. Fourth, Iraqi and Iranian military leaders agree that weapons of mass destruction should not be employed against Muslim population centers. Ports and airfields that lie in close proximity to Muslim populations must be attacked in other ways. However, all weapons can be used against ships at sea.

In phase I, Iran deploys its MIG 29 fighters, new tactical ballistic missiles (TBM) and ground-launched cruise missile (GLCM) batteries to key points along the Persian Gulf coast from which strikes can be launched against ships within 100 miles of the Iranian coastline and against targets in the Emirates.[18] When these forces are in place, Iranian amphibious and air-mobile forces concentrate at five points along the coast inside the Gulf to prevent alerting U.S. strategic intelligence to their activities while Iranian diesel submarines position themselves inside the Gulf near the entrance to the Straits of Hormuz. Iranian ground forces to include 500 T-72 tanks disperse to three general areas which are defended by recently modernized Iranian air defense forces. These points include Tehran, two areas just inside Iran near Ahvaz and Bushehr, and Bandare Abbas in the southwestern region of the country. At the same time, Iran and Iraq divide their ballistic missile forces into mobile and fixed launchers, both heavily protected and dispersed. Mobile units are given additional protection by elite special forces units. Iraq deploys its TBM forces to the northwestern corner of Iraq near Rutbah and Tikrit. Iran concentrates its TBM and cruise missile forces in the southern portion of the country. Iraqi ground forces do not move from their planned exercise locations near Karbala and An Nasiriyah until the disposition of both Iranian and Iraqi TBM and ground-launched cruise missile forces is completed.

In phase II, Iran quietly begins to seed the Straits of Hormuz with approximately 500 sea mines from its islands and ships near the Straits.[19] When the first 500 mines have been launched, Iraqi ground forces move into their attack positions south of the Euphrates River and prepare to launch a surprise attack to seize Kuwait City, King Khalid Military City, and the Saudi ports and airfields on the Gulf Coast—Al Jabayel and Dahran. Iranian naval infantry and special forces prepare to seize the remaining ports and cities of the Gulf Emirates which lie inside the area defined by the Persian Gulf. Oman is initially excluded from this action in the hope that it can be persuaded to remain neutral and deny American access to Omani ports and airfields. The same condition applies to Jordan (Syria, Turkey, and Pakistan have already assured Tehran and Baghdad that they will not interfere in any fight Iran has with the United States and the Emirates).

Phase III begins with the launching of TBM and GLCM strikes to disable harbors, airfields, and American prepositioned equipment sites. Having weaponized a limited number of warheads for chemical munitions, the Iraqis want to use these early against targets on the peninsula to establish the credibility of this threat for American and allied forces. Simultaneously, Iranian and Iraqi forces attack on the ground and across the Gulf to seize the objectives mentioned earlier. After much discussion, the senior military leaders of both states agree to 13 January 2003 as the earliest date for execution. The Iranians make no mention of the fact that they have a limited number of low-yield nuclear warheads for their TBMs and cruise missiles.

Before the Iraqi and the Iranian National Defense Councils agree to the proposed plan and date for the operation, questions arise concerning Jordan's possible role as a bridgehead for U.S. and allied military action. The Iraqis acknowledge this as a possibility but argue that the offensive through Kuwait can be executed quickly enough to make a later American offensive from Jordan irrelevant. They also point out that King Hussein of Jordan is in ill health and that several Palestinian organizations will cooperate in the effort to subvert Jordan's internal order if King Hussein grants the United States access to his country. The Iraqis are also quick to remind the Iranians of the importance of keeping Oman out of the conflict. If Oman decides to provide access to the Americans, Iran's hold on the Straits becomes tenuous. There is also much discussion about the incomplete C3I networks in both states. However, with Arabia in chaos and American access to the Gulf Ports and prepositioned equipment sets denied, both parties are confident of success.

The View from U.S. Central Command

Knowing the fragile nature of the Gulf States' political structures and keeping in mind the U.S. President's public commitment to the government of Kuwait that U.S. forces will fight to prevent another Iraqi occupation of the country, the Commander-in-Chief of U.S. Central Command (CINC-CENT) sets aside plans for the defense of Saudi Arabia and Kuwait that presuppose U.S. access to airfields and harbors on the Saudi Arabian Peninsula. Although nothing in the U.S. intelligence summaries as of 1 January points to a massing of Iraqi or Iranian ground combat forces near Kuwait, the deployment of the two countries' TBM and GLCM batteries to points along the Euphrates and the Iranian coastline near the Straits of

Hormuz convinces him that some form of armed action is imminent. When he receives reports of a mine sinking an oil tanker in the Straits of Hormuz on 3 January, CINCCENT asks CJCS for assistance in establishing a U.S. military bridgehead in Jordan. In the meantime, he reads with special interest the U.S. intelligence community's appreciation of the Iraqi enemy:

> The Iraqi command should not be expected to take rapid advantage of a favorable situation or to carry out any maneuver with speed or precision. The movement of Iraqi ground forces is extremely slow and there are long delays in the issue, transmission and execution of orders. When fighting the Iraqis, U.S. Forces may attempt maneuvers which would be impermissible against a European or North Korean opponent.[20]

Reassuring words, but CINCCENT knows that this conflict will not begin as it did in Desert Storm. This time, the war will begin with the engagement of stand-off weapon systems as sensors come into range. Because the ensuing conflict will be a fluid one in which electrooptical countermeasures and antisensor weapons will fight for information dominance as the United States–led coalition and its opponents attempt to dominate greatly expanded battlespace by maneuvering for a decisive positional advantage, providing early theater ballistic missile defense of critical air and sea ports of entry will be critical. The fact that the Iraqi and the Iranian TBMs are already targeted creates an initial advantage for the force that initiates the conflict which CINCCENT cannot easily offset. At the same time, decisive American action to gain the initiative in this war will not be a deliberate attack to penetrate linear defenses, but the establishment of a robust American C4I structure in the region that can orchestrate a sudden, rapid, paralyzing blow to blind and unhinge the opponent while attacking friendly forces are protected from the enemy's attempt to strike a similar blow. These thoughts prompt CINCCENT to take the following actions on 4 January:

He informs CJCS of his intent to launch immediate *offensive* operations against Iraq and Iran from Jordan and the Indian Ocean in the event of hostilities. He recommends to CJCS that U.S. forces in Kuwait prepare to fight to retain Kuwait. In CINCCENT's view, successful defeat of a short-warning Iraqi and/or Iranian attack depends on offensive action by U.S. forces in Kuwait and throughout the region. CINCCENT argues that Kuwait City must be retained for the same strategic purpose for which Tobruk was defended by the British in 1941 (see Figure 5.1). Whatever gains Iraq and Iran make in the Gulf, they will be unable to consolidate these gains as long as Kuwait City and its surrounding area threaten Iraqi and Iranian forces on

Figure 5.1
Operation Crusader

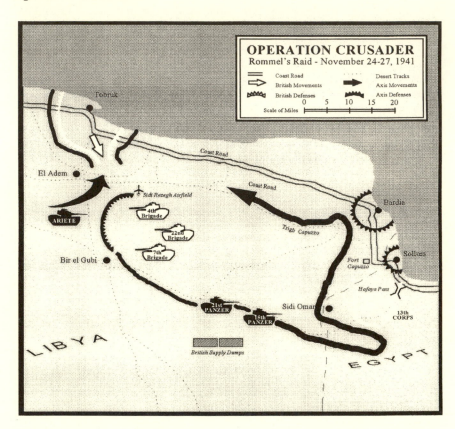

Despite British numerical superiority in the North African theater, German and Italian
   forces under the command of Colonel General Erwin Rommel launched an offensive
   in April 1941 that drove British forces 800 miles from Benghazi in Western Libya to
   Sollum along the Egyptian frontier. In the course of the retreat, the British
   Commander, General Wavell, decided to fight to retain the port of Tobruk with 20,000
   British and Austrialian troops. Wavell's decision to establish "fortress Tobruk"—
   certainly a gamble—was eventually to rescue Egypt from Axis occupation and turn
   the tide of battle. While Rommel's forces were strong enough to out-fight the larger
   British Army in the desert, they were incapable of coping with 20,000 British troops
   in Tobruk that could be supplied and supported from the air and the sea without
   significant Axis interference. The siege of Tobruk dragged on for eight months until
   the winter of 1941. But the British decision to retain control of Tobruk diverted Axis
   military strength from a decisive Axis attack that would have placed the Suez Canal
   in German hands.

the peninsula. An Iraqi–Iranian offensive which does not result in the capture of Kuwait City will fail as assuredly as the German–Italian offensive to take Egypt did in 1941. Reflecting on this experience, CINCCENT reasons that the combined offensive efforts of U.S. Ground Forces already in Kuwait along with the double envelopment of the peninsula through the attacks of two JTFs—one from Jordan and the other from the Indian Ocean—will have the same effect on Iraqi and Iranian operations in the Gulf region. Knowing that this will involve the deployment of two Joint Task Forces to two separate areas within the same theater, he adds the following requests to his message:

- That CJCS approve the immediate deployment of a Light Recon-Strike Group to Jordan with the object of cooperating with Jordanian forces to secure Jordan's border with Iraq, and that the III Corps Deep and Rear Battle Command Posts be included early in the deployment to Jordan.

- That CJCS move the Army Preposition Afloat (AWR3) in its entirety under U.S. Navy escort through the Red Sea, from which it can ultimately disembark its equipment in Aqaba, Jordan.

- That CJCS release the Airborne-Air Assault Group stationed in Italy for immediate self-deployment to Jordan.

- That the 1st MEF be designated JTF South and begin preparing operations to open the Straits of Hormuz with the objective of breaking through to Kuwait City from the sea.

- That the III U.S. Corps Commander be designated to command JTF North.

- That the Army's JFLCC deploy immediately to Egypt, from which it will move forward to command and control JTF North and JTF South. CINCCENT will retain overall command within the theater, but CINCCENT concludes that the JFLCC will add greater depth to the command and control of the two Joint Task Forces. Until JTF South begins operations to come ashore, the JFLCC will concern itself only with the Ground Component of JTF North.

- That the Army National Guard elements in the Strategic Reserve Corps be mobilized for deployment.[21]

- That Commander, U.S. Ninth Air Force, the Joint Force Air Component Commander, develop a plan for deep strike operations from CONUS, Egypt, Jordan, and sea-based platforms to achieve the strategic objective of isolating any attacking Iraqi and/or Iranian forces south of the Euphrates and on the western side of the Persian Gulf from their C4I and sustainment systems. CINCCENT suggests strategic objectives with the following priority: (1) Destroy/neutralize Iraqi/Iranian TBM and GLCM capability; (2) destroy/disrupt Iraqi/Iranian C4I; (3) destroy/neutralize Iraqi/Iranian air forces; (4) provide air support to the U.S. and allied forces defending Kuwait City. Although CINCCENT notes that all of JTF North's deep strike assets will be considered in the context of planning these deep operations, he directs the JFACC to allocate a portion of his fighters to JTF North in support of the forces defending Kuwait City.

The JFACC is irritated by the proposal to provide any close air support in the first phase of the campaign, preferring to allocate all assets to strategic strike. Centralized control of air assets is a basic tenet of air campaign planning.[22] He argues that deep strikes against targets of strategic military importance should take precedence and urges CINCCENT to request that (five) more Air Force wings deploy to join the air forces already in the theater no later than 16 January. The JFACC indicates that with these additional resources, he can comply with the CINC's directive. The CINC grudgingly agrees.

On 6 January after several days of consultation with the Secretary of State and the President, the Jordanian Ambassador in Washington, D.C., finally communicates Jordan's agreement to the U.S. proposal and U.S. Army and Air Force deployments to Jordan begin immediately. Jordan also closes its border with Saudi Arabia to prevent terrorist groups from entering the country. Careful not to force Iraq's hand sooner than desired, CINC-CENT presses for the rapid deployment of the APA from the Indian Ocean to the Red Sea and the Airborne-Air Assault Group from Italy to Jordan. By 9 January, the airlift to move the light Recon-Strike Group into Jordan is complete and the Group is moving to the Iraqi border.

On the same day, the APA arrives in Aqaba, Jordan, from Diego Garcia. The APA ships return to sea after disembarking (two) Heavy Combat Groups, (two) JTF Support Groups, and 30 days' supplies.[23] The trip through the Red Sea, however, is not without incident. Two Russian-built diesel submarines operating presumably from bases on the Sudanese coast launch torpedoes that sink one commercial container ship and damage a U.S. Aegis-class cruiser. Fortunately, the CVBG is shadowing the movement of the APA and is able to destroy one submarine before it can escape to Sudanese waters.[24] Whether these are Iranian submarines that somehow managed to evade detection or Sudanese forces is unknown. Afterward, the APA heads through the Suez Canal for Italy, where the ships load equipment for (two) more Heavy Combat Groups and additional supplies on 12 and 13 January before beginning the return trip to Jordan on 14 January. The airlift continues in the effort to move an Aviation Strike Group (4 AH64 Bns) from the United States to Jordan.

However, only 60 percent of the U.S. Army's theater missile defense forces in Egypt and Jordan are operational on 10 January with the result that Amman remains unprotected from Iraqi missile strikes until 15 January, when 100 percent of the theater missile defense systems will be operational. In response, CINCCENT urges that additional Aegis-class destroyers position themselves in the Gulf of Aqaba, the Red Sea, and the Mediterranean to provide anti-TBM defense coverage until the Army's THAAD Group is fully operational. Without this coverage, the damage to port facilities in Aqaba could be severe.[25] He also asks the NCA to deploy the USAF's experimental airborne laser. Mounted in a large commercial airframe, this aircraft is designed to orbit over the region to engage tactical ballistic missiles in their boost phase. Although experimental, the CINC reasons, it may be able to augment the missile defense effort over Amman.[26]

On 9 January 2003 Saddam Hussein watches a videotape from an Iraqi UAV orbiting over Amman, Jordan, showing U.S. forces disembarking from C-17s[27] at a Jordanian air base and urges the Iranian National Defense Council to begin its offensive operations immediately. At home, Hussein begins moving Iraqi forces into attack positions on the south side of the Euphrates. Because Russian intelligence informs Iran and Iraq that U.S. Marine Amphibious Forces will not be ready for an all-out assault for at least another 10 days, the Iranians refuse to act until 13 January as originally planned. Sensitive to his need for Iranian support, Hussein abandons his effort to press Iran for an earlier attack and returns to his preparations for the 13 January offensive. The stage is now set for a new Gulf War.

CINCCENT's View from Cairo, Egypt

Although Iraq's activities are consistent with a series of Iraqi maneuver exercises conducted since the lifting of sanctions, CINCCENT is convinced that Iraq's current moves are in preparation for a real offensive. CJCS is cautious but agrees to move one of the Army's Rocket Artillery Groups from Fort Sill, Oklahoma, to Jordan. Even with TRANSCOM's improved airlift capability, however, this means that the Rocket Artillery Group will not be deployed and ready to sustain offensive operations before 17 January.

On 13 January, CINCCENT awakes in Cairo at 5:00 A.M. (local time) to a message from the JTF North Commander in the Jordanian desert which reports that all U.S. prepositioned equipment sites in the Gulf region have been hit with fifty-three theaterwide TBM strikes. The accuracy of the strikes suggests that the enemy has access to a commercial global positioning system. Fortunately, the U.S. site in Kuwait was already empty and there

were very few U.S. and Kuwaiti casualties. However, the Kuwait City and
Amman, Jordan, airports along with all major Saudi Arabian and Emirate
airfields, were hit by a mix of TBM warheads containing conventional high
explosives and toxic agents of an unknown type.[28] Worse still, rebellious
Arabian troops in eastern Arabia have closed the border with Kuwait. As a
result, Kuwait's population has no alternative but to stay in Kuwait City.

Though there are no reports of Iranian air-mobile assaults on the Emirates
or of Iraqi invasion of Kuwait, satellite photos provide evidence for the
westward movement of these forces. In the same message traffic, CINC-
CENT receives authorization from the President to begin combat operations
against both Iran and Iraq. The objective of these operations, states the
President, is the destruction of Iraqi and Iranian weapons of mass destruction, the destruction of attacking enemy ground and air forces, and the
restoration of "legitimate government and stability" in the Gulf region.
CINCCENT is further authorized to employ all military means short of use
of nuclear weapons.

14 January: CINCCENT Counterattacks

Reading the reports of the damage inflicted on the airfield facilities in
Amman during the early morning hours of the 13 January, CINCCENT
realizes how vulnerable his ports, airfields, and logistics will be if he cannot
reduce their exposure to enemy surveillance and weapons of mass destruction. He directs the JFACC to begin operations against Iraq immediately.
Since the Rocket Artillery Group will not be operational for another 3 days
and Iraqi ground forces in northern Iraq are far weaker than in the south,
the JTF North Commander suggests that by positioning his forces in Jordan
closer to the Iraqi border, the three MLRS batteries in these Groups can add
their firepower to the joint suppression of air defense. At the same time, he
urges the JFACC to employ his stocks of sensor-fused munitions against
the Iraqi forces attacking Kuwait. The JFACC agrees, and the first phase of
the air campaign begins with B-2 bombers carrying 32 tons of sensor-fused
munitions toward southern Iraq.

Keeping in mind CINCCENT's initial guidelines for the development of
the air campaign, the JFACC launches the first strikes shortly after dark on
13 January. However, the air strikes on suspected air defense sites in and
around Baghdad, Basra, Ahvaz, Bandere Abbas, and Tehran, along with
other suspected key command, control, communications, and transportation
nodes, result in an unexpected development. When the initial strike packages are sent in, it is assumed that the vast numbers of American surveillance

and airborne warning systems will detect the phased array radars and assist the fighters in destroying them. More important, the U.S. airborne jamming capabilities are thought to be so overwhelming that a C5A could fly through the Iraqi and Iranian air defenses without being detected. This, however, does not happen.

First, the EAC2 aircraft are lost. Then thirty-one more aircraft to include F-15Es and F-16s are mysteriously lost to enemy air defense missiles including Russian SA-10s.[29] A similar experience is repeated in the Straits, where forty-three Navy F/A-18s are lost. In response to these losses, the JFACC suspends further attacks until he can employ the 590 Tomahawk missiles (TLAMs) in theater to destroy every possible radar and air defense site in and around Basra, Baghdad, and the Straits.[30] In the meantime, he diverts fighters to attack Iraqi troop concentrations in the southern Iraqi desert. Attacks with inertially guided sensor-fused munitions are conducted by B-2 bombers from 50,000 feet, but the effects on the widely dispersed Iraqi combat formations are difficult to assess. It appears that these attacks slow the pace of attacking Iraqi ground forces and drive them further into the open desert, where dispersion offers protection. When Iraqi formations are found in assembly areas or in column along roads, sensor-fused munitions turn out to be much more effective than when they are dropped on already dispersed combat elements.[31]

When asked by CINCCENT whether low-level fighter attacks could be coordinated with Army rotary wing aviation assets in Kuwait, the JFACC agrees, but warns that the tactical air defense threat has also increased with the presence on the battlefield of an improved version of the SA-16—a Russian Stinger equivalent. He notes the recent AH64 losses in an attack helicopter deep operation to destroy reserve Iraqi artillery and armor concentrations 50 miles east of Rutbah.[32] CINCCENT listens but is still unsure whether the expenditure of three hundred TLAMs against "possible" air defense sites is the best answer to the air defense threat. He takes the JFACC and flies to a site near Amman, Jordan, for a meeting with the Joint Forces Land Component Commander on 15 January.

At the meeting, the JFACC explains that the real threat of the Iraqi and Iranian electronic long-range detection threat of this new integrated air defense system is a passive receiver. The JFACC informs CINCCENT that this is a huge problem because U.S. aircraft have no way of knowing whether they are being tracked passively. Worse, recent experience with F-117 attacks on Baghdad and Tehran indicates that the enemy definitely has stealth tracking technology. Although this makes little difference to the B-2s, which operate at altitudes of 50,000 feet, enemy air defense systems can apparently track and engage F-117s at altitudes of 20,000 to 30,000 feet.[33] CINCCENT is furious. Dominant battlespace knowledge has turned out to be an illusion!

In addition, the passive detection sites do not radiate at all, making it extremely difficult to identify or locate them! In fact, any attempt to jam or destroy these sites when U.S. fighters find them may be exactly what the passive array needs to locate and identify those fighters.[34] U.S. and allied fighter pilots have already discovered that the jamming tactics used against the traditional phased array radars are practically suicidal. The fighter pilots who survived are being paraded before the media in Baghdad. In view of these events, the JFLCC concludes that the air offensive will have to wait for the coordinated actions of the Rocket Artillery Group (four MLRS/ATACM battalions), Army Special Forces units, and Airborne-Air Assault Group to neutralize or destroy Iraqi air defenses west of the Euphrates before the air offensive continues. He points out that Marine forces will have to execute similar operations from the sea to liberate sea-based aviation from the same threat in the Straits of Hormuz.

Watching these events unfold on 13 and 14 January from his Deep Battle CP in Jordan, the JTF North Commander also learns of an Iraqi Air Force fighter attack on U.S. troops near Amman. Although all twenty-five Iraqi fighters are destroyed by U.S. fighters and Army air defense assets, this is a sobering experience that leads him to consider a different course of action to support the JFACC.[35] First, the JTF North Commander recommends converting the defensive screen of the Light Recon-Strike Group along Jordan's border with Iraq into a limited offensive operation to penetrate into northern Iraq. With the southern flank protected by friendly Jordanian troops, he reasons that by advancing quickly on multiple axes to destroy the linear in-depth disposition of Iraqi ground forces, he can offset the temporary numerical disadvantage and accelerate the destruction of Iraqi TBM sites west of the Euphrates River. Iraqi forces in the area have no more than 500 tanks. And most of these are in static defensive positions (see Figure 5.2).

Using sophisticated Air Force attack operations together with a battalion of Rangers and the Army's Special Operations Aviation Regiment, the JTF North Commander is confident of finding and destroying the TBMs, as well as the outlying air defense sites. This is important because the Iraqi air defenses are also protecting the launch sites for as many as thirty TBMs a day against Amman, Aqaba, and the Suez Canal. Theater antimissile defenses have been remarkably successful, but the shield is not leakproof: Seventeen missiles have penetrated TBM defenses and reached the port of Aqaba and the Suez Canal.

In addition, the JTF North Commander argues that a limited penetration would both divert Iraqi military resources from the attack on Kuwait and

Figure 5.2
USCENTCOM Scheme of Maneuver

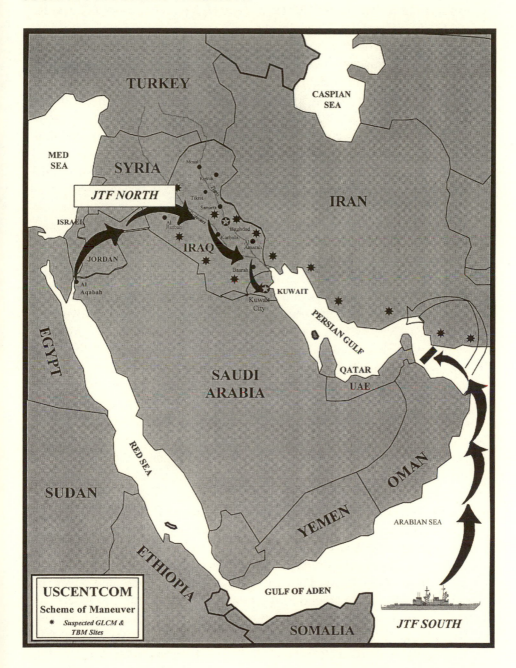

position the MLRS/ATACM batteries closer to central Iraq, where they can launch deeper attacks against Iraqi air defenses. Thanks to real-time links to surveillance satellites, JSTARS, and the UAVs at Group and JTF levels, the JTF Commander is certain that he can coordinate this operation directly with the JFACC to match the right weapon system with the right target. Because of enormous pressure from the President to reverse the apparent defeats of the first forty-eight hours, CINCCENT and the JFACC agree that this course of action should be attempted immediately. Planning gets under way at the JTF Deep Battle CP while the JTF commander goes forward to colocate with the Recon-Strike Group commander until the remaining Heavy Combat Groups arrive from Aqaba.

This decision turns out to be fortuitous. As the Recon-Strike Group moves forward on 16 January, space-based infrared systems spot Iraqi ground forces as they assemble to attack the JTF's air–ground penetrations into the country. Digitization of the battlespace in the air and on the ground allows both land-based and sea-based aircraft to focus their attention on the concentrations of Iraqi ground troops that are revealed by JSTARS, Guardrail, and other types of electronically collected intelligence while the Recon-Strike Group avoids direct contact and speeds to their rear. Before Iraqi mobile GLCM batteries can be withdrawn for protection over the Euphrates River, the batteries are discovered by combinations of UAVs and Comanche[36] teams searching in areas where Army Special Operations Forces report launches have taken place. Although some of these batteries are dummy formations, most are not. After the Rangers and attack helicopters from the Recon-Strike Group destroy the surrounding air defense assets, the GLCM batteries are, in turn, destroyed by ATACM strikes or precision guided missiles and munitions delivered from Air Force fighters. Elements from the Airborne-Air Assault Group augment the Rangers and the 160th Special Operations Aviation Regiment. Occasionally, when no alternative exists, RAH66–equipped Army Special Operations elements employ their own missiles to accomplish the mission.

With the arrival of two more Heavy Combat Groups from Aqaba late in the evening of 19 January, the JTF North Commander obtains permission from CINCCENT to attack on 20 January through and around the defensive positions of Iraqi forces between Rutbah and the Euphrates River. In addition to the Light Recon-Strike Group already in Iraq, he has (four) Heavy Combat Groups, (one) Aviation Strike Group (forty-five AH64s and twenty-seven RAH66s), a Rocket Artillery Group (108 MLRS/ATACM launchers), and three JTF Support Groups (JTF sustainment). Ignoring the larger concentrations of Iraqi ground forces east of Rutbah and along the main highway to Baghdad, he sends the Heavy Combat Groups in a double envelopment with instructions to reach the bridges over the Euphrates at Ar Ramadi and Karbala as soon as possible.

Having "atomized" the Iraqi forces defending Iraq's border with Jordan with the Recon-Strike Group and elements of the Airborne-Air Assault Group between 16 and 20 January, the JTF North Commander decides to establish a blocking position with his Airborne-Air Assault Forces near Karbala behind the shattered Iraqi defenders while the Heavy Combat Groups are moving forward through and around Iraqi forces. He directs the Airborne-Air Assault Group Commander to prepare his elements and the two German Paratrooper Brigades in theater for an attack during the night of 21 January. He describes this operation as an attack to penetrate to Karbala to take advantage of the confused state of the Iraqi forces. He also hopes that this will divert the Iraqi command's attention from its main attack to seize Kuwait. Knowing that his ability to conduct this air assault operation will necessitate the neutralization of Iraqi air defenses in the area, he turns again to the JFACC.

With the extended range ATACM, MLRS, and AH64 longbow attack helicopters, the JFACC is certain that the air defenses around Karbala can be obliterated. Then, he points out, the rocket artillery assets will be in range of Baghdad's air defense sites. The JTF North Commander agrees and discusses how to employ the unmanned aerial vehicles, RAH66 helicopters, and satellites systematically to establish precise locations for the passive arrays. Flying only 15 feet above ground, the RAH66s are undetectable to the passive arrays.[37] In fact, the greatest threat to the new Comanche is not a high-tech weapon at all; it is an undetected line of sight air defense gun that emits no signal. While this threat is rare, it can be deadly at close range once an air defense site is under attack. As the sites are identified, either cruise missiles from sea-based platforms and Air Force fighter-bombers or ATACM missiles can engage the targets acquired by nearby Comanche teams. Unfortunately, it will be hard to tell whether this approach is working. Until an assessment reveals the degree to which these detection systems have been neutralized or destroyed, air strikes against key command and control locations in and around Baghdad and Basra will remain hazardous. Fortunately, satellite intelligence from the area around Karbala suggests that the area is not heavily defended by these systems and that a Joint Army–Air Attack to neutralize potential air defenses around the city should be easy to arrange. Hearing this, the JTF North Commander turns over this operation to his Deep Battle Commander to plan the JSEAD operation with the JFACC and contacts his Close Battle Commander in Kuwait City.

From his Close Battle Commander, he learns that the initial Iraqi thrust into Kuwait was on the high-speed avenue of approach from Basra. Iraqi forces, however, encountered the dense air-delivered antitank minefields just north of Al Jahrah and were forced to swing northwest around Kuwait City into the open desert. Orienting their fire on the city's outlying defenses, where Iraqi unmanned aerial vehicles identified what appeared to be Kuwait's main defensive belt, they were surprised by the arrival of large numbers of American armor and attack helicopters in their rear areas and on their flanks. JTF North's Close Battle Commander indicates that some 24 hours of TBM strikes has ended, and that the Iraqi command structure—to judge by the attacks with tanks that began to build up in the early morning of 15 January—is only now finally aware that their initial thrust south from Basra failed (Figures 5.3 and 5.4).

Although Iraqi air defenses succeeded in protecting the attacking Iraqi armor and TBM sites during the initial phase of the operation, deep strikes through the holes in Iraqi air defenses created by advancing ground forces in northern and central Iraq to disrupt and confuse the Iraqi command structure are now beginning to show some effect. Only one RAH66, eleven AH 64s, fifteen M1A1s, nineteen M3A2s, and seventeen LAVs and AGSs have been lost to enemy fire. In the case of the tanks, it appears that Iraqi Gazelle helicopters armed with improved HOTH antitank missiles were able to launch their missiles against the M1A1s before U.S. attack helicopters destroyed them.[38]

The battle in Kuwait and southern Iraq, the Close Combat CP reports, is now assuming a new confusing pattern. American air–ground combat teams are seeking elbow room for maneuver in the daylight, while RAH66s, AH64s, U.S.AF fighters, and MLRS batteries strike Iraqi TBM and C4I sites at night. With the fire-controlled, radar-equipped RAH 66, targets that frequently escape detection by J-STARS and UAVs are acquired and categorized quickly. Through the digital interface with the Rocket Artillery Group and the Air Force, target hand-offs and dissemination occur almost instantaneously.[39] In the vicinity of An Nasiriyah, a team of two RAH66s knock out most of an Iraqi artillery brigade and logistics unit with ATACMs from the MLRS battery in the Recon-Strike Group. Farther north on the outskirts of Basra, a deep special operations team with improved data modems (IDMs)[40] designates what turns out to be a TBM storage site for attacks by fighters that now roam the skies south of the Euphrates River virtually at will. The Iraqi command structure responds in the only way he can—by attempting to wear down the defenders in Kuwait City with rocket and TBM strikes while committing his remaining armored forces south of

Figure 5.3
Iranian Plan of Action

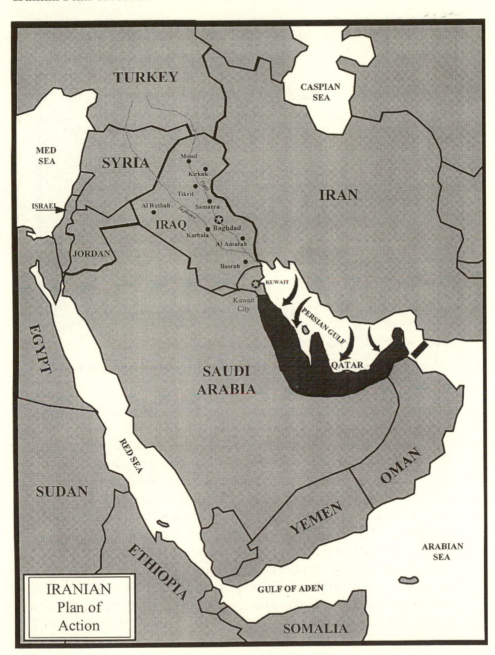

IRANIAN
Plan of
Action

Figure 5.4
Battle for Kuwait City

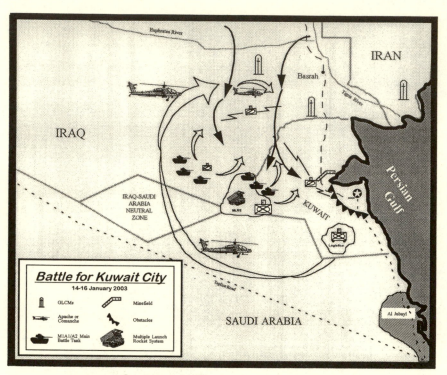

the Euphrates for an end-run around U.S. forces in the open desert of southwestern Iraq and Kuwait.

This last attempt to drive the defenders of Kuwait City from their positions succeeds only in revealing to space-based sensors the general locations of Iraq's last remaining TBM launchers. When RAH66 teams arrive to find and fix the batteries, the JFACC is quick to respond with a rain of precision-guided munitions on the launchers. As the missile and rocket fire slackens on 17, 18, and 19 January, the Close Battle Commander informs the JTF North Commander that Kuwait's crisis has passed.

With the Heavy Combat Groups ready to attack and most of the JTF Support and Rocket Artillery Groups in place, the JTF Commander begins moving all of his forces west toward the Euphrates. Watching the Combat Groups pick their way through Iraqi defenses and minefields that did not show up on JSTARs, the Aviation Strike Group Commander hears request after request to the JFACC for close air support go unanswered. Because of the close nature of the fighting and the concern for the safety of friendly ground troops, the JFACC is directing air strikes from sea-based and land-based platforms well beyond the fire support coordination line (FSCL).[41] As a longtime air cavalry pilot, the Aviation Strike Group Commander knows that an aircraft must be within a 5,000 to 8,000 meter slant range in order to determine whether a carefully camouflaged armored vehicle is a tank, a dismounted crew-served weapon, or simply a dummy position. Recognizing which elements are friendly and which are enemy is even tougher during rapid advances because friendly and enemy armored forces are intermingled. Further, the same air defense threat that limits Air Force fighters is preventing the Aviation Strike Group from executing the continuous attacks against deep Iraqi reserve troop concentrations for which the Group has trained. This prompts him to adopt a new approach to close air support.

The Aviation Strike Group Commander begins rotating AH64 companies forward to the attacking Heavy Combat Groups. He concludes that with four AH64 battalions, he can easily commit two battalions to the close fight while keeping two more in reserve for possible deep operations at night. Kiowa Warrior teams organized with the Recon Squadrons of the Combat Groups assume operational control of the companies and help position the arriving AH64 companies so that they can direct their fire from behind the line of advancing friendly troops against enemy targets that cannot be attacked by either high-flying, fast moving jet fighters or ground combat troops.[42] This informal arrangement permits AH64 companies from the Aviation Strike Group to work directly with the commanders on the ground, and under this decentralized operation, the Strike Group Commander achieves a response time to calls for close air support of less than 15 minutes.[43] When the AH64s arrive on station, combat identification systems and common digitization of the battlespace facilitate the situational awareness that prevents fratricide. Comanches quickly update the AH64 companies on the progress of the battle and the location of the forward line of troops. As the battle develops, these air–ground combat teams also capture or destroy Iraqi air defense sites that confirm the JFACC's assessment that a nationwide integrated passive array is responsible for downing dozens of U.S. fighters.

For almost 30 hours, the Airborne-Air Assault Group maintains control of the main route over the Euphrates to Baghdad, forcing the retreating Iraqi forces to cross points further south. At the same time, the 7,000 U.S. and German troops in Karbala have acted as a magnet for Iraqi forces from Baghdad with the result that U.S. attack helicopters and fighters have had a field day attacking the Iraqi troop concentrations as they move out from under the protection of Baghdad's still robust air defenses.

But now the JTF Commander wants to regain contact with these troops on the ground. He also wants to ensure that the Heavy Recon-Strike Group in Kuwait does not pause. He directs the JTF CP in Kuwait City to move the Heavy Recon-Strike Group to points along the river where the Iraqis are attempting to cross. The Close Combat Commander objects to this on the grounds that the troops are exhausted. CINCCENT who is tied into the discussion thanks to a real-time C4I structure intervenes to insist that the Recon-Strike Group attack regardless of its condition. He explains that U.S. forces must win a decisive battlefield victory in the eyes of the world to prevent other regional actors like Turkey or Syria from being tempted by earlier U.S. losses to intervene on the side of Iraq and Iran. This would also compel Israel to fight in a widening regional conflict.

When the forward security outposts of the Airborne-Air Assault Group Recon Squadron make physical contact on the ground with the RAH66 pilots of the Light Recon-Strike Group for the first time in 48 hours, the JTF commander is relieved. The task now, he believes, is to establish contact in the air and on the ground between his remaining Combat Groups in Kuwait and north central Iraq. He decides to attack Baghdad directly with the Airborne-Air Assault Group, the Light Recon-Strike Group, and four Heavy Combat Groups. With the failure of Iraqi forces to capture Kuwait City, the U.S. forces in Kuwait can regain control of the oil fields and parry any unlikely Iraqi counterattacks from Basra. In the meantime, the arrival of French troops in Jordan and the Sinai ensures that the long lines of communication from Aqaba and Egypt will not be threatened by growing unrest in Egypt or terrorist attacks from Saudi Arabia. The Egyptian unrest is a by-product of radical religious elements, who, encouraged by the TBM strikes along the Suez Canal, demand the removal of all U.S. and allied aircraft from Egypt. Though the Iraqi and Iranian TBMs cannot reach targets in Central Egypt, the Egyptian government is still concerned about missile strikes on the Aswan Dam and willingly tightens security around U.S. antimissile defense sites and air bases.

Encouraged by the rapid advance of JTF North, the JFLCC asks CINC-CENT to reinforce this success with another Airborne-Air Assault Group and the one remaining Light Recon-Strike Group from the Pacific. JTF North's Commander recommends that these elements fly directly into Samarra, where the air defenses are destroyed and a local airstrip is still in good shape. The JFLCC asks CINCCENT for the use of the Rangers and the Special Operations Aviation Regiment[44] for the task of seizing the airstrip from the Iraqi troops in the area. He plans to follow up their assault with the insertion of the second Airborne-Air Assault Group and the second Light Recon-Strike

Group. This will cut off Baghdad from the north and force the Iraqis either to fight for Baghdad or to retreat to Iranian territory. After a sudden, short attack by Air Force fighters on suspected and known enemy locations in the area, the Rangers will assault the airstrip during darkness. As soon as they have established control of the airstrip, C-17s will begin landing the first squadron of light armor while the Recon-Strike Group's Air Attack Squadron deploys from staging areas in Jordan to protect the landings.

The JFLCC knows that when the offensive against Baghdad begins, these air-mobile forces will have to fight their way into that part of the city where Saddam Hussein and his command structure are located. For this reason, the JFLCC begins to doubt that he has enough airborne infantry for the job. Ideally, when the U.S. and German airborne-air assault infantry close in on any political–military strongpoints, the Iraqis will be driven down into cellars or underground bunkers by the volume of fire from AGS and 155 millimeter artillery, but the JFLCC knows from experience how easily the Iraqi defenders can cut down opposing infantry in a city's streets. Detaching the hybrid artillery battalions from the four Heavy Combat Groups to provide additional reinforcing fires for the Airborne Infantry is one measure that will assist the effort. With more time, he could also mount a significant psychological operations campaign to try to reduce opposition. Unfortunately, there is little time and there is no choice. The roughly 12,000 American and German paratroopers will have to carry the brunt of the battle for the allies. Political considerations dictate a rapid termination of the conflict and this requires U.S. and allied forces to enter Baghdad before 26 January.

CINCCENT agrees with the JTF North Commander's proposal and directs the JFACC to move part of his force to Jordan, where the major airport outside Amman is no longer contaminated. From Jordan, a major joint attack to destroy Baghdad's air defenses that will culminate in the seizure of key military and political C2 centers in the city can be launched. He asks CJCS to deploy another corps/JTF headquarters—the XXVIII—to assume control of part of these elements for an attack before 25 January, to forcibly install the Iraqi government in exile in Baghdad. CJCS refuses the request and directs CINCCENT to attack no later than 25 January with the forces he has. A British Air-mobile Brigade arrives in Jordan on 22 January, brightening the picture, but CINCCENT wonders what else is happening in the world that CJCS is not sharing with him.

JTF South's Operation

On 4 January JTF South's Commander sets in motion the forces that will eventually establish U.S. and allied control of the Straits to capture the islands where Iran has established extensive antiair and antiship defenses. After 10 January, these defenses allow the Iranians to exert complete control in the air and on the sea for 150 miles in every direction from the Straits. For the Marine Expeditionary Force to accomplish its mission, these conditions must change. In pursuit of this objective, the MEF Commander's first challenge is to unite the Marine Expeditionary Brigade from California with its equipment in Diego Garcia as quickly as possible. During Desert Shield this force was flown by commercial air to Al Jubayl, where it assumed responsibility for defending the approaches to the Saudi port.[45] Although the Marines could have gone ashore at Aqaba as the Army did, the CINC's plan to envelop the region from two directions simultaneously makes this impossible. Moreover, employing the Marines ashore in the same way as the Army is, in the opinion of the President, a misuse of the Marine Corps. Thus, CINCCENT's plan entails the use of Marine Amphibious Forces to seize the two key Iranian-held islands in the Straits before attempting to seize the port of Bandera Abbas on the Iranian coast.

CINCCENT's intelligence assessment indicates that these areas are the real hub of Iranian military effort in the Straits and that clearing the Straits of mines will be impossible without gaining control of these areas.[46] The MEF Commander would prefer to go ashore in Oman and establish control of usable airfields and port facilities there, but the Sultan of Oman, like leaders of other Islamic states in the region, has declared his neutrality and refuses to cooperate with the United States and its allies. On 9 January, CINCCENT informs the MEF Commander that the government of Kenya will provide port facilities in Mombasa to the Marines. Although not ideal from the perspective of geographical proximity, it is close enough to support the link-up of the Marines with their equipment. The "full-up" Marine Expeditionary Brigade which departs for the Straits on 19 January includes twenty to twenty-five ships with a reinforced battalion landing team as its ground combat element. It looks roughly like this:[47]

14 MEB GCE (17th RLT)	*14 MEB ACE (MAG-35)*	*MEB CSSE (BSSG-14)*
(6,608 Marines)	(5,910 Marines + 500 Navy)	(3,101 Marines)
3 Infantry battalions	Amphibious Group ships of all types	6+ Support battalions
1 Field artillery Bn	V22s, heavy lift helicopters	
1 Tank co.	Stinger and Hawk air defense units	
1 LAV co.		
1 Recon co.		
1 Combat Engineer co.		

Though uneasy with CINCCENT's operational directive, the MEF Commander plunges ahead with a plan to gain control of the Straits from the Iranian armed forces. Knowing that the TBM batteries present almost no threat to his operations, he seeks to take advantage of the Marines' best warfighting technology. Predator UAVs begin immediate sweeps throughout the area to provide a real-time picture of Iranian defenses. Fighter pilots from the carriers begin flying their planned missions on "power scene." This allows them to rehearse their missions on high-resolution video equipment that utilizes the best satellite photography to recreate the enemy terrain and environment digitally. Most important, the plan calls for an over the horizon assault from the place where it is least expected: the Iranian coast. Instead of striking directly into the Straits or from the Arabian side of the Gulf, the Marines will fly into Iran, seize the islands, and eventually take Bandere Abbas from the Iranian side of the Gulf. Though this is admittedly a risky course of action, it promises the advantage of surprise. Thus, the JFLCC supports the MEF Commander's plan and CINCCENT approves.

With the news of Iran's assault across the Gulf to seize the oil fields on the lower peninsula, carrier-based air begins a series of attacks to destroy Iranian air defenses and to cripple Iranian C3I nodes. Initially, the carrier-based fighters are considered for use against deep targets in the southern Arabian peninsula and Iraq, but the JFACC is unable to support the Navy's fighters with in-flight refueling assets and maintain the tempo of land-based air strikes from Egypt and Italy. Unable to reach deep targets, the carrier-based fighters concentrated their attacks against the Iranian air and ground defenses in and around the Straits.[48] The results are similar to those of the Air Force attacks, but more severe. Possessing large numbers of SA 10 Russian air defense systems as well as radars using varied frequencies and different radar waveforms of various complexity, turning radars on and off to confuse the intelligence collection effort or to complicate targeting—all of these countermeasures result in the losses of many American aircraft and pilots over the Straits. To turn this situation around, the JFACC launches eighty Tomahawk missiles at several identified or suspected air defense and Iranian C3I sites on Abu Musa, Tunbs, Jask, and Bandar E Abbas.[49] By 21 January, this approach appears to achieve a condition of local U.S. air superiority over the Straits with the result that Navy fighters are able to launch strikes against the islands and the port of Bandere Abbas.

This development prompts the MEF Commander to schedule the Marine assault to begin "from over the horizon" before dawn on 22 January. Marines in V-22s will launch from amphibious carriers to fly inland at speeds of 400 knots around the port of Bandera Abbas to execute an air-mobile assault on the two islands from the Iranian mainland. This will avoid most of the Iranian coastal and air defenses, which will be coping with fighter attacks from two carrier battlegroups in the Indian Ocean. This also takes advantage of the V-22 range and speed to provide greater security for the eighteen Marine infantrymen in each V-22. The clandestine insertion of Navy SEAL and Marine Force Reconnaissance teams 12–18 hours before the main attack begins will provide additional intelligence to confirm UAV observations as well as to identify lightly defended landing areas and beaches. Once ashore in Iran, landing craft, air-cushions (LCACs) will be launched from amphibious carriers and other ships to reinforce the Marine position ashore. Tracked amphibious assault vehicles will follow once the coastline is secure. Because the Marines' 200 ton LCACs cannot carry more than one 70 ton M1A1 tank at a time, the majority of the Marines' M1A1 tanks will have to be ferried ashore on barges or off-loaded in the port after it is secure.

On 22 January at 0400 hours, eight V-22s carrying 144 Marines lift off from one Wasp-class LHD and one Tarawa-class LHA to begin the attack to seize the islands in the Straits. They disappear into the night and report no contact with either Iranian air defenses or aircraft. Iranian radars are off and Navy and Marine fighters over the target area report no activity in the projected landing zones. Although nothing has been heard from the SEAL teams that went ashore 12 hours ago, the absence of air defense activity and the reports of no significant enemy movement from JSTARS and the UAVs is reassuring. When the V-22s reach the landing zones on the islands of Abu Musa and Tunbs, they are able to disembark their forces without much interference. After a brief battle with Iranian infantry, the Marines gain complete control of the islands! After completing the air insertion, however, Iranian line-of-sight air defense guns destroy two of the V-22s as they pause in midair to make the transition from vertical to horizontal flight. Also Iranian rocket artillery launches several attacks on the islands from positions on the mainland. Still, the MEF Commander is elated and communicates the news of the Marines' success to CINCCENT. CINCCENT urges the MEF Commander to reinforce his success as rapidly as possible.

This elation does not last long. On 20 January, the Russians passed a note through their operatives in Tehran to Iranian military intelligence that three U.S. "carriers" were sited east of the entrance to the Persian Gulf. The Russian information includes course, heading, and last known location for the ships. As in Iraq, the redundancy offered by conventional telephone cables, coaxial cable, and fiber optics defeats American air and missile power's attempts to target critical Iranian C3I nodes effectively. Because the Iranian and Iraqi systems are really "nodeless," missiles and bombs on one particular target do not assure the destruction of the C3I system. As a result, this information reaches the Iranian Military Commander in Bandere Abbas in time to be of value. While remembering that Iran has a total inventory of only sixty-seven cruise missiles, the Iranian Commander decides that these targets are important enough to justify their use. The prize of sinking a large U.S. carrier is worth the entire inventory! Just after midnight on 22 January, eleven light trucks carrying twenty-three missiles depart for a position on the Iranian coast just 50 miles from the Marine amphibious carriers.[50] Three of these missiles are fitted with low-yield nuclear warheads (less than 5 kilotons).[51]

At 0400 hours, the trucks arrive in position, set the missiles on their launchers, and drive to a secluded location some 2 kilometers away. From a nearby ground station, an Iranian intelligence officer watches several video screens. Each screen displays an image of the Iranian coast and the seas churning in the Straits. At 0500, the Iranian officer sights several ships in the area where the Russian intelligence had indicated there were two carriers. Certain that these are his targets, he signals the cruise missile battery commander, who returns to the launch site to adjust the targeting data. Then, from the small headquarters van mounted on the back of his commercial truck, the battery commander launches all twenty-three missiles at 0555 hours in quick succession.

Thanks to the UAVs overhead, both sides are able to watch the results of the attack in real time. Three missiles fail to reach the target area, but the remaining twenty do find the ships. Although fleet antimissile defenses shoot down nine of the in-bound cruise missiles, five of these cruise missiles strike a Wasp-class LHD, an amphibious ship 844 feet in length with a mix of V22s, three LCACs, and 1,875 troops aboard. One of these missiles carries a low-yield nuclear warhead.[52] All the Marines and sailors aboard are either wounded or killed as the ship sinks in less than a minute. Fortunately, the rest of the missiles either fail to detonate or strike the Whidbey Island–class dock landing ships instead of the Tarawa-class LHA, which is nearby. A simultaneous attack by twenty-five of Iran's fifty MIG 29 fighters is defeated by thirty-four F/A-18 E/F from the Navy's two carrier battlegroups in the Indian Ocean with the loss of only two F/A-18 E/Fs.[53] A guided missile frigate moving to the aid of the stricken ship is damaged by Iranian air attack but does not sink.

Shaken, but undeterred, the MEF Commander decides to position his force 100 miles farther south in closer proximity to the CVBG in the Indian

Ocean. Of course, this places the main body of Marine Forces nearly 200 miles from their original objectives, but it places the Marine amphibious ships beyond the range of the Iranian surveillance and, ideally, the ground-launched cruise missile threat. It is at this point that the V-22 makes a critical contribution to the operation. Although intended for deep insertions of Marine forces farther inland, the V-22s with superior range and speed now move Marines at night to locations along the Iranian coast where the mobile cruise missile detachments are operating.[54] Aided by marinized UAVs and fighters, the Marines fight a series of short, violent actions with Iranian Naval Infantry and Special Forces units that are guarding the GLCM batteries. By 26 January the Marines succeed in eliminating the GLCM threat from the Straits and begin to move along the coast toward Bandere Abbas. However, before the Marine main body can come ashore, the Navy will have to complete the tedious job of removing or destroying some 500 sea mines that block the Straits. When CINCCENT asks the Naval Component Commander how long the operation will take, the Admiral indicates several weeks.[55]

Horrified at the news from Southwest Asia, the President wants to suspend all further operations from the sea to regain control of the Straits but is persuaded by CJCS to permit further Marine operations to eliminate the cruise missile threat from the Straits. The President is bewildered by what has happened and is unsure how this military debacle can be presented to the American people in a balanced fashion. In the space of a few minutes, the numbers of American casualties to this point (less than a thousand) are more than triple what they were. Fortunately, the arrival of JTF North in Baghdad on 25 January and the installation of a new friendly government there on 26 January moderate public reaction to the disaster in the Straits. Hussein is killed in an aircraft shot down by Air Force fighters while it attempts to fly east toward Iran. JTF North combined the enabling joint capabilities of mobility, command, control, communications, computers, intelligence, surveillance, and reconnaissance to execute dominating maneuver in an operation to attack directly the Iraqi enemy's center of gravity: Baghdad. Predictably Iraq's forces melt away with the news that Hussein is dead. Even more important, the Sultan of Oman is overthrown by a pro-Western faction that quickly grants access to the United States. The Marines go ashore unopposed on January 27 to establish a base for additional Air Force fighters from the United States. However, the good news that both JTFs are prepared to renew decisive offensive operations is quickly obscured by developments on 29 January: Russia publicly announces its readiness to intervene in the Middle Eastern conflict if U.S. Ground Forces seize control of Iran's oil fields.

This bad news is accompanied by an intelligence report of Russian troops massing to support a Russian-sponsored military coup in the Ukrainian Republic.[56] In response to Polish, Slovak, and Hungarian requests, the V Corps Commander in Germany is directed by the President to move V Corps' three Heavy Combat Groups and one JTF Support Group to Poland. Germany condemns the Russian moves in Eastern Europe and mobilizes its armed forces.[57] In the meantime, the American troops belonging to two more Heavy Combat Groups, one Rocket Artillery Group, and one Heavy Recon-Strike Group are ordered to deploy by "federalized" commercial air from their bases in CONUS to Germany, where they will draw prepositioned equipment. Recognizing that of five remaining Heavy Combat Groups in the Active Component only three are available in CONUS for immediate deployment, the President suspends of the movement of more U.S. forces and equipment to the Southwest Asian theater.[58]

OBSERVATIONS

Southwest Asia was chosen only because the area is now somewhat more familiar to Americans than North Africa, Eastern Europe, Korea, or Southeast Asia. However, similar events could have occurred in those places too. It is no exaggeration to suggest that the implications for the U.S. Armed Forces of a scenario like the one outlined here are significant. Technology changes the ways in which conflicts are conducted, won, or lost. Technology also shapes or influences events by amplifying American strengths and minimizing the effects of mishaps, mistakes, or technical failures (friction).[59] In the right hands, modern military technology increases the American Armed Forces' ability to diminish its adversary's capacity for independent action, but in the wrong hands it cannot compensate for the absence of human insight, understanding, or effective leadership. This is because technological advances cannot eliminate ambiguity, uncertainty, chance, and the forces of chaos from the field of conflict.[60]

In the U.S. Army there is an old saying: "Intelligence is almost always wrong!" There is little in the historical record to suggest that this saying is any less true today than it was a hundred years ago. It is still unclear whether the American intelligence community is actually capable of either mapping out critical enemy strategic and operational capabilities or explaining enemy intentions and actions. At most, intelligence analysts can point with certainty to the high probability that future adversaries will work hard to exploit "niche" vulnerabilities in the American force structure through the use of mines in littoral waters, TBMs, GLCMs, and sophisticated air defenses. This will allow enemy ground forces to outpace the American military response if U.S. Ground Forces either are not already ashore, as was the case in Kuwait during 1990, or cannot arrive in time. This observation reinforces the need to organize both air assault and heavy ground combat forces to deploy rapidly and fight effectively within a joint framework. It also means forward-stationing Army ground forces in critical regions like Southwest Asia.

Despite the development of American deep-strike attack weapons, capable of attacking targets hundreds of miles in the enemy rear, the results of the close battle—the area where the combatants are in direct contract—will remain critical to the outcome of the war. If war in the future will be a contest between regional powers that will seek to exploit new information age military technology for limited regional aims, it will still involve closing with the enemy and killing him at close range. It will not be possible to destroy all of the enemy's forces before they get to the battlefield, and so it will continue to be necessary to engage and defeat the enemy's forces in battles when the two sides are in sight of one another. The tendency over time in land warfare is to disperse ground forces and concentrate the effects of weapons rather than troops. This makes it very inefficient as well as expensive to allocate one PGM (Precision Guided Missile) to every enemy ground system. Moreover, merely killing the enemy's fixed sites will not win the war. Unless the information age Army is able to fight and defeat opposing forces in face-to-face combat, the ability to launch deep strikes will be of limited strategic value in future conflicts.[61]

An enemy who cannot see its deep targets fails to cope with the rapid overland advance of the Army's close combat formations. The faster and deeper Army air–ground combat teams advance into enemy territory, the less dangerous and effective the enemy's weapons of mass destruction become. "All-arms" formations smaller than the current divisions thrust forward behind a screen of manned and unmanned reconnaissance and stand-off weapon systems. Air–land forced entry operations are made possible today by new aviation technology, and new sophisticated light armor and recon–attack helicopters. It is now possible to launch such an operation from the United States and reach halfway around the world in less than 24 hours.[62]

Once enemy and friendly troops begin the close battle, it is difficult to rely on Air Force fighters for close air support. The difficulties in directing accurate fire from altitudes in excess of 15,000 feet against ground targets that are relatively close to friendly troops that are also camouflaged, scattered, moving, and defended by antiaircraft systems cannot be overstated. Current and future generations of fighters simply fly too fast and too high to discriminate between friendly and enemy forces in close combat. The constraints and limitations on the application of air power at night or in adverse weather only make these matters worse. Digitization may succeed in partially solving the combat identification problem, but in the interim there is little prospect of sufficiently removing the fog of war to prevent fratricide from the air. Beyond these points, the Air Tasking Order (ATO) process works well for planned strategic strikes, but its 48–72 hour planning cycle does not lend itself to quick reaction strikes or close air support missions. There is also another reason.

American and allied Air Forces will be fully engaged in an all-out deep strike effort to suppress, neutralize, or destroy the enemy's weapons of mass destruction when future ground offensives are just beginning. In fact, this was the conclusion drawn from the Yom Kippur War by the Commander of all the regular Israeli Forces in the Golan region. Rafael Eitan, the former Israeli Defense Force Chief of Staff, went so far as to suggest that in the early phase of future offensive operations Israeli Ground Forces would have to become self-reliant in the context of close air support:

> The air force must not be involved in support missions for the land forces until it has assured itself reasonable freedom of operation by destroying the enemy's missile networks. This being so, the land forces must be prepared to bear the burden in the war's opening stages, and not pin their hopes on the performance of the aircraft.[63]

It would make sense in the new strategic environment to shift the funds committed to close air support capabilities from the Air Force into Army programs for attack helicopter modernization and artillery stand-off weapon system development.[64] The Air Force response time to Army requests for close air support has risen consistently since the end of World War II, and there is no evidence to suggest that this will change in the near future. Furthermore, relieving the Air Force of the close air support mission would conform to an Air Force requirement to concentrate its attacks against deep targets in the first phase of any future conflict.

"Army deep fires" from improved MLRS rocket systems destroy a variety of enemy targets, including air defense sites, TBM sites, C4I installations and reserve troop concentrations—some with a single missile. These capabilities augment, supplement, and magnify the impact of airpower in the theater of war.[65] C4I integration through the structures outlined here is essential to ensure that air and ground forces are mutually reinforcing and supporting. Moreover, in contrast to those of airpower, the response time and accuracy of these systems are unchanging. Joint C4I structures like the proposed C4I battalion are vital to the exploitation and use of these systems in operations to suppress, neutralize, or destroy enemy air defenses.

Airpower tends to operate in surges of firepower and does not apply constant pressure against enemy forces. It is also very vulnerable to periodic swings in technology. In the Gulf War, American airpower operated in an environment where it had a relative advantage over Iraqi ground forces. In the years ahead, passive detection and tracking systems, speed of light antiaircraft systems, tactical ballistic missiles, and cruise missiles will change warfare in ways not yet comprehended. However, technological surprise poses special perils to airpower where sudden, one-sided supremacy in aerospace defense, lasers, and smart weapons could create spectacular shifts in the balance of military power.[66]

An enemy able to neutralize U.S. airpower as a result of either breakthrough air defense technology or TBM strikes will not succeed if Army Ground Forces are designed to cope with this contingency and can assist the air component to overcome the threat. Airpower enthusiasts conveniently forget that the Egyptians gained a 6 day respite from the effects of Israeli air superiority in 1973. In this short time, over 100,000 Egyptian troops with 1,000 tanks and armored fighting vehicles were able to cross the Suez Canal and nearly overrun the state of Israel. The Israelis have never forgotten the lesson that overreliance on any one arm of combat or weapon system is ill advised. Just as new antitank capabilities and new air defense technology surprised Israeli Defense Forces in 1973 during the Egyptian offensive to retake the Sinai, modern information age technology in the hands of innovative military leaders can potentially reduce or neutralize the effectiveness of high altitude air strikes. Passive radar systems are evolving to the point where they are sensitive, accurate, and persistent enough to locate and identify aircraft at long range. Because passive detection sites do not radiate, it is extremely difficult to identify or locate them.[67] Clearly, the consequences of relying on airpower to achieve strategic aims without ground forces in this 2003 scenario would have resulted in certain defeat for U.S. forces.

In this regard, missiles, however revolutionary in character, are still like bullets: once fired, they cannot be retrieved. Just as it is unwise to rely too much on airpower, it is equally unrealistic to expect stand-off missile systems to win wars. When the inventory of expensive missiles is gone, their role is over. Therefore, their use should be reserved for critical periods and for targets especially difficult for other weapons to handle.[68] As sensor-to-shooter technological enhancements make fires more responsive, it will be necessary to ensure that an expensive Tomahawk missile whose warhead is intended for a hardened target is not allocated for use against softer, more mobile targets. For these reasons, government-sponsored research and development programs in Europe, Japan, and China are working to create new, less expensive cruise missile systems of increased range and striking power. As more inexpensive cruise missiles become available, reliance on manned aircraft to conduct deep operations will probably decline. This is true for Army as well as Air Force aircraft.[69]

Inexpensive unmanned aerial vehicles equipped with thermal imaging technology for night targeting linked to terminally guided missile systems are also proliferating.[70] The mobile cruise missile batteries firing sea-skimming missiles with ranges in excess of 80 miles that were central to the defeat of forced entry operations from the sea in this setting will be present for the next conflict whether it occurs in Southwest Asia or in the straits between Taiwan and China. When these points are considered in connection with the penalties in performance suffered by naval aircraft compared with land-based aircraft (the aerospace engineer's rule of thumb is that catapult launches and arrested landings impose a 1,200 pound penalty for additional structural weight), these observations raise serious questions about the viability of the U.S. Navy's new concepts for littoral warfare.[71]

In future conflicts and crises, carrier and amphibious battlegroups will have to adjust constantly for a wide range of emerging threats: shallow water submarines, stand-off missiles, underwater mines, space-based surveillance, and unmanned aerial vehicles. Prudent response to these threats influences where naval and amphibious forces operate, and that, in turn, establishes how far inland naval and amphibious forces can influence the action.[72] Sea-based forces are ideal targets for weapons of mass destruction when they attempt to execute forced entry operations from the sea.[73] The concentration of several thousand sailors, airmen, and Marines in an amphibious or Nimitz-class aircraft carrier risks single-point failure in future warfighting. In contrast, dispersed, highly mobile ground forces present poor targets for these weapons and land-based aviation can operate from protected locations beyond the range of these weapons.

Provided that ground forces organize to disperse, historical evidence indicates that casualty rates in land warfare do not necessarily increase when weapons of greater lethality appear. In the last century, it was not unusual for armies to lose between 10 and 20 percent of their strength in a single day. But despite the increasing destructiveness of weapons during World

War II, this loss rate dropped to around 1 to 3 percent a day. Loss rates for Israeli forces during the 1973 war were estimated at 1.8 prcent per day.[74] Loss rates for U.S. Ground Forces during the 4 day ground war with Iraq were less than 1 percent. Why? As weapons become more dangerous, armies reorganize to disperse and to increase their mobility, reducing the density of troops in jeopardy.[75] Sea-based forces that rely on large, expensive industrial age platforms like aircraft carriers and amphibious carriers have to depend on a vast array of costly defensive systems to survive the proliferation of less expensive missiles, mines, and land-based aircraft. These fiscal and technological constraints on naval power interact and add up in ways that simply reinforce another important trend in military affairs: the long-term military superiority of land-based ground forces, missiles, and aviation.

These points further reinforce the enduring requirement for United States–sponsored alliance structures and the forward-basing of U.S. Army contingents to overcome these constraints. Without Army contingents positioned in areas of vital strategic interest, U.S. forces are unlikely to gain access from the sea in future crises or conflicts. At the same time, naval forces that must position hundreds of miles away in order to operate beyond the reach of the enemy's weapon systems are unlikely to act as a persuasive deterrent. In addition to being extremely high-risk combat tactics, forced entry operations from the sea are capital intensive.[76] Most important, not only do forward-deployed ground forces defend America at a distance and demonstrate America's determination to honor its overseas commitments, they provide proof of a visible and credible link to America's ultimate strategic power.[77]

The force described here would have to be examined against a range of warfighting criteria and command arrangements in simulation before any decision were made to adopt this specific force design; however, the implications of this warfighting structure and scenario for the Army's future role in the context of joint warfare are significant. Of these, probably the most important is that the U.S. Army is positioned to be a core element of most future joint operations. Beyond this, there are others:

- The Army's senior leadership must rethink its commitment to preserving all current echelons of command and control.[78] If it did, the Army could reorganize its current forces to field corps-based JTFs by transforming its ten divisions into twenty-five to thirty Groups like the ones outlined here. This would help to shape the Army's organization within the trendlines by clearly establishing the urgent requirement for additional rocket artillery systems, advanced rotor-driven aircraft, tactical ballistic missile

defense systems, armored vehicular survivability equipment, light survivable air-delivered armor, modularity in tactical logistics, and improved
C4I.

- Reorganizing the Army's forces along the lines suggested in this scenario
  would seem to be essential in a strategic environment in which the time
  for mobilizing and massing forces to attack is likely to be quite short. The
  political fragility of future American-led coalitions under the weight of
  regional conflict and the impact of instantaneous communications on
  public perceptions of military operations will not improve this situation.
  For these reasons, the readiness and ability to deploy quickly will be more
  important than ever before. The speed and tactical surprise of units from
  the same divisions in the 1989 invasion of Panama clearly contributed to
  their success. In both cases, the first troops began to be airlifted less than
  18 hours after the order was given.[79] However, Army troops in the future
  will have to be armed with the required C4I capability, sophisticated light
  armor, advanced recon–attack helicopters and rocket artillery and still
  move just as quickly in order to both survive and win in action! This means
  funding and deploying all of the equipment and systems in the *Mobility
  Requirements Study* including the C-5 upgrades, the C-17, fast sealift, and
  Army Prepositioning Afloat.[80] It also means reexamining the protection
  afforded to facilities for prepositioned sets of Army equipment around the
  world. In some cases, sites will have to be either hardened or positioned
  where they will be protected from the type of attack described in this
  scenario.

- The question of how much force to assemble is no more important than
  the question of how quickly that force can be deployed in a major crisis.[81]
  Prepositioned equipment accelerates the readiness of arriving combat
  troops to fight and commits allies to cooperation. Enhancing current
  additional prepositioning of Army (APA) equipment afloat should be
  considered, but this does not mean abandoning plans to preposition Army
  equipment in allied states. Prepositioning ashore secures the strategic high
  ground in pivotal states. Early entry ground forces will, however, have to
  be equipped, trained, and prepared to decontaminate prepositioned equipment sites if they are attacked with chemical or biological agents as in the
  scenario described.[82]

- To obtain a real advantage from rapid deployment, however, Army forces
  must be structured, equipped, and trained to execute offensive operations
  almost immediately on arrival in a theater of conflict. The U.S. Army's
  passion for centralization, pooling of resources, and conducting war by
  remote control, which contributed to the long lead times needed by Army
  forces to prepare and launch offensive operations in Vietnam and Southwest Asia, cannot shape operational thinking in the future.[83] Compared

with those of Desert Storm, the numbers of Army troops and equipment are lower. Operationally, the distances covered are greater.[84]

- Striving for speed and decisive force on the strategic level goes beyond rapid deployment. This means that the nation cannot afford to trade forces on land for the promise of forces delivered from the sea over the beach. To do so means risking the certainty of another war in the Gulf. The 1991 war to regain control of Kuwait cost the United States–led coalition at least $60 billion. An additional $25 billion was spent in the reconstruction of Kuwait. Compared with the costs of responding repeatedly to future crises as the Armed Forces did in 1994 and 1995, the estimated cost of establishing an Army ground presence of less than 5,000 troops (a Recon-Strike Group or Heavy Combat Group) in Kuwait—roughly $300 million to $400 million per year—is modest in comparison. Kuwait and the GCC states would also share some of this burden.

- The assertion that Kuwait is indefensible constitutes an American confession of impotence in a confrontation with reactionary regimes that threaten not only regional stability, but global economic prosperity as well. For reasons that are reminiscent of German insistence on the stationing of U.S. ground forces in Central Europe after World War II, today's Gulf Arab elites understand that U.S. ground forces represent a tangible commitment to regional stability that neither Iraq nor Iran can afford to ignore. Just what the United States might do to protect its ground force in Kuwait would figure prominently in any Iraqi or Iranian plan to attack Kuwait and the Arabian Peninsula. This is, after all, the essential feature of deterrence.[85]

- In contrast to the air–ground team of the MEF,[86] the Army is capable of combining its elements for operations with all of the services at the Corps/JTF and Group levels. With few exceptions, it is simply a question of organizing existing Army assets differently to exploit new technology and human potential more efficiently and effectively. Organizing to support the implementation of a joint C4I structure is already in blueprint in the form of the Defense Information Infrastructure (DII) Master Plan and its associated Defense Information System Network (DISN) Joint Capstone Requirements Document. The C4I battalion structure would be linked through the Global Command and Control System to this new overarching architecture; thereby significantly enhancing the joint information content available to Army Ground Forces.

The questions, then, are the following: How can current Army doctrine and training with their heavy emphasis on detailed planning, lengthy deliberation, and maintaining control of forces be reoriented to a new information age force design which depends for its effectiveness on joint

C4I, "war-ready" combat forces, and operational flexibility to win? And how can the Congress be persuaded of the strategic and economic benefits of a national military strategy built primarily around American land-based air and ground forces for control of events on land without jeopardizing American dominance at sea?

NOTES

1. J. R. Wilson, "Simulation Bites the Budget Bullet: Powerful Computers Bring New Levels of Reality," *International Defense Review*, 1 April 1995, p. 44.

2. A JWARS office has been established to develop the JWARS program. Theoretically, JWARS will significantly enhance analytical support to the acquisition process by providing a common joint model from which all services, OSD, and Joint Staff will conduct capability tradespace assessments. JWARS is being designed with an object-oriented, open architecture that incorporates C4, ISR, and information warfare enablers, in addition to direct warfighting capabilities.

3. Robert Holzer, "Trainers and Simulators," *Defense News*, 2 October 1995, p. 26.

4. Pat Cooper and Robert Holzer, "U.S. Military Leaders Consider More Realistic Models for C4I," *Defense News*, 6 November 1995, p. 26.

5. "NRC Panel to Army: Use Care in Mixing, Matching Technologies," *Aerospace Daily*, 1 November 1995, p. 187.

6. Stephen T. Hosmer, *Effects of the Coalition Air Campaign Against Iraqi Ground Forces in the Gulf War*, MR-305-AF (Santa Monica, Calif.: RAND Corporation, 1994), 58. The Gulf War Air Power Study noted that of 163 Iraqi tanks examined by battlefield analysis groups, between 10 and 12 percent had been struck by air-delivered munitions. According to Stephen Hosmer, the three Republican Guard Divisons in the Kuwait Theater of Operations as of 1 March 1991 left behind in their prewar deployment areas 166 tanks, 103 Armored Personnel Carriers (ACPs), and 99 artillery pieces. As percentages of prewar deployments these amounted to 21 percent tanks ($n = 786$), 28 percent AQPCs (736), and 32 percent artillery (308). This offers further confirmation that at least 70–80 percent of the Republican Guard losses were inflicted by advancing ground forces. However, this would not be suggested by any of the current models. Also see General Accounting Office Report to Congress: *Operation Desert Storm—Evaluation of the Air War* (Washington, D.C.: Government Printing Office, July 1996).

7. Paul K. Davis and Donald Blumenthal, *The Base of Sand Problem: A White Paper on the State of Military Combat Modeling* N-3148-OSD/DARPA (Santa Monica, Calif.: RAND Corporation, 1991), 22.

8. Colin S. Gray, "The Changing Nature of War?" *Naval War College Review* (Spring 1996): 11.

9. Israel's antitactical ballistic missile system, the Arrow Missile, still in the experimental stage, will probably be deployed by 1999. The Israeli human and

electronically collected intelligence system would be of enormous value in the effort to place the U.S. Theater Missile Defense Group into operation quickly.

10. Jeff Erlich and Theresa Hitchens, "Counter Proliferation Efforts Await Requirement Review: DoD Programs Are on Hold Until at Least 1998," *Defense News*, 6–12 November 1995, p. 20.

11. Amir Attaran, "Soviet Nuclear Droppings Get Hotter," *Wall Street Journal*, 23 January 1996, p. 14. Fred H. Lawson, *Critical Issues: Opposition and U.S. Policy Toward the Arab Gulf States* (New York: Council on Foreign Relations Press, 1992), 12–30.

12. This scenario assumes that the Heavy and Light Recon-Strike Forces could be equipped with the Comanche between now and 2003. For similar reasons, it assumes that the MEF is at least partially equipped with the V-22. See David S. Harvey's "Awaiting Anticipated Modernization," *Rotary Wing International* (January 1996): 24.

13. "The Threat in Turkey," *Providence Journal-Bulletin*, 31 December 1995, p. C-14.

14. Charles Aldinger, "Russian Defense Chief Warns NATO Not to Expand," *Washington Times*, 5 January 1996, p. 15.

15. "Time for Change in Saudi Arabia," *New York Times*, 4 January 1996, p. 20.

16. Wing composition is not uniform in the Air Force. This scenario assumes that there are roughly seventy-two fighter aircraft in each wing along with C3I assets, B-1s, and B-52s.

17. See John M. Collins, "Prepositioned Weapons, Equipment and Supplies: Overview and Evaluations," *CRS Report for Congress* (Washington, D.C.: Congressional Research Service, Library of Congress, October 27, 1995: 1–5. This program includes the C-17 and C-5 aircraft, fast sealift, and the Army Prepositioning Afloat (APA) program or Army War Reserve 3 (AWR-3). The current interim APA accommodates 123 M1A1 Tanks, 154 M3A2 Armored Fighting Vehicles (AFVs), 100 armored personnel carriers, 24 self-propelled 155 millimeter Howitzers, 9 Multiple Launch Rocket Systems (MLRS) together with 15 days of essential supplies loaded aboard five refurbished roll-on/roll-off (RO/RO) ships. The APA is presently located at Diego Garcia together with additional ships containing supplies and hauling assets for a three division contingency corps to sustain operations for 30 days 100–150 miles inland. The APA will expand from a total of 14 ships to 16 ships by FY1999. The new ships will include a second heavy lift propo ship and eight new Large Medium Speed (24 knots) RO/ROs, increasing storage space from 807,000 to 2,000,000 square feet. Thus, the capability to receive and support follow-on forces in reduced time from the United States and Europe will improve commensurately. This scenario assumes that the size of the APA has increased on schedule to allow for the numbers of equipment items to support the deployment of two Heavy Combat Groups and two JTF Support Groups.

18. See "Iran's Anti-Ship Missile Forces," *Iran and "Dual Containment," A Net Assessment* (ed. Anthony Cordesman and Ahmed Hashim) (Washington, D.C.: Center for Strategic and International Studies, 1995). Iran has purchased eight Soviet-made SS-N-22 "Sunburn" or "Sunburst" antiship missiles. They have a range of 100–120 kilometers and relatively sophisticated guidance systems that are resistant to countermeasures. Also, the Naval Branch of the Republican Guards utilize the Chinese Silkworm with a range of 80–90 kilometers. It climbs to 145 meters (600 feet) after launch, then drops to a cruise profile of 30 meters (100 feet). There are two variants. One uses IR passive homing and the other active radar homing systems.

19. Michael R. Gordon and Bernard E. Trainor, *The Generals' War* (Boston, Mass.: Little, Brown, 1994), 345. Initially, the Navy discounted the Iraqi capability to mine any water but shallow water. The Navy was wrong. The Iraqi sea mine belt was roughly 5 miles wide and reached 30 miles from the shore into the Gulf waters.

20. Rowan Scarborough, "Perry Questions Plan to Defend Gulf Area: Sees Gap in Protection of S. Korea," *Washington Times*, 5 January 1996, p. 1.

21. The Strategic Reserve Corps is a concept for the integration of that portion of the Army National Guard into a corps structure for early access and deployment under Active Component command and control. The details of this proposal are included in the chapter "Streamlining Defense to Pay for Strategic Dominance."

22. Commander Albert Hochevar, USN, Major James Robards, USA; Major John Schafer, USAF, and Major James Zepka, USAF; "Deep Strike: The Evolving Face of War," *Joint Forces Quarterly* (Autumn 1995): 85. This is a good primer for those who think that any real "joint" doctrine exists in this area.

23. See Appendix C concerning the APA and sealift times.

24. Robert J. Murray, "Russia's Threat Beneath the Surface," *Wall Street Journal*, 25 August 1995, p. A8.

25. See "Aegis Ships Head for Hawaiian CEC Experiments," *Navy News & Undersea Technology*, 8 January 1996, p. 1.

26. Bradley Graham, "Pentagon Plan to Delay Antimissile Programs Draws Heated Opposition on Hill," *Washington Post*, 7 March 1996, p. 12. Rowan Scarborough, "Israel Missile Defense Sparks U.S. Debate: Billions Needed for Troubled System," *The Washington Times*, 9 March 1996, p. 1. Bill Gertz, "Plea for Missile Defense in Korea Fails," *The Washington Times*, 15 February 1996, p. 4.

27. Heather J. Eurich, "Aggressive C-17 Production Rate Would Provide Savings—MDC," *Defense Daily*, 11 March 1996, p. 368.

28. See Mary Williams Walsh, "German Linked to Libyan Arms Deal," *Los Angeles Times*, 28 February 1996, p. 2. The article discusses German suppliers of poison gas to the Third World.

29. The SA 10 is an exceptionally capable command-guided antiaircraft missile. Its range is in excess of 100 kilometers and it can be linked to a variety of

radars, including Flap Lid, Big Bird, and Clam Shell. New Russian variants for sale on the open market reportedly incorporate Western microcircuitry and new target acquisition technology. See *FM (Army Field Manual) 100–2–3* dated 1991. Also see Zaloga's book *Soviet Air Defence Missiles: Design, Development and Tactics* (London: Janes Defence Studies, 1989), with CACDA 1991–93 updates.

30. Robert Holzer, "U.S. Navy Eyes Cruise Missile Dearth: Procurement May Leave Service's Commanders Short-Handed," D*efense News*, 8–15 January 1996, p. 4.

31. "Air Force Studies Ability of Air Power to Blunt an Armored Invasion," *Inside the Air Force*, 9 February 1996, p. 11. This article inflates what this technology can currently accomplish. Recent test results forecast more limited expectations. However, this technology is one that deserves continued attention.

32. AH64 is the primary attack helicopter of the Army. It is a dual-engine aircraft equipped with Hellfire antitank missiles, a 30 millimeter chain gun, and rockets. Its target acquisition designator sight and pilot night vision sensor allow it to fly and operate at night and in poor weather. It weighs 17,650 pounds and has a top speed of 155 knots. *An Analysis of U.S. Army Helicopter Programs* (Washington, D.C.: Congressional Budget Office, December 1995), 12.

33. Brendan McNally, "Czechs Ponder 'Stealth Tracker' Sale to Iran; Plane Comes After Government Eases Export Rules," *Defense News*, 12 July 1993, p. 1. Also see article by Bill Sweetman, "The Future of Airborne Stealth," *International Defense Review* (March 1994): p. 39.

34. Lt. Col. James R. Brungess, USAF, *Setting the Context: Suppression of Enemy Air Defenses and Joint War Fighting in an Uncertain World* (Maxwell AFB, Ala.: June 1994), 170–71.

35. "Deadly Returns," *Boston Globe* (16 February 1996), p. 13. This essay discusses arms shows in the Middle East and the possibility that U.S. arms sales of sophisticated aircraft and missiles may be fueling the conflicts that the United States wants to contain.

36. The RAH66 Comanche is the first helicopter designed specifically for the role of armed reconnaissance. The Army plans to buy 1,300 RAH66s, with the first arriving in the force during 2004. In this scenario, the arrival date has been advanced to 2003. *An Analysis of U.S. Army Helicopter Programs* (Washington, DC: Congressional Budget Office, December 1995), 18.

37. James T. McKenna, "First Flight Boosts Comanche Program," *Aviation Week and Space Technology*, 15 January 1996, pp. 44–45. Most of the RAH66's most endearing qualities are classified, but some of them may be inferred from the comments in this brief essay.

38. Dr. George W. Gawrych, "Attack Helicopter Operations: Attack Helicopter Operations in Lebanon," in *Combined Arms in Battle Since 1939*, ed. Roger Spiller (Leavenworth, Kans.: Command and General Staff College Press, 1992), 37. Israeli tanks in the Bekaa Valley during 1982 had no on-board survivability

equipment and were operating without friendly recon or attack helicopters in the air. The results were disastrous.

39. Cpt. David A. Dykes, "Does Longbow Apache Really Make a Difference?" *Army Aviation*, 29 February 1996, p. 35.

40. John Robinson, "Squadron Commander Sees New Modem Improving Bombing Accuracy," in *Defense Daily*, 21 February 1996. This device compresses the time required to transmit target locations to fighter aircraft and significantly improves target accuracy.

41. Gen. J. H. Binford Peay III, "The Five Pillars of Peace in the Central Region," *Joint Force Quarterly* (Autumn 1995): 33. General Peay indicates that the JTF command and control apparatus is now capable of orchestrating both land-based and naval air attack.

42. The Kiowa Warrior is an upgraded version of a Vietnam era airframe. The helicopter has a gross weight of 4,500 pounds, a top speed of 120 knots, and a cruising range of 215 miles. It is equipped with air-to-air Stinger missiles, Hellfire antitank missiles, a machine gun or 2.75 inch rockets. *An Analysis of U.S. Army Helicopter Programs* (Washington, D.C.: Congressional Budget Office, December 1995), 10.

43. David S. Harvey "Awaiting Anticipated Modernization," *Rotor Wing International* (January 1996): 24. The OH58D was the Army's first aircraft with digital communications. The armed upgraded version is a major player in Task *Force XXI* tests. The planned upgrades include a more powerful central computer process, a digital map, radio communications enhancements, integrated GPS/inertial navigation, and an improved data modem.

44. The 160th Special Operations Regiment is an aviation regiment designed for close cooperation with the Army's Ranger battalions. It is equipped with the most modern and sophisticated rotary wing technology in the world. Unfortunately, most of its capabilities are classified.

45. E. H. Simmons, "Getting Marines to the Gulf," *U.S. Naval Institute Proceedings* (May 1991): 51–54.

46. Admiral William D. Smith, " Seapower: There Is No More Vital Research Than That Involving Defenses Against Theater Ballistic Missiles," *Defense News* (January 1996): 54.

47. LTG John H. Cushman, USA (ret.), *Command and Control of Theater Forces: The Future of Force Projection* (Cambridge, Mass.: Harvard University Center for Information Policy Research, March 1995), 45.

48. Steven Uehling, "The Case for the F/A-18E/F Just Doesn't Fly," *Navy Times* (September 1995): 39. This article touches on the F/A-18's range problem. It will actually have less range and carry less ordnance than the A-6E it is supposed to replace.

49. "Tomahawks Strike 85% of Their 242 Intended Targets in Gulf War," *Defense Daily*, 3 April 1991, pp. 17–19. For a wartime assessment of the Navy's

cruise missile requirements see Beth Jannery's "Future Korean War Would Require 1,113 Tomahawks, Navy Estimates," *Inside the Navy*, 2 October 1995, p. 5.

50. Steven Zaloga, "Russian Strategic Cruise Missiles," *Jane's Intelligence Review* (May 1996): 198. Zaloga talks specifically about variants of the Raduga Kh-65SE export cruise missile on sale at the Dubai Air Show in 1993. This system can be air- or ground-launched. The RK 55 is also a missile similar to the American Tomahawk designed to be launched from a truck.

51. Tim Weiner, "Cruise Missile Is Test-Fired from a Ship by Iran's Navy," in *New York Times*, 31 January 1996, p. 5. The missile fired was Chinese-made with a range of 15–120 kilometers. It carried a 700 kilogram warhead.

52. K. Scott McMahon and Dennis M. Ghormley, *Controlling the Spread of Land-Attack Cruise Missiles* (Marina del Rey, Calif.: American Institute for Strategic Cooperation, January 1995), 12.

53. Uehling, "Case for the F/A-18E/F," 39.

54. Michael Towle, "Bell's Outlook Is Healthy with Osprey, Study Says," *Fort Worth Star Telegram*, 28 August 1995, p. 1. Although large and powerful, the Osprey is three to four times the size of a UH60. This tends to force reliance on large-deck Marine Amphibious Carriers.

55. L. Edgar Prina, "Sea Power from Over the Horizon to Over the Beach: Amphibs Move to Center Stage in Contingency Plans," *Early Bird Defense Supplement*, 13 November 1995, p. B-11. Also, see John Robinson's essay "Navy Crafting Mine Warfare Campaign Plan," *Defense Daily*, 23 September 1995, p. 138.

56. Mark Helprin, "For a New Concert of Europe," *Commentary* (January 1996): 30–33.

57. Joseph Fitchett, "Germany Moves to Shoulder Europe's Post-2000 Military Burden," *Herald Tribune*, 7 December 1995, p. 3.

58. Donald Blinken, "America's Stake in NATO Expansion," *Wall Street Journal*, 5 July 1996, p. 6.

59. John R. Boyd, "A Discourse on Winning and Losing," unpublished manuscript, 175–89.

60. John Robinson, "Deployment Highlights Hopes, Future Challenges for Pioneer UAV," *Defense Daily*, 24 January 1996, p. 105. This essay discusses the problem of overreliance on surveillance without manned reconnaissance in Bosnia. Similar observations about the difficulties with overreliance on JSTARS in Bosnia have been communicated to the author by members of the J-5's staff returning from regular trips to the region.

61. Hirsh Goodman and W. Seth Carus, *The Future Battlefield and the Arab–Israeli Conflict* (New Brunswick, N.J.: Transaction Publishers, 1990), 161.

62. LTG William E. Odom, USA (ret.), "Shift in Military Resources Could Leave National Security at Sea" in *The San Diego Union-Tribune*, 7 August 1994, OP-ED page.

63. Ariel Levite, *Offense and Defense in Israeli Military Doctrine*, JCSS Study No. 12 (Boulder, Colo.: Westview Press, 1990), 119.

64. Earl Tilford, *Crosscurrents: The Air Force Set-Up in Vietnam* (Maxwell AFB, Ala.: Air University Press, 1993), 183. Tilford indicates that whenever the Army has suggested this, the Air Force has moved quickly to promise better support in the future to prevent lose of funding for more planes. Then nothing changes.

65. George Durham and Michael D. Holthus, "Field Artillery 'Dumb' Rounds Lethal Against Tanks," *Armed Forces Journal International* (May 1991): 37–41.

66. John Allen Williams, "The U.S. and Soviet Navies: Missions and Forces," *Armed Forces & Society*, 10, no. 4 (Summer 1984): 524.

67. Lt. Col. James R. Brungess, USAF, *Setting the Context: Suppression of Enemy Air Defenses and Joint War Fighting in an Uncertain World* (Maxwell AFB, Ala.: Air University Press, 1994), 171.

68. Quoted by Paul Kozemchak in *Swords and Shields: NATO, the USSR and New Choices for Long-Range Offense and Defense*, ed. Fred S. Hoffman, Albert Wohlstetter and David Yost (Lexington, Mass.: Lexington Books, 1987), 268.

69. John Robinson, "UAVs Could Replace Several Manned Aircraft, Owens Says," *Defense Daily*, 29 February 1996, p. 303.

70. "Q & A: Admiral William A. Owens, Vice Chairman of the Joint Chiefs of Staff," *San Diego Tribune*, 17 December 1995, p. G–5.

71. Jan S. Breemer, "The End of Naval Strategy: Revolutionary Change and the Future of American Naval Power," *Strategic Review* (Spring 1994): 40–53. John Robinson, "Navy Vision Sees Greater Role in Conventional Deterrence," *Defense Daily*, 28 February 1996, p. 295.

72. "Crises and Constraints," paper prepared for the Air Force Chief of Staff, December 1995, pp. 4–5.

73. Robinson, "Navy Vision Sees Greater Role," 295. If anything, Robinson argues that the Navy has gone overboard with this latest round of "From the Sea" publicity to capture large parts of the defense budget.

74. James J. Schneider, "The Theory of the Empty Battlefield," *RUSI Journal for Defence Studies* (September 1987): 37–44. Also see T. N. Dupuy's "History and Modern Battle," *Army* (November 1982), 28.

75. Goodman and Carus, *Future Battlefield*. 265–66.

76. Prina, "Sea Power from Over the Horizon to Over the Beach," B-11. Eventually, the Marines plan to organize their force around a total of thirty-six new ships including twelve large-deck amphibious carriers. The costs are staggering by any measure. Also see GAO Report *Navy Carrier Battle Groups: The Structure and Affordability of the Future Force* (Washington, D.C.: U.S. Government Printing Office, February 1993), 19. Annual cost in FY96 dollars of a Nimitz-class carrier is roughly $3.7 billion. Add this to the cost of construction— $1.7 billion to $2 billion—and it is easy to imagine what twelve 40,000 ton amphibious carriers will cost the taxpayer.

77. James Berry Motley, *Beyond the Soviet Threat: The Army in a Post–Cold War Environment* (Lexington, Mass.: Lexington Books, 1991), 25.

78. Because the Army's rigid patterns of career progression and professional development are inseparable from the division-centered force, the elimination of the division/brigade echelons in this design also creates time at the Army Lieutenant Colonel and Colonel levels for assignment to Joint Staffs in Washington and the unified commands before consideration and selection for "Group" command. At present, the Army's career management system leaves little time for joint assignments or advanced civil education.

79. Richard Halloran, "An Army for the Twenty-First Century," *The United States Army: Challenges and Missions for the 1990s*, ed. Robert L. Pfaltzgraff, Jr. and Richard H. Shultz, Jr. (Lexington, Mass.: Lexington Books, 1991), 255.

80. Gen. Peay, "Five Pillars of Peace," 31. Gen. Peay points specifically to the APA and includes the three ships that carry USAF supplies as well. Also see David Fulghum's essay "Defense Studies Back Large C-17, C33 Buys," *Aviation Week & Space Technology*, 18 September 1995, p. 26. The tactical and operational utility of these aircraft was studied in several still-classified scenarios. The results are impressive.

81. Michael O'Hanlon, *Defense Planning for the Late 1990s: Beyond the Desert Storm Framework* (Washington, D.C.: The Brookings Institution, 1995), 55.

82. Holly Porteus, "Grappling with the BIO Genie," *International Defense Review* (March 1995): 32–34.

83. Martin Van Crefeld makes this observation about the U.S. Armed Forces in Vietnam, *Command in War*, 258.

84. One Airborne-Air Assault Group, one Heavy Recon-Strike Group, one Light Recon-Strike Group, three Heavy Combat Groups, one Rocket Artillery Group, one TBM Theater Defense Group, two JTF Support Groups, and one Engineer Group. These Groups comprised 654 M1A1/A2 Tanks, 622 M2/3A2 Bradley Fighting Vehicles, 140 product improved LAVs, 126 Armored Gun Systems, 17 MLRS batteries, 12 Paladin/AFAS batteries, 60 RAH66 Comanche helicopters, 75 AH64 Apache (attack) helicopters, 93 UH60 Blackhawks (assault), 12 Patriot and MEADs batteries, and about 3,000 wheeled vehicles. Of these items, the Crusader 155 SP howitzer, AGS, PAC3 Patriot, and RAH66 Comanche are not yet fielded in the Army inventory.

85. Positioning a force of brigade strength in the region will strategically fix this force. Yet where else does the Army expect to fight? Two divisions are strategically fixed in Europe, where the probability of a major conflict is currently low. A third Army division is strategically fixed in Korea, where a powerful South Korean Army is in place to defend the peninsula. If the NCA will not expand the Army force structure to cope with a real, long-term strategic threat to vital U.S. and allied interests in Southwest Asia, then the Army should consider the internal reallocation of its forces to meet the need for a ground presence in the region. In this connection, an Army presence in Southwest Asia could be linked to the establishment of a Joint and Combined Multinational Training Center in Southern

Kuwait that existed to integrate regional Arab as well as other allied forces with the U.S. commitment to preserve Kuwaiti sovereignty and access to the oil fields. There is reason to believe that in the interests of regional stability the Gulf Arab elites would support such an initiative. To date, the military performance of the Gulf State coalition forces has been disappointing. The creation of a Joint and Combined Multinational Training Center in the region could significantly improve this situation. More important, allied UK and French forces could be included in this training structure. This would impart more than cohesion to the region's United States–led coalition structure. The periodic presence of coalition forces in Kuwait would also reinforce the deterrent effect of an Army ground presence on both Iran and Iraq.

86. *The Military Balance, 1993–1994* (London: Brassey's, 1994), 33–35.

6

Shaping Landpower
for Strategic Dominance

The preceding account of a future conflict in Southwest Asia shows that it is no longer meaningful to speak of individual service doctrine or operations. Ground forces are part of an integrated joint force that includes sensors, remote targeting capabilities, stand-off weapon platforms, and surveillance systems. The second point is that there are no technological single-service silver bullets in military affairs. Successful strategy is still the effective organization and application of power. These observations are important because the persuasion in victory that a new silver bullet has been revealed that is largely independent of time and circumstance is a delusion to which many military and political leaders have fallen victim.

When a British Army annihilated an opposing Sudanese Army in 1899 with the help of several machine guns, military observers of the day expressed the view that the machine gun was the new principal weapon of the age—a new silver bullet. But the machine gun could not and did not win World War I. New tactics and new countermeasures—the tank—defeated the machine gun. In the 1930s, the manned bomber became the silver bullet. Britain's Prime Minister, Stanley Baldwin, believed this so strongly he implied that to hold a different opinion was stupid and even dishonest![1] Of course, the Prime Minister was wrong. Antiaircraft guns, the proximity fuse, and above all men in fighter planes downed hundreds of manned bombers. Today's exponents of strategic airpower are no less strident in their claims that they have found a military silver bullet in the form of new stealth aircraft with precision-guided missiles.[2]

Yet, as we have seen, silver bullets do not win wars. It is the combinations of weapons, and above all their skilled and practiced use, which result in victory. This suggests that overreliance in war on supposed silver bullet weapon systems that can be inexpensively countered once their technical characteristics are understood should be prevented, especially if the acquisition costs are high. This reality has been evident in warfare for many years. Modern aircraft depend heavily on electronic jamming to protect them against radar-guided antiaircraft systems and infrared-guided missiles. The survivability of large aircraft carriers and amphibious ships depends on antiship missile defenses, which must perform perfectly within a few seconds of a missile alert. In both cases, very expensive platforms can be destroyed by relatively inexpensive weapons when the platforms' auto-mated detection and response systems are neutralized in yet another round of the endless measure–countermeasure cycle. This problem is complicated by several factors: the rising costs of weapons platforms, long lead times for development and acquisition of new systems, and accelerated pace of the measure–countermeasure cycle.

In terms of the current changes which are being brought about by the impact of new military technology and political upheaval, policymakers are really much closer to the beginning of the RMA in which they find themselves than to its end. The problem for policymakers is compounded by events in the international arena. For instance, competition between nations for control of the earth's resources combined with the tendency of human populations in the developing world to increase up to the limits imposed by the food supply will create tensions that could require the U.S. Armed Forces to undertake sustained occupation duties in regions of conflict.[3] Thus, the changing nature of the international system itself requires a continuous assessment of the relationships that actually link new technology's military potential to national strategy and military doctrine. This involves the search for a national military strategy that does not spread American military resources too thinly across the globe, but rejects isola-tionist calls to withdraw from overseas engagements in favor of sole reliance on airpower from the land or the sea, and a strategy that does not emphasize types of armed forces independently of the criteria by which the warfighting utility of military power is normally judged. In this perspective, overreliance on one category of weapons creates a dangerous dilemma for policymakers who want to build forces capable of fighting decisively in a variety of conflict settings.

In a strategy that emphasizes the selective use of military power to protect U.S. security, American military strength should be organized and deployed differently than it is today. The selective use of military power suggests a readiness to buttress the stability of key states around the world, operating to prevent regional crises and conflicts rather than reacting to them. Apart from preventing a great power war that could destroy civilization, nothing in U.S. foreign policy could be more important.[4] Americans have also fastened on a formula for going to war in which American casualties are minimized and protracted armed conflicts are prevented. For this formula to work again as it did in the Gulf War, adoption of a military doctrine that has a decisive foreign policy intent is key to signaling the seriousness of American interests in war and peace.[5]

As mentioned previously, military establishments achieve a revolution in military affairs when they successfully exploit technology, organization, training, and leadership to attain qualitatively superior fighting power as well as dramatic positional advantages in time and space which the enemy's countermeasures cannot defeat. In a military doctrine at the outset of a new RMA, all the attributes of national military power still have a vital role. Airpower and seapower shape the battlespace and create the foundation for battlespace dominance. Naval forces secure the movement of critical ground forces through the world's sea lanes and augment military power ashore with sea-based air- and missilepower. Land-based airpower not only attacks to disrupt and degrade the enemy's capacity to wage war, but protects and delivers ground forces to critical points inside the battlespace.

Landpower plays a critical role. The presence of U.S. Ground Forces in areas of strategic importance to the United States commits allies who augment American military power and guarantees American political, economic, and military access to the region. The readiness of American ground forces to deploy quickly and fight both from bases in the United States and from allied territory eliminates doubt in the minds of potential opponents whether the United States can or will intervene.[6] When fighting breaks out, U.S. Ground Forces strike into the enemy's heartland to terminate the conflict on terms which the United States and its allies will accept. However, to play their part, not only must they be organized within a joint framework to strike a paralyzing blow against an opponent, Army Ground Forces must also be postured, trained, educated, and modernized to do so as well. For the U.S. Army to play its role it must be proactive, coming into play before the peace is lost.

NEW THINKING ABOUT WARFIGHTING DOCTRINE

Military doctrine, the collective body of thinking and writing that describes how a military organization expects to fight, is designed to support national strategy by assuring that military establishments are organized and postured at all times to further national goals.[7] Military doctrine underpins national military strategy by rationalizing the development and use of military power on every level: tactical, operational, and strategic. To the military professional, the existence of a genuine military doctrine is of great value. It provides a body of knowledge rooted in military experience on which to draw for the solution of contemporary military problems. Moreover, the existence of a warfighting doctrine and its universal application in the sphere of military affairs mean that all officers, noncommissioned officers, and soldiers will be trained and educated along roughly the same lines. In addition, the basic tenets of a warfighting doctrine can be applied not only to field forces, but also to research and development and to production of military equipment. Thus, a warfighting doctrine exerts a potentially unifying influence and supports the coordination of operations, tactics, training, and modernization.[8] The notion here is that any discussion about warfighting doctrine is part of the larger debate about the role Army Ground Forces should play in a future conflict. In the Southwest Asia scenario, the tactical and operational performance of the Army's Combat Groups was designed to highlight aspects of warfighting that are firmly rooted in the doctrinal thinking of an Army shaped for high mobility and rapid improvisation in the new strategic environment.

In the waning years of the 20th century, several factors are converging to create the capability to execute dominating maneuver on a new, unimagined scale. These factors include the increased accuracy and destructiveness of modern ordnance, greatly enhanced surveillance and reconnaissance capabilities, strategic range of American land-based air- and landpower, and American control of the high seas. Adjustments in joint tactics and operational methods will have to be made to cope with these new factors, but a new American operational structure for future conflict is emerging.

The power of modern technology to integrate systems that can facilitate a more efficient exchange of information may be one of the most important factors in the Army's plan to reorganize for future war. Instead of perfecting separate weapon and communication systems, the current RMA emphasizes technologies and command structures that meld computers, weapons, communications, and surveillance systems. Not only does this observation imply that the future conduct of war will be more fluid, opportunistic, dynamic, and lethal than ever before, it also shifts warfare's focus away from overreliance on the physical ability of individual weapon systems to destroy vast numbers of targets. Although this does not diminish the value of precision engagement as a concept for locating and striking enemy targets, it does reject the assumption that as a more refined instrument of attrition warfare, "precision engagement alone" makes positional advantage irrelevant. Victory in war is rarely the result of the victor's superior technology.[9]

The Southwest Asia scenario suggests that future victory in land warfare will depend on the ability of Army Ground Forces to deploy quickly and advance rapidly in great strength into the depths of the enemy's territory. This action fundamentally neutralizes the enemy's military capability, ensures a rapid collapse of his command system, and terminates the conflict. In describing the doctrinal implications of the Army organization for combat proposed in the preceding chapters, an image of a joint, simultaneous attack in depth in which speed of movement and decision are paramount emerges.[10] In effect, the importance of preventing the enemy from bringing his weapons of mass destruction to bear against friendly operational centers of gravity combined with the need to achieve a much higher operational tempo in future air–ground offensives elevates the traditional ground combat tactics of infiltration to the operational level in land warfare. In broad outline, this observation suggests a new operational structure for military strategy in the information age. This structure appears to comprise four overlapping operational phases.

In the opening or initial entry phase, missilepower and airpower are critical. Precision guided missiles and air strikes are launched early in the campaign to disrupt and degrade enemy C4I. Every lethal and nonlethal system that can contribute to both suppression of enemy air defenses and strikes against militarily and politically significant targets in depth are mobilized in support of this effort. In the Army, these forces include Rocket Artillery Groups, Aviation Strike Groups, Special Operations elements, as well as deep strike–capable assets that are organized with the Army's close combat formations. Even Airborne-Air Assault elements or Recon-Strike elements are subordinated to the JFACC for missions to suppress or neutralize air defenses and weapons of mass destruction which cannot be attacked in any other way. However, rather than seeking to strike every potentially important target in a given theater in the hope of achieving total paralysis, the strategic aim of this operational phase is to achieve partial paralysis at key points inside the battlespace. This operation involves simultaneous attacks to dismember and isolate forward-deployed enemy combat forces in preparation for the attack of the Combat Groups into the battlespace. Knowing that the shock to the enemy's C4I systems will be greatest in the first hours of the strikes, the Combat Groups are postured to attack much earlier than was the case during Desert Storm. If this phase is preempted by the enemy, then a similar operational phase will be necessary to regain the initiative.

As the preparatory/initial entry phase (2 to 14 days) draws to a close, the infiltration/penetration phase begins when a mix of highly mobile "all-arms" Combat Groups smaller than the current divisions thrust forward behind a screen of manned and unmanned reconnaissance and stand-off weapon systems. For the advancing Combat Groups, the tactical objective in this phase is not to assault frontally or destroy defending enemy combat formations, but to penetrate the enemy's defenses simultaneously at several different points. For example, the Airborne-Air Assault Group evades contact with all of the enemy's forward-deployed elements and seizes lightly defended, but operationally significant objectives in depth or on the flanks. Penetration operations do not entail direct frontal assaults into the teeth of enemy defenses. The Recon-Strike Group leads the attack by guiding follow-on Heavy Combat Groups around or through the enemy's defenses and by neutralizing or disrupting enemy counterattacks to stop the Heavy Combat Groups.

Regular infusions of focused logistical support which are delivered quickly and precisely by ground and aerial means are key to the success of this operation. This suggests that in many instances less support needs to be delivered more precisely and rapidly for greater overall effect. Aerospace denial continues to be a minimum condition for success during this phase. This means that if attacking American Air Forces cannot achieve air superiority or air supremacy throughout the theater of conflict,[11] then denying the enemy the opportunity to attack U.S. Ground Forces through the use of air defense elements, anti-tactical-missile systems, and fighter aircraft will still permit American offensive operations on the ground to begin.[12]

Throughout this operational phase the Combat Groups move like irregular swarms spaced in breadth and echeloned in depth, moving to gaps and weaknesses revealed or created by organic armed air–ground reconnaissance and indirect fires. The zones of attack for individual Combat Groups may be anywhere from 20 to 80 kilometers in width and 50 to 200 kilometers in depth. Rocket Artillery, Aviation Strike Groups, and Air Force fighters dispersed throughout the battlespace focus their fires on vulnerable enemy formations to accelerate the forward momentum of the attack. Thanks to an integrated multiservice C4I structure and the proliferation of Army aviation elements in every Army warfighting formation, the Combat Groups are unconcerned with uniform rates of advance, alignment of their formations, and open flanks. Attacking air and ground formations share a common sense of situational awareness and augment one another's fighting power.

Manned reconnaissance elements find and target static defensive positions containing enemy armored vehicles or dismounted troops. Surveillance, to be useful, needs manned reconnaissance to confirm and refine its
data. Thus, the increase in air–ground combat formations equipped and
trained for armed reconnaissance within the Groups prevents limited armed
reconnaissance from slowing the Groups' advance. Technological advances
in microcircuitry, communications, and reconnaissance allow these penetration attacks on the tactical level to be translated simultaneously into
exploitation operations on the operational level. Because the Groups are
self-sustaining, their operational reach is considerably greater than was the
case during the Gulf War.

After penetrating the enemy's defenses, the Heavy Combat Groups drive
deep into the enemy's rear areas, where the enemy's weapons of mass
destruction are either quickly destroyed or incapacitated. In this exploitation
phase of the attack, the operational theaterwide offensive is transformed
from a series of breakthroughs in the air and on the ground where the enemy
defense has lost its coherency into large-scale exploitation attacks along
multiple air–ground axes to seize operational objectives in the enemy's rear
areas. In striking contrast to the way the Army fought in the world wars,
Korea, and Desert Storm, enemy elements are discovered, then neutralized,
destroyed, or bypassed as the operational situation and the tactical mission
warrant. As the exploitation attacks succeed, the conflict termination phase
begins with the occupation and administration of key areas. In the past
decade, as civilian populations in underdeveloped states have exploded, the
size of American and allied armies has declined significantly. Military
operations to restore and maintain order and stability place armies squarely
at the juncture of these two trends. As practiced in recent decades, such
operations are troop-intensive, with the required forces on the ground
related closely to the size of the populations in the area of operations.[13]

Thus, future regional conflict is neither a one-act play nor a series of
discrete operations. Rather, dominate maneuver begins with the attacks of
strategically dispersed forces. These attacks gather strength through a series
of consecutive, overlapping phases of offensive action involving all the
arms of combat. By exploiting the combination of armed reconnaissance
and overhead surveillance, air and ground forces attack without pause to
seize and maintain the initiative. This implies never allowing the enemy to
recover from the initial shock of the first attack. Because of the ambiguity
of the situation that results from simultaneous deep and close attacks, the
enemy is unable to react in time and cannot regain a coherent picture of the
conflict.[14] The four overlapping phases can be summarized as follows:

- Preparatory/initial entry phase: In this phase, air, land, and sea forces move from a condition of strategic dispersal to strategic concentration while all forces either conduct or prepare to conduct joint, simultaneous attacks in depth. The minimal precondition for success during this phase is aerospace denial. This means that the arriving or assembling ground forces must be protected from the enemy's weapons of mass destruction through both passive (dispersion/stand-off) and active means (theater missile defense/air superiority over U.S. forces). Early in this phase, sea-based weapon systems and C4I, intercontinental land-based air and ground forces are critical. Strategic knowledge of the enemy's operational intentions and capabilities is an important element of this comprehensive joint response to regional conflict or crisis. Centralization of strike assets to maximize force protection and damage to the enemy will be an important feature of operations in this phase.

- Infiltration/penetration phase: All operations in the infiltration phase will be highly opportunistic in character. That is to say, autonomy and independence at the tactical level will have to be supported by decentralization on the operational level. This will facilitate the use of all arms in the context of discovering, defeating, or destroying the enemy. Advanced surveillance and armed reconnaissance, integrated C4I, enhanced mobility, accurate weapon and navigation systems, as well as superior human talent and potential, allow for the rapid penetration and infiltration of an enemy's military defenses regardless of his deployment scheme. Thus, the principle of centralization of control over strike assets in the first phase has to give way gradually to decentralization of control over strike assets in the follow-on infiltration phase.

- Exploitation phase: Today, new technology extends the deep attack to the enemy's heartland in a very short period over great distances. Existing and future improvements in force protection, lethality, mobility, and information collection and dissemination will compress this operation into days or hours, depending on the size of the geographic region involved. As this phase is ending, the national command authorities will begin to examine options for the rotation of fighting forces to reconstitute and replace these forces with fresh elements from the continental United States. Some of these forces will consist of Army National Guard formations.

- Termination: It is probable that the disintegration of the opposing state apparatus during the exploitation phase will result in the termination of hostilities in the areas where exploitation attacks are in progress and before a formal arrangement is made. In many cases, the fact that spreading democracy and human rights is a concomitant strategic aim of any American-led offensive, the potential to supplant enemy opposition with the cooperation of the noncombatant population should not be underestimated. However, this also means that Army Ground Forces must be prepared to administer and control large populated areas of enemy territory until legitimate indigenous administration can be restored.

This picture of future warfare suggests the need for change in the way Army forces are postured for both overseas presence and rapid deployment from the United States. Because of the threat of weapons of mass destruction and the fragility of future alliance structures under crisis conditions, an extended preparation of Army Ground Forces for an offensive in close proximity to the enemy's forces is extremely risky. Army Ground Forces cannot expect to build up their combat power in the future as they did in the Gulf War without being challenged. Otherwise, U.S. forces will be presented with a fait accompli as enemies attempt to outpace the American military response. More important, the national command authorities cannot afford to grant a more substantial enemy time to organize his own forces or to disrupt the deployment of American forces.[15] Simultaneously, it is equally dangerous to concentrate combat power in any one region too early. This means that Army forces must be capable of moving rapidly from widely dispersed staging areas overseas and in the continental United States, deploying into a crisis or regional conflict and initiating an attack, all without pausing.

OPERATIONAL READINESS

The prevailing military response to the operational challenge of sudden and often unanticipated regional crises or conflicts is twofold. First, an Army presence must exist in those regions of the world where unimpeded American political, economic, and military access is vital to American security. This military strategy heightens the importance of forward-positioning Army combat power in pivotal states. Peace requires the enhancing of crisis stability, both through unilateral moves concerning the movement and readiness of the Army's combat forces and through negotiation with the opponent from a position of military strength. Second, to facilitate the Army's rapid response to future crises and conflicts, Army forces overseas and in CONUS need an operational link that enhances readiness and deployability. Because operational success in the information age will depend on the Army's readiness and capability to conduct dominating maneuver within a joint framework, the Army will have to make it possible for the regional CINCs to have ground forces at their disposal that can respond quickly and decisively to regional conflicts and crises.

To date, this has been very problematic for the Army. With only ten divisions and two armored cavalry regiments (one of which is really very lightly armed), the Army has been hard pressed to provide the regional warfighting CINCs with the Army forces they need in times of peace and war. These forces include engineers for peacetime civil engineering projects; air-mobile infantry, light armor, and attack helicopters for crisis response; and heavy combat troops and rocket artillery to forge a powerful offensive capability in war. Having made the decision to posture the Army for deployment from the continental United States (CONUS), the National Command Authority (NCA) has unintentionally prevented the CINCs who will command the Army's combat power in war or crisis from exercising much influence over the training and preparation of these forces for deployment to their respective theaters. The consequences of this arrangement for war planners, logisticians, and U.S.TRANSCOM is significant. The same four or five divisions are routinely included in multiple war plans with the result that the CINCs are always competing for access to the same units.

No observer of the last four years would deny that the most striking feature of the new strategic environment is the dependence of the national command authorities on the readiness of U.S. Ground Forces to move quickly and decisively. This was certainly true in October 1994 when the 24th Infantry Division had to move troops and equipment in a matter of days to Kuwait in response to what appeared to be a possible short-warning attack by Iraqi forces. The need to move ground forces quickly was demonstrated again during operations in Haiti and Bosnia. This places emphasis on combat forces-in-being, not understrength units dependent on infusions of soldiers from other Active Component units or reserve formations. Preemption is not an option in a force structure that lacks the manpower to launch combat operations from a standing start. In other words, achievement of the ability to project Combat Groups to areas of American strategic interest requires a cultural change in the basic concepts of training readiness that have dominated Army thinking for decades.

The Group structure adapts the Army's force readiness to the new environment. Combat Groups both in the United States and overseas can be assigned on a rotating basis to the operational command and control of the regional CINCs for a "standing start, come as you are war" environment. In a smoothly functioning military system organized around the "Group" concept, this approach does more than closely link the warfighting forces to the CINC who will employ them. The information age Army permanently assigns one warfighting Corps headquarters each to USEUCOM,

USCENTCOM, USFK/CFC, and USACOM. These four fully manned Army Corps headquarters, in conjunction with resources from all of the services, would become the basis for "standing" JTF headquarters in each major geographical region as well as a CONUS-based contingency corps under USACOM in its force provider role.

This approach would have been impossible just a few years ago. However, with the creation and modernization of the Army Prepositioning Afloat (APA) (see Appendix C) set, the prepositioned sets of Army equipment in strategically pivotal regions of the world, and air transport modernization and expansion (C-5A/C-17), Army Ground Forces are now global weapons with global reach. This approach could also be extended to the Marine Corps in the context of standing MEF-based JTFs in maritime theaters. In USPA-COM and USACOM/USSOUTHCOM,[16] the Marine Corps could establish a standing MEF-based JTF under CINC command and control which the Army and other services would support as required. These areas are dominated by water and are ideally suited to the type of operation for which the Marine Corps has been structured.

The proposal to transform Army Corps Headquarters into the basis for permanent Joint Task Force Headquarters supports more than just joint warfighting. It conforms to the long-term aim of supplanting service component operational, administrative, and logistical commands in the regional unified commands with multiservice Joint Force Operational and Logistics Commands (JFLC). Scrapping the service-pure component commands allows the Joint Task Force structure to be organized around functional areas of responsibility (this is effectively what General Schwarzkopf did during Desert Storm when he appointed MG Pagonis as his JFLC). This approach imparts greater flexibility to the JTF while allowing the assignment of command and staff responsibilities to the organizations with the preponderance of forces employed.[17] In an emergency involving the use of force to preserve free passage of shipping through the Malaccan straits near Indonesia and Malaysia, a MEF-based JTF Headquarters would be supported by whatever Army, Air Force, and Navy forces were necessary for success. In the event that operations in the Sudan or Egypt required the use of force, a USEUCOM Corps-based JTF Headquarters would receive similar multi-service support.

Moreover, instead of relying on a small portion of the Army's forces to execute critical regional warfighting tasks, the CINCs can expect the Army to provide a predictable mix of Combat, Combat Support, and Combat Service Support Groups from the entire ground force to the operational command and control of the CINC on a rotational basis. These Groups would be available for two purposes: First, they would always constitute the forces that would deploy first to combat under control of the regional JTF headquarters in the CINCs' theater. And, second, they would provide troops to conduct joint training and to execute missions in the context of peacetime engagement. Finding time in the course of regular training to preserve Service Core Competencies is always a challenge. But finding time to conduct realistic joint training with the other services is extremely difficult within the contemporary Army training framework. In this proposed Army training system, joint training can be executed under the supervision of warfighting CINCs during phases when units have already completed core competency training and are ready for deployment. And, finally, this concept rests on the foundation of a new information age training system that supports the short-notice deployability of these forces.

For example, one-third of these Groups can be involved at any given time in one of three 180 day operational readiness cycles in peacetime. On a strategic level, this means that one third of the Army's total combat strength in the continental United States could be considered ready for rapid deployment. This is a larger percentage of the force than is currently the case. These cycles would each encompass 180 days and their structure would resemble the following:

Training Cycle

In this phase collective training would be conducted from the lowest levels and build to a combat training center rotation roughly halfway through the cycle. Training deficiencies noted in the rotation would be addressed during the last half of the cycle. In addition, the battalion through corps/JTF staff levels would prepare for and execute a simulated exercise at the operational (corps/JTF) level at the end of the cycle. The regional CINC to whom the Group is assigned for the Deployment Ready Cycle would presumably shape this training and preparation.

Deployment Ready Cycle

In this cycle the Group is ready for deployment. Its equipment is sustained at its highest readiness status. Its soldiers and small units would hone their individual skills in such areas as gunnery and marksmanship and conduct small-scale collective training at local training areas. Early deploying forces planned for response to an initial major regional contingency as well as forces for operational contingency deployments would be identified and drawn from Groups in this cycle.

Reconstitution Cycle

This phase is devoted to individual, equipment, and unit renewal. Activities in this cycle would include military and civilian individual education, periodic medical and dental treatment, individual leave, periodic equipment servicing and overhaul, equipment upgrades, changes of command, personnel reassignment, and postsupport functions.

Adherence to this cycle construct would result in a number of benefits for the readiness of the soldiers and their units. The certainty of knowing when he must be ready to deploy is a source of great confidence to both the soldier and his commander. General Reimer, Army Chief of Staff, has noted that to accomplish the Army's missions, large numbers of soldiers have to execute back-to-back deployments and experience extended separations from their families:

> On average, American soldiers assigned to a troop unit now spend 138 days a year away from home. Many special units, such as military police, air defense and transportation, have been carrying a heavier load. Operations tempo is high. Thus, leaders must help reduce stress in units. One way to do this is predictability.[18]

The soldiers deploying on short notice to combat or other operations within the framework of this cycle concept would always deploy with all aspects of their Combat Group performing at peak efficiency. In addition, CONUS posts with only one or two units in the Deployment Ready Cycle at any one time would be able to maximize the efficient use of their infrastructure for training and troop support. The Army's current system encompassing early deploying and late deploying divisions induces a de facto tiered readiness system within the CONUS force. The permanent "haves" are the divisions which are positioned to go early in the war plans. They are given priority for personnel, equipment, and training funds. They are also routinely overcommitted and their training readiness often suffers as a result. In the best of circumstances these divisions can quickly deploy one maneuver brigade at the peak of readiness and a second at a reduced state of readiness. The third brigade flows later, but in a condition far from the top of its form.

The permanent "have not" units, low on the Army's priority list and late in the MRC deployment timelines (TPFDL), are routinely underresourced. The morale of soldiers and leaders within such units suffers because they are challenged to be as ready as the tier 1 divisions, but are deprived of the means to achieve it. Under the current Unified Command Plan (UCP), U.S. Army Forces Command (FORSCOM), the Army Component Command for USACOM is the headquarters to manage this cyclical approach to prepare Army forces for rapid, short-notice deployment. The bottom line is that a minimum of six or seven Combat Groups, one Engineer Group, and one JTF Support Group would be ready for immediate deployment to a theater of conflict at all times. In addition, for the period the Groups are in the deployment ready cycle, they can be utilized by the warfighting CINCs for specific regional tasks. On a reduced level, this construct may also be applicable to Reserve Component (RC) units. The position of RC elements on the deployment timeline could be tied to their annual training cycle, placing them highest immediately after their annual training.

What forces remain in the United States and are not already assigned in the course of the readiness cycles to USEUCOM, USPACOM-USFK/CFC, USCENTCOM (see Figure 6.1), or USSOUTHCOM consist of what are effectively "swing assets" (Army Special Forces are excluded from this discussion and are not subject to reorganization). This simply means that these elements can be swung to any theater of conflict as part of an existing JTF or a second corps-based JTF if that becomes necessary. These are the combat power multipliers—rocket artillery, attack helicopter, and antimissile defense forces that can be plugged into any JTF.[19] A Light-Recon Strike Group, an Airborne-Air Assault Group, or an Engineer Group could be added to a Marine Expeditionary Force in the Pacific. Had this system been in place during the last 12 months of the Bosnian conflict, part or all of a Rocket Artillery Group could have deployed to Croatia's Adriatic coast, from which it could strike targets in the joint suppression of Bosnian Serb air defenses or as artillery support for the Bosnian Federation's forces. This was unnecessary in 1995 but may become critical in a future strategic environment where sophisticated air defense technology is proliferating. Consequently, these assets are consolidated into the CONUS-based Decisive Force Corps for operational training and deployment.

This strategic reorganization of the Army to conduct dominating maneuver in a joint context assumes that future crises or conflicts will erupt suddenly and with minimal warning. For instance, in the event that a major regional contingency seemed imminent in Korea, this structure would allow for the rapid deployment of sufficient force either to deter an attack or to halt one. This situation could result in a decision by the National Command Authorities immediately to deploy three Heavy Combat Groups, two JTF Support Groups, and one Engineer Mobility Group to Korea where the Groups would draw equipment from the APA and from prepositioned equipment sites. If conditions in Southwest Asia suggested the simultaneous need to strengthen deterrence there, one Heavy Combat Group from this pool of ready forces could fly to Southwest Asia, where it would fall in on

Figure 6.1
Army Overseas Presence

ARMY OVERSEAS PRESENCE

USEUCOM
1 ALL ARMS CORPS/JTF
3 HVY COMBAT GROUPS
1 ENGINEER GROUP
3 JTF SUPPORT GROUPS
1 C4I GROUP
  (GERMANY)
1 AVIATION SUPPORT GROUP
1 AIRBORNE-AIR ASSAULT
  GROUP
  (ITALY)
(35-40,000 Troops)

USCENTCOM
1 ALL ARMS CORPS/JTF
1 HVY RECON-STRIKE GROUP
  (KUWAIT)
(5000 Troops)

USFK/CFC (USPACOM)
1 ALL ARMS CORPS/JTF
1 HVY RECON-STRIKE GROUP
1 ENGINEER GROUP
1 THAAD GROUP
1 JTF SUPPORT GROUP
1 C4I GROUP
  (KOREA)
(25,000 Troops)

CONUS-BASED ARMY

USACOM
FLEXIBLE DETERRENT CORPS/JTF
6-7 AIRBORNE-AIR ASSAULT GROUPS
2 LIGHT RECON-STRIKE GROUPS
2 AVIATION SUPPORT GROUPS
1 ENGINEER GROUP
3-5 JTF SUPPORT GROUPS
1 C4I GROUP

These formations would be stationed at Fort Bragg, NC, FT Campbell, KY, FT Drum, NY, FT Lewis, WA, FT Wainright, Alaska, and FT Polk, LA.

USACOM
DECISIVE FORCE CORPS
10-12 HVY COMBAT GROUPS
3 ROCKET ARTILLERY GROUPS
3 AVIATION STRIKE GROUPS
4 ENGINEER GROUPS
1 THAAD GROUP
2 JTF AIR DEFENSE GROUP
5-9 JTF SUPPORT GROUPS
1 C4I GROUP

These formations could be stationed at FT Hood, TX, FT Carson, CO, Fort Riley, KS, FT Stewart, GA, FT Sill, OK, FT Bliss, TX, FT Rucker, AL, FT Leonardwood MO, FT Meade, MD.

This represents a reduction of 20,000 to 25,000 Troops assigned to USEUCOM and 27,000 to 25,000 Troops assigned to USFK. It also adds 5,000 to USCENTCOM.

This means that 6-7 Combat Groups, 1 Engineer Group and 1 JTF Support Group could be kept ready for immediate deployment to APA and Prepo Sites year-round.

=

2 AIRBORNE-AIR ASSLT GROUPS
1 LIGHT RECON-STRIKE GROUP
4 HEAVY COMBAT GROUPS
1 ENGINEER GROUP
1 JTF SUPPORT GROUP

IN THE EVENT OF A MAJOR REGIONAL CONTINGENCY, WITHIN 30 DAYS THESE ELEMENTS COULD BE RAPIDLY REINFORCED BY 1 AVIATION STRIKE GROUP, 1 ROCKET ARTILLERY GROUP, 2 + JTF SUPPORT GROUPS AS WELL AS ADDITIONAL COMBAT GROUPS.

NOTE: *CORPS/JTF SUPPORT GROUPS WILL VARY IN STRENGTH (2500-5500 TROUPS) AND CONSIST OF A VARIETY OF ELEMENTS—MILITARY POLICE, CHEMICAL, MEDICAL, ETC. C41 GROUPS WILL CONSIST LARGELY OF SIGNAL AND MILITARY INTELLIGENCE. THERE WILL BE MORE GROUPS AT THEATER/ARMY LEVEL THAT ARE NOT SHOWN HERE.*

prepositioned equipment in order to reinforce the Army presence in the region. If necessary, a further reinforcement of the U.S. and allied position in Southwest Asia by air transport of a Light Recon–Strike Group could be executed if it were warranted. If, however, war in Korea seemed unavoidable, a Rocket Artillery Group (four MLRS/ATACM Battalions), an Aviation Strike Group (four AH64 Battalions), and additional JTF Support Groups could be flown to Northeast Asia in a matter of days.

The fact that the Combat Groups' battalion/squadron-level structures are uniform in their composition and warfighting orientation also offers the opportunity to keep combat units together for longer periods than is currently the case. This has never been easy. Professional armies like the U.S. Army and the British Army lose about half of their enlistees after 3 or 4 years, but it is possible to integrate new enlistees quickly into relatively stable unit organizations.[20] As a result of the consistency of the Group structure, battalion-size elements could be periodically rotated from CONUS to overseas locations for 12-month unaccompanied tours. Units from CONUS would simply fall in on the overseas equipment sets, while the overseas unit would return to its home station post. Soldiers and their families could establish homes and family support networks in the United States, where they can expect to live for many years.

Rising military marriage rates in the last decade have led the U.S. Army to adopt an expanding program of family support, which is difficult to sustain under the present fiscal strain. In an era of diminished financial resources, there is much to be said for a home-basing system and for encouragement of military families to live off-post in civilian communities where they may, as long-term residents, build the networks of social support that modern families require.[21] There is no estimate of the savings that could be realized from reducing the numbers of dependent American families living overseas. However, by combining this 1 year unaccompanied overseas rotational system with a reduction of Army forces in one pivotal state, Germany, the Department of Defense could realize considerable financial savings over the long-term.

Reduction of some of the Army's Europe-based force from 65,000 to roughly 40,000–45,000 would also allow for the addition of 5,000 troops to Southwest Asia. A reduction in Korea of perhaps 5,000 troops may also be possible under this proposal. Although these proposals may initially be viewed with concern by many of our allies who are accustomed to equate American power with numbers of committed combat troops, they will be more enthusiastic when they understand that these changes will actually enhance America's responsiveness to regional conflict while adding to its overall striking power.

This agile strategy for the employment of Army Ground Forces in the modular Group structure recognizes the distinction between a "two near-simultaneous MRC" force and a force that is actually structured to fight and decisively win one MRC while conducting economy of force operations in a second potential theater of war. "Win–hold–win" (today's de facto strategy) requires that regardless of LRC entanglements, "2nd MRC halt forces" get in quickly to the second theater. The outlined force structure enables this. Historically, the nation's armed forces have treated one theater of war as a "decisive force theater" and a second theater as an "economy-of-force" theater. During World War II, the National Command Authorities treated the European Theater as the decisive force theater and the Pacific Theater as the economy-of-force theater.

TRAINING

At this point, it should be apparent that a doctrine based on dominate maneuver is an approach to war that relies for its success in war more on the quality of its officers, noncommissioned officers, and soldiers than on any particular weapons technology. While it admits the possibility that a JTF may have to defend against an attacking enemy, the doctrinal thinking implicit in an American concept for strategic dominance regards the defense as a temporary condition from which a Joint Task Force goes on to the offensive. Rather than relying on the cumbersome mobilization arrangements of the Cold War Army, the JTF-based Army is positioned on the frontiers of American strategic interest, primed to move with a minimum of notice and preparation.

The search for an overarching doctrinal framework for training Army Ground Forces to deploy and fight in the new strategic environment, however, is no easy task. During the 1980s, when the Soviet threat dominated American military thought, the Army leadership implemented a series of revolutionary training programs that began the demanding process of institutionalizing competence at the soldier, platoon, company, and battalion levels by demonstrating in great detail what was required to be trained. Few American soldiers were untouched by the combat training center experience, the battle command training program, and a host of other training initiatives. All of these programs played a major role in shaping the Army that performed brilliantly during Desert Storm.[22]

In a fundamental sense, gaining and maintaining the initiative in a new period of potentially revolutionary change involve training to achieve higher levels of unit readiness and finding people who can integrate all the arms of combat in the midst of a new RMA. Thus, reorienting current military thought to keep pace with the transformation of war is essential to accommodating technologically induced change and modifying warfighting structures. In this context, contemporary Army training with its heavy emphasis on detailed planning, lengthy deliberation, and strict control of forces seems at variance with the RMA trendlines.

Army training is in many ways still profoundly influenced by a philosophy of training that emerged in the 1970s and contains tactical ideas and rests on assumptions about the contemporary Army that discourage improvisation in the face of diverse missions. In many ways, Army training continues to restrict the autonomy of subordinate officers and noncommissioned officers.[23] Without intending to do so, training actually tends to mute the decisiveness of the offense and to ignore the impact on maneuver forces of the increased range, lethality, and accuracy of new weaponry. There is little emphasis on the fact that a small, well-drilled, and coordinated air–ground combat team with instantaneous links to stand-off weapon systems (like rocket artillery) can be counted on to accomplish more than a larger, traditionally trained industrial age force. The reluctance to emphasize independent action, initiative, and use of battle drills in small unit tactics, though, is not really a new problem.

On St. Valentine's Day 1943, 30,000 Americans confronted 11,000 Germans in combat for the first time during World War II at a place called Kasserine Pass in Tunisia. American and British air forces dominated the skies over North Africa. When the battle ended, the U.S. II Corps had lost 183 tanks, 194 half-tracks, 208 artillery pieces, 512 trucks, and more supplies than existed in all the depots in Algeria and Morocco and 20 percent of its strength, or 6,300 troops. The British lost nearly 1,000 men trying to prevent the collapse of the American front; in contrast, the Germans sustained only 989 casualties.[24] At the time, America's senior military leaders were both surprised and disappointed by the outcome.

The U.S. II Corps Commander, Major General Lloyd R. Fredendall, was among the officers named in General George Marshall's letter to Eisenhower who had distinguished themselves as meticulous planners and expert trainers in the interwar period. In fact, Major General Fredendall completed the General Staff College at Leavenworth as a "distinguished graduate." He later graduated from the Army War College and was promoted to Brigadier General relatively early by the standards of the day.[25] For that matter, the

American troops under his command who had landed 4 months earlier at Oran had performed successfully and seized their objectives in less than 3 days. The fact that French armed opposition to the American landing was modest compared with what the Germans could present or that his subordinate commanders had acted largely on their own during the landings was never mentioned. Though Fredendall remained in his command post aboard ship offshore, he gained a reputation as a forceful commander who succeeded in battle. Fredendall's distinguished service medal awarded by Eisenhower a month after the landings spoke of his "brilliant leadership and resolute force" and his demonstration of the "highest qualities of leadership."[26] Kasserine changed all that.

The battle of Kasserine Pass was very different from the fight at Oran. Major General Harmon, who played a key role in rescuing the III U.S. Corps from total disaster at Kasserine and who later commanded the 1st Armored Division, prepared a report on the battle for General Marshall that addressed several problems. He noted that while American soldiers were well trained on an individual level, they were not trained to operate as cohesive teams. Consequently, German superiority in battle drill and teamwork was partly responsible for the American defeat. Too many American fighting formations were ad hoc organizations with the result that they were easy prey for more experienced and cohesive German units. Harmon also complained about the quality of battlefield leadership. He advised General Marshall that measures were needed to correct the leadership deficiencies that had contributed mightily to the defeat of American forces:

> We must be ruthless in weeding out and changing officers and men around so that the leaders are in positions of leadership and the others, regardless of their personal qualifications, are put elsewhere. Up to the time of battle itself, we are inclined to stress administration, paper work and tactical knowledge above the flare for leadership. In this we are wrong. . . . A well trained and coordinated division and any unit, for that matter, works on the same principle as a championship football team. Each man must know his job, there must be perfect teamwork, and there must be good substitutes to replace injured men without weakening the team. There must be no favoritism, and selection must be ruthless.[27]

In fairness to Fredendall, most of the American senior officers, including Eisenhower, were not certain what constituted effective warfighting, particularly after 20 years of peace. Thus, Fredendall was not alone in an environment in which new technologies and techniques were emerging more quickly than he and many senior leaders of his generation could digest them. Not only did most senior American officers fail to understand the tactical value of radio communications and airpower, they also lacked any appreciation for the rapidity and complexities of mobile armored warfare. Fredendall's decision during the action at Kasserine to remain remote from the scene of the action by following the battle on a map in his command post was completely consistent with the way the U.S. Army waged war in France during the last months of World War I, but it was a critical mistake in World War II. The rest of the story is too well known to repeat here, but it is worth noting that although Fredendall had superior resources, as well as advance notice of German plans and intentions thanks to Ultra secret intelligence intercepts, his determination to fight a centrally controlled, set-piece battle resulted in one of the Army's worst defeats in this century.[28]

In practice, the contemporary Army still treats warfare as an activity that can be carefully orchestrated. As a result, simulated combat at the training centers still accustoms too many leaders to look at war more in terms of the plans and preparations to fight than of the results that can be achieved in action. Because of the concern with synchronization in operational and logistical planning, not enough attention is devoted in training to the missed or seized opportunities for battlefield success which may result from subordinate initiative and new fighting techniques and tactics. Writing in 1932, in an article appropriately entitled "New Questions of War," a Russian, Marshal Tukhachevskii, argued:

> Small units cannot afford to wait for orders; nor do they have the right to do so. They must act boldly and decisively on their own initiative. It is in reliance on this spirit of initiative and acting without orders that the commander planning the battle issues his orders and directs the action. Clearly, then, there is no paradox here. Tactical command and control is in its very essence a mixture of control and self-control. Doctrinaire officers, blind to the living nature of the modern battle, want "strict planning" of the actions of their forces. But these actions are determined not only by their orders, but by the actions of opposing infantry soldiers, machine gunners and tanks as well. These doctrinaire officers may be "in command." but they are not in control of the course of events; they are irretrievably behind the times. Firm control of one's troops by no means always signifies real control in battle. Frequently, firm command may even run counter to development of the tactical process. Commanders who seek to control their entire battle firmly, on a tight rein, are apt to hold back the offensive during a penetration or pursuit and thus damage their chances of success.[29]

Tukhachevskii expressed these thoughts at the beginning of an earlier RMA. Consider how much more important the training, discipline, and leadership of small units are now when their independence from the center, as well as their striking power and range, is so much greater![30] In many cases, the tasks that ordinary soldiers are being asked to perform now involve decisions which previously would have been made by officers. To expect a relatively inexperienced and possibly poorly trained soldier to decide in a few seconds whether or not to fire his stinger missile at jet aircraft or to attack a column of armored vehicles with his air reconnaissance troop is to ask for trouble.[31]

Although there is plenty of confirmation in the historical record that soldiers, noncommissioned officers, junior officers, and commanders can make such decisions, there is also a lot of evidence to suggest that they will only make the right decision if they are trained, selected, and encouraged to do so.[32] The German Army units that contained the Allied forces in the Normandy beachhead in an environment of overwhelming Allied air superiority did not depend on extensive or elaborate guidance from higher headquarters to guide their actions. Neither did the Russian troops who defended Moscow in the dark days of December 1941. Had they done so, Moscow would probably have fallen to the advancing Germans. The application of tactics involves much more than matching the right weapon system with the right target. Tactics entail combining and using technology with a human dimension. And continuous changes in technology place a premium on tactical innovation and adaptiveness.

As the experience at Kasserine demonstrated, great practical difficulties face the wartime commander who ignores the truth that warfare is really exploratory in nature and who develops a plan that restricts the tactical initiative of his subordinates in battle. The pressure exerted in war by technology pushes the human mind to the limit. Computers, satellites, and electronically collected and transmitted information make more intelligence available to a commander at any level more than he can possibly digest in the time available. As time goes on, this tendency will only get worse.

Training within the framework of the Army's many warfighting simulations advocates thorough planning as the best solution to this problem. This involves exploring all of the contingencies and developing decision trees and execution matrices. But no amount of planning will confer on the commander the ability to foresee all of the contingencies, nor will the planning constructs abstracted from the battlefield before the battle begins ever coincide precisely with wartime conditions. Even when the enemy cooperates (and that is rare), the plan will always fall short because of limitations on the accuracy of data and time. Therefore, as much as the Army seeks to train commanders at all levels to plan well, it needs to induce leaders at every level to think quickly, adapt to changing circumstances, and junk plans that seldom survive contact with the enemy. Defeat in battle stems more from the leader's failure to adapt to rapidly changing circumstances than from the failure to plan every action deliberately or the influence of new technology. This observation magnifies the importance of finding leaders who demonstrate in tough, realistic training that they are likely to excel in the chaotic environment of warfighting.

In the current training environment, the U.S. Army spends lavishly for every brigade-size training rotation at the National Training Center. Although it is fair to say that the combat training centers provide rotational units with the most realistic peacetime training available, the "Kasserine-style" defeats sustained by many Blue Force (BLUEFOR) units are not encouraging. What is worse, however, is the "lose and learn" theory that is used to rationalize defeats. This mentality displaces winning as a worthy goal and is based on the assumption that objectively evaluating the performance of leaders in the field environment is neither possible nor desirable.

To the soldiers who fight the simulated battles, however, a win or a loss in training is described in absolute terms. It is to say, in paraphrase of Vince Lombardi's legendary dictum, that for our soldiers winning at the Training Centers isn't everything, it is the only thing that counts. For obvious reasons, a battalion or brigade commander is at his worst if he tells his soldiers at the end of a training rotation, "We trained safely and we learned a lot," when the soldiers know perfectly well that they were defeated in every encounter with the opposing force (OPFOR). The ordinary American soldier is exceptionally bright and has surprisingly good instincts for what is true and what is not. American soldiers instinctively grasp the fundamental fact of military life that in combat, winning is everything!

Measuring the performance of units at a training center only on the basis of wins and losses against the OPFOR is risky. It potentially misinterprets both the underlying purpose of the Army's training centers and the nature of the profession itself. The quality of the performance does count. But legitimizing repetitive losses by emphasizing the process at the expense of results is riskier. Nothing illustrates this better than the comments of Lieutenant General A. E. Percival when he attempted to explain his behavior in the face of Japanese attacks on Malaysia and Singapore after his release from Japanese confinement: "I had learnt on exercises we had held in England not to commit your reserve until you are quite sure you are dealing with the real thing."[33] Unfortunately for Percival, the Japanese attack was the real thing. Percival was physically brave, physically fit, and a first-class staff officer. He was unassuming, considerate, and conciliatory, with a good mind. But Percival was not a commander who would take risks, so he could not imagine that a potential enemy commander would do so. After the fall of Singapore to a Japanese force that was smaller than the British Army defending Singapore, many British officers to Field Marshal Alan Brooke, the Chief of the Imperial General Staff, expressed the view that "officers were being promoted to higher command because they were proficient in staff work—which was quite wrong—and urged that fewer mistakes of this nature should be made in the future."[34]

In peacetime, the commander who makes the fewest mistakes is usually judged to be the best. In war, the commander who compels the opponent to make the most mistakes usually wins.[35] If finding and developing leaders during prewar training who will excel in wartime are important, it follows that a field environment which is conducive to the emergence of such people is critical. For the nation's ground forces the following are key questions. How can prewar training be structured to prepare units to cope with a turbulent environment in which the only constant is change itself? And can it be structured to determine when or whether a leader is effective in this chaotic environment? One way is to structure training in a manner that compels commanders to break the rules in order to win. Another way is to avoid presenting units with impossible tactical missions. Demanding that units charge head-long into the teeth of the enemy's prepared defenses with woefully inadequate fire support is not something the U.S. Army does in wartime. Why do it in peacetime training?

Tactical training which emphasizes speed of movement, simple rehearsed battle drills in response to predictable situations, and rapid improvisation in the face of the unexpected is the first step toward preparing soldiers in peacetime for the conduct of dominating maneuver in wartime. Instead of reading or being told that in war information is often confusing and conflicting, training must accustom leaders to work in this type of environment. The truth is that the maxims of war and regulations which set forth the rules of war go no deeper than the memory, "and in the excitement of battle the memory is useless; habit and instinct are alone to be relied on."[36]

The emphasis on rapid response, innovation, and intelligent leadership from the front is not an excuse for sloppy thinking or planning. It is simply time to reevaluate the ways in which the Army goes about conducting deliberate attacks and defenses in the context of Army training. Unmanned aerial vehicles (UAVs) and attack helicopters must be part of any future training environment. Training operations should include the use of rocket artillery and precision-guided munitions to neutralize an enemy's defensive positions while friendly air assault infantry and armored forces maneuver to the flanks and rear of the enemy's defenses with the object of destroying its mobile reserves. These actions comprise the tactics of dominate maneuver.

It is also possible to create opportunities in the conduct of battles for the unit commander and his soldiers. If they seize these opportunities and win, the command climate, morale, and training of the unit would appear to be in good shape. If, however, the soldiers and their leaders are paralyzed with the fear of failure induced by an oppressive or controlling commander who crushes initiative, then there is a problem.[37] Finally, if the unit repeatedly dashes itself to pieces against the enemy (this frequently happens) because the commander, though charming and likable, is incapable of extracting performance from his troops, then there is another problem.

These points are not impossible to discover, but few armies learn them in peacetime. The people who know are the soldiers, noncommissioned officers, and junior officers who routinely accompany units in training (observer–controllers) and the soldiers in the OPFOR who operate against many different units. The RAND Corporation's analysts, who have nearly ten years' experience with the National Training Center, as observers with no formal relationship to the units in training provide some of the most interesting observations. Moreover, they know which units win and why.[38] The Battle Command Training Program provides an additional opportunity at the operational level for related exposure and scrutiny. Currently, there is no way to ensure that these insights will have an impact on the selection of future leaders for further advancement. This suggests the need for the inclusion of reported observations and insights from more than one source. As Major General Harmon described to General Marshall in 1943, "There must be no favoritism, and selection must be ruthless."[39] Findings from multiple sources must be presented to promotion and command selection boards.[40]

In sum, the U.S. Army has a historic opportunity to do what few professional military establishments have done before—sift out those who cannot lead in action before the war starts. It will not be 100 percent effective, but it will be an improvement over what has happened in the past. In addition to the NTC and the excellent computer-based warfighting simulations which are conducted by brigade, division, and corps staffs as part of the Army's Battle Command Training Program, another area deserves attention—joint training.

The centrality of tactics and operational methods to future war has important implications for jointness. It is clearly not the individual weapons possessed by one side or the other that matter as much as their effective integration and application in combat. Because technology is changing so rapidly, large-scale multiservice joint maneuvers must be held every 3 to 5 years in order to determine whether the forces are adequately trained and prepared to execute wartime missions. There is a tendency today to put too much faith in computer-based simulations that reduce warfare to a mathematically driven process. Computer simulation is not enough. Human endurance, human intelligence, and human skills must be tested to ensure that technology is not developing faster than the human mind can absorb it. Examining the performance of individual battalion-size fighting units is vital, but it will not suffice to prepare the nation's ground forces for warfare beyond the year 2000.

Of all the major powers between the world wars, the U.S. Army had the least effective approach to training for future conflict. Between World War I and 1941, the Army conducted no multidivisional maneuvers. The only place where American officers could even theoretically train for warfare with large units was in the war games of the 1 year course at the Command and General Staff School at Fort Leavenworth. Truman Smith, who had observed the German Army in the 1920s before attending the U.S. Army Staff College, described Fort Leavenworth training as "archaic." According to Smith, Patton, Wood, Harmon, and many subsequently famous wartime commanders, it was a concept of training that viewed future warfare as a series of mathematical formulas.[41] Predictably, it was the American soldier who would discover in the opening battles of World War II how rapidly war was changing and how much American doctrine and training methods had ossified.

Joint training exercises cost money. But Congress should not balk at a proposal to deploy 40,000 to 50,000 troops somewhere in the world every 3 to 5 years to guarantee that the information age force does not end up like the interwar Army of the 1930s. Joint training involving three or more Combat Groups, Fighter Wings, and offshore Naval Forces must be planned and executed often enough to ensure that U.S. forces can still outpace prospective enemies to deter or win conflicts. There are other reasons for regular, joint training exercises. A JTF-based information age Army must actively cultivate informed and intelligent leadership at all levels. This is because jointness is really about both ends and means. Thus, Army training in the context of joint operations should be a process of stressing the importance of strategic ends over the service operational and tactical means of achieving them. Though this observation may seem to be a self-evident truth to the civilian analyst or political appointee without military experience, it is not nearly so obvious to the professional military. Even in war, service parochialism is seldom discarded. This was so much the case in World War II that Field Marshal Rommel felt compelled to address the issue in the context of German Army officer training:

> The greatest efforts must be made in the field of training to counteract the separatist tendencies of the various services and arms of the services. It happens again and again that the air force or the army begins to play its own private political game. This struggling for power is rather like sawing off the branch on which one is sitting. One must be particularly vigilant to ensure that no kind of Corps ambition develops. *Anything which may deflect from unity of purpose, from the will to pull together, must be utterly eradicated.*[42]

Had the reader not been told that the author of this statement was Rommel, the reader might have mistaken the passage for an American CINC's description of events in Korea, Vietnam, or the Gulf War! Of necessity, officers spend their early years in a nearly service-pure environment. This is not an accident. Learning the tools of the trade and knowing the character of warfare at the tactical level and the nature of the Americans who serve in the armed forces' enlisted ranks are all essential features of professional military development. After 8 years of service or more, however, a systematic effort must begin to determine who can grasp the complexities of modern warfare on the operational level and who should be selected for further advancement to serve at the operational level.

EDUCATION

Military education in the General Staff Colleges and War Colleges of the armed services is designed to equip officers with the analytical tools to translate strategic goals into achievable military objectives along with the expertise to plan, move, and employ forces to achieve these objectives.[43] Thus, education is viewed in professional military circles as an essential feature of preparation for senior leadership. In this connection, one of the greatest advantages of a lean, JTF-based professional Army over a mass mobilization force should be its superior leadership. Anyone who has a modest appreciation of the technical knowledge, analytical insight, disciplined mental faculties, and numerous military instruments manned by highly trained professional soldiers necessary for the effective conduct of modern military operations must admit that these qualities cannot be taken for granted.[44] Since the JTF-based Army is founded on the assumption that war at the operational level will always be joint, this suggests that military leadership on the operational level requires much more than hard work or tactical experience. Still, establishing the special qualities of professional-ism above the tactical level that differentiate the outstanding officer from the officer of average abilities is not easy in peacetime.

"We professional soldiers are traditionally laggard in facing and adopting changes," General James Gavin wrote in 1947, "especially radical changes that upset proven methods and the ways in which we have been doing things for years past."[45] LTG Gavin, however, was clearly an exception to his own rule. Gavin rose from Captain (O-3) in 1941 to Major General (O-8) and command of the 82nd Airborne Division in 1944. Like many of his contem-poraries—Ridgway, Harmon, Wood, and Quesada—he was an innovator. He transformed a portion of the outdated prewar American Army into the modern force that won the Second World War. After the war, he initiated the development of helicopter tactics and modern missile artillery and was an early critic of Army and Air Force operations in Vietnam.[46] Students of innovation and the processes of change in large institutions describe people like General Gavin and many officers of his generation who advocated and effectively implemented change as sharing certain personality attributes or characteristics. Among these attributes are a higher degree of intelligence, more favorable attitudes toward change, more individual education, and a more favorable attitude toward risk taking.[47] As mentioned earlier, some of these attributes can be discovered in the right training environment, others through education.

Making the military educational experience relevant to contemporary and future warfare is not easy. Before his appointment as Chief of Staff in 1939, General Marshall felt strongly that the Army's educational institu-tions were dominated by concepts and thinking that were outmoded. Con-vinced that most decisions in battle must be taken swiftly, on minimal information, Marshall believed that military education ought to emphasize dealing with the unexpected and practicing the art of improvisation. "I found that the technique and practices developed at Benning and Leavenworth would practically halt the development of an open warfare situation, appar-ently requiring an armistice or some understanding with a complacent enemy."[48] When LTC George Patton and Major John Wood openly ques-tioned the validity of the solutions to tactical problems presented by the Army General Staff College, Marshall sided with Patton and Wood. How-ever, by 1939, the thinking in the Army's educational institutions was so anachronistic that little could be undertaken to reverse it. General Marshall simply closed the General Staff and War colleges and relied instead on officers like McNair, Patton, Arnold, Wood, and Harmon whose views on warfare had been formed outside the mainstream by the same kind of independent, professional self-study of military affairs which General Marshall had undertaken throughout his career.

The situation today is not the same as it was in 1939. Funding for joint training at the operational level is on the rise and all of the services have developed programs for advanced military studies. But there is room for more change with regard to the way officers are selected and prepared for further education as future senior leaders at the joint level. Today, the officer evaluation report is the only evaluative tool. One way to infuse military education with greater rigor would be to subject officers to written evaluation as a prerequisite for admission to the Army's General Staff College. A written examination would require officers in the grade of captain who have successfully completed company, battery, or troop command to study the profession seriously. Under this system, any captain who has successfully completed command could take the examination annually until the officer met the examination criteria for entrance to the Staff College. Assuming that roughly 1,500 or more captains take the test in any given year, a qualifiying test performance rate of 20 percent would result in the admission of 300+ students a year to the program. However, if after three attempts, the officer could not meet these criteria, he should not be admitted and should not be allowed to advance to positions of high command and influence in the profession of arms.

Skill in the operational art of joint warfighting demands that officers read, study, and think about warfare. In order to institutionalize excellence in the profession of arms above the tactical level, systematic operational studies impelled by meaningful evaluation are necessary. It is important that contemporary study at the General Staff College consist of serious and demanding work with an emphasis on understanding the operational situation and the military–political options in a variety of operational settings. Because this approach involves more than regurgitating Army-pure school solutions on multiple choice exams, the types of studies in operational art conducted at the Army's School for Advanced Military Studies may be a model for military educational experience throughout the system.[49]

The other half of the military education process involves conceding that, however important to a military career, in-house military education is not enough. This suggests that the same officers who are selected for specialized education for future service at the operational or joint level should be offered a year of graduate schooling. This would allow the officer to complete a master's degree in a discipline of value to the officer and to the Army. In a report to the German Army High Command after World War I, it was suggested that the General Staff had been filled with tacticians—no technologists, analysts, or grand strategists. Realizing that the old War College was incapable of providing the education that was needed for a new generation of officers to cope with a new revolution in military affairs, the postwar German military leaders decided to send German General Staff students to civilian education courses at German universities as part of their General Staff education and training.[50] For officers like Guderian, Student, Kesselring, and many others, this opened up a whole new world in which aviation, automotive technology, rocketry, geopolitics, and radio communications presented new solutions to the problems of warfare. It is probably one reason that Germany's wartime commanders were initially far ahead of their contemporaries in the British, American, French, and Russian armies in their understanding of military strategy and technology.

Military educational institutions lost their monopoly as providers of professional military information and knowledge long ago. Had Marshall relied on the generation of officers who had thrived in the interwar environment of military education to win World War II, the war might have dragged on for years without result.[51] For that matter, the contemporary challenge of unconventional warfare and peacekeeping can be much more efficiently met through officer education at the graduate level than through the creation of new OOTW-specific military structures and training. Early attempts by the American military establishment in Vietnam to come to grips with counterinsurgency as a special form of conflict were unsuccessful for reasons that had nothing to do with the military's technical expertise. American field commanders were often too intent on the military aims of unconventional warfare to see that they were undermining the much more important political objectives of the Vietnam conflict.[52] If victory in Southeast Asia had been a function of dedication, commitment, and unbelievably hard work; if sheer attention to detail, long hours of effort, and the right attitude could have done it, then the Army's leaders would have won the war in a few weeks.[53] As American military and political leaders discovered in Somalia, Haiti, and Rwanda, problems of political and economic development can be understood only when viewed in their historical context and successful tactics and strategy require a sophisticated understanding of both problems and solutions.[54]

Because some will still question the utility of higher civilian education as well as the wisdom of the abolishing single-service war colleges, it may be useful to illustrate these points with an example of what a difference careful selection for the right educational experience can make in the preparation of officers for operational command in war. One of the Second World War's most brilliant field commanders who demonstrated an exceptional appreciation for land warfare was an Air Force officer, Field Marshal Albert Kesselring, who commanded ground forces in the Italian campaign with far greater success than virtually all of the American and British Army generals who fought against him. In fact, Kesselring's brilliance as a field commander contributed in no small way to the decision to abandon Churchill's plan for further attempts to strike at Germany through northern Italy and Austria.[55] For those with an interest in joint operations, the question is, How was a German Air Force officer able to command all of those German ground forces successfully?

In addition to Kesselring's natural ability as a commander and leader, one reason may be that Kesselring had a conceptual grasp of warfare that was widely understood by his contemporaries in the Army.[56] This is to say, Kesselring and his Army contemporaries shared a coherent view of the future battlefield which enabled Kesselring to move in and out of Army and Air Force senior command positions as necessary. Although he and Rommel had disagreements, Rommel did not question his competence to command at the operational level. On one occasion during the fighting, when Rommel was forward in action during a critical period, Rommel's Chief of Staff asked Kesselring to assume temporary operational command of a portion of the Italian and German ground forces in North Africa. Major General von Mellenthin, the celebrated author of *Panzer Battles,* describes Kesselring's conduct of operations in glowing terms.[57] Later, when Kesselring commanded German ground forces in what is now widely regarded as a highly successful economy of force campaign to delay and disrupt Allied attempts to strike at Germany through Italy, he was esteemed by both his Army contemporaries and his enemies for his brilliance.[58] Kesselring, who was a product of von Seeckt's postwar hybrid educational system stressing military–technical education along with civilian university coursework, said of the importance of his years in the German Army's institutions of higher learning in Berlin: "Professionally, the Berlin years were a schooling for me. What could have replaced the debates, often held in my room, in the presence of Lieutenant General von Seeckt, who knew so well how to listen and then sum up in a way that always hit the nail on the head?"[59]

Today, the possibility that a U.S. Air Force officer could command and control U.S. Army ground forces in a major theater of war would strike many in uniform as unrealistic. In 1994 an Air Force Lieutenant Colonel wrote: "Would soldiers be comfortable executing a scheme of land warfare designed and controlled by an airman acting as the land component commander? Of course not, and that's why airmen look to another airman, the JFACC, to plan and control the air operations."[60] Yet are the qualities of human intelligence, understanding, and leadership required to command and control service means at the operational level in war really dependent on an individual senior officer's service background?

What was true for the interwar German Armed Forces is true today for the U.S. Armed Forces. In the postindustrial age, knowledge is critical. Knowledge and understanding do not reside in books, databanks, or software programs. Knowledge is always embodied in a person, carried by a person: created, augmented, or improved by a person. The shift to the knowledge-based society and information age military establishment positions the educated person in the center.[61] Knowledge is essential to the emergence of a coherent view of warfare on the operational and strategic levels across service lines. Knowledge of modern technology, strategy, economics, and history is indispensable to senior officers charged with the responsibility to devise true joint doctrine for operational warfighting. If the services could pool their resources in support of one exceptional War College and augment this experience with additional civilian graduate schooling, a dramatic step could be taken in the direction of developing future Joint Commanders like Kesselring.

The Lieutenant Colonel level is the point at which most officers have served long enough to have an image of what they think warfare is really like. Because the Group structure eliminates the Colonel level command requirement from career progression, graduating Lieutenant Colonels can be assigned to joint headquarters while they await selection for further education and promotion to Colonel. Once selected, these same officers can complete further military and graduate education before returning to a Group where they can perform duties as Chiefs of Staff before competing for selection to Group Command. With the time to prepare and educate themselves adequately for command and staff work on the operational level, an exchange program that sends Army officers to the other services for 12 months could also operate successfully within this Group framework.

If the services do not move in this direction, however, then the turmoil surrounding which service gets to do what in every potential contingency will continue. Without the consensual support of the officers who must implement it, a joint warfighting doctrine on the operational level is unlikely ever to have much impact.[62] American service culture militates against this process, but the attitudes born of narrowness that obstruct interservice cooperation can be overcome through careful selection of the right people, the right training, and the right mix of military and civilian education.

MODERNIZATION

To this point, the discussion of the role of ground forces in the new strategic environment has been limited to warfighting, readiness, training, and education. It is important to remember, however, that the entire system of Army Ground Forces—from the type of warfighting equipment procured through the Army's tactics and logistics—must be optimized for the new strategic environment too! In addition to selecting the correct wartime tactics and objectives for American soldiers, technological innovation can protect soldiers from the effects of future conflict. Clearly, the effort to convert theoretical military capability into actual military power through force modernization is a complex challenge. Fortunately, the Army faces fewer constraints than, say, the Navy, which cannot quickly or inexpensively recapitalize itself with smaller, faster surface combatants.

In keeping with the principle that people, not things, are decisive in war, the thinking behind force modernization must be to "equip the man; not man the equipment." Frequently, the enthusiasm for new technology that promises a quantum leap in capability or the desire to prolong the life of equipment that is obsolescing quickly can lead to unnecessary expenditures.

Because the Department of Defense typically purchases in low volumes, with production stretched over many years, it cannot tap into cost savings achieved by economies of scale in the private sector.[63] At the same time, the connection between cost and effectiveness is no longer as clear as it once may have been. Sometimes simpler, inexpensive systems outperform more expensive equipment. Sometimes the opposite is true.[64] Moreover, once munitions become more accurate and lethal, the advantages of expensive weapons platforms to deliver them begin to disappear. Thus, measures to improve, enhance, or fundamentally revolutionize force protection, sustainment, mobility, lethality, and information collection, analysis, and dissemination should seek to avoid systems that are prone to countermeasures, especially if the acquisition costs are high.[65]

These points notwithstanding, improvements in firepower, precision strike, and mobility will count for little if tactical logistics is allowed to obstruct organizational change or to constrain the operational reach of Army Ground Forces in the future. Future warfare places great emphasis on the operational reach of attacking ground forces to strike deep into enemy territory. The concern for operations dominates most military analyses. However, the logistical dimension has contributed more often to military success in the last hundred years than tactical finesse.[66]

This suggests that a modernization program to confer greater reach on ground forces must involve a reduction in the quantities of fuel that are consumed during movement. Engines that can meet the needs of an army shaped for dominating maneuver exist in the commercial sector. This approach could also result in a further reduction in the numbers of fuel trucks that are needed to support armored forces. With this point in mind, the Army's focus in this area already involves reducing the volume and weight of equipment to enhance deployability, sustainability, and mobility. The AGS, RAH66, CH47 upgrades, and UH60 modernization programs are good examples of this thinking. Palletized load systems, integrated family of test equipment, logistics over the shore, and combat service support control system (CSSCS) are all designed to streamline and speed sustainment operations. Logistics is also an area where the Army may be able to benefit from increasing integration with and reliance on the commercial sector. A rugged commercial chip mounted on the engine block of a car, for example, must withstand temperatures, vibrations, and shocks equal to those imposed on a chip mounted in a tank (and indeed the commercial chip is much cheaper, far more reliable, and years more advanced). Similarly, in software terms, the highly sophisticated computer models used in military system target recognition are today being developed in the commercial sector for inventory identification in automated factories.[67]

Force protection consumes planners, who must find ways to move forces safely as well as quickly. Integrating Army aviation into every "all-arms" Combat Group is one important feature of force protection. Comanche's stealthy form and breakthrough communications and targeting technologies are a key feature of force protection. Equipping armored fighting vehicles with electronic countermeasures that initiate actions to defeat stand-off missile systems in the same way aircraft are protected is another. However, tactical ballistic missile defense is probably more urgent than any other effort in this area.

Five years after twenty-eight Americans were killed in the Gulf War by a missile that is now obsolete compared with the missiles that are in the hands of today's potential opponents, there is still no effective theater missile defense system.[68] As the Southwest Asia scenario suggests, force protection during the preparatory phase of future conflict is vital to operational success. Proposed changes to funding for ballistic missile defense are not helpful in this regard. Cutting the Army's Theater High Altitude Area Defense program from $4.7 to $3 billion is imprudent. Adding money to the Navy's Theater Wide (upper tier) program and to the Air Force's effort to develop an airborne laser for boost phase intercept as a hedge against enemy breakthroughs makes sense. But underfunding the Army's ongoing antimissile defense program could delay fielding of new systems for 3 years.[69] The long, sad history of ballistic missile defense from the 1950s through today cries out for an American renunciation of the pattern of accepting "good enough" rather than perfect. American lives depend on ending American procrastination in this area.

Information is always an important feature of force protection as well as an important strategic goal in all future military operations. Digitization is in many ways the centerpiece of this effort. The concept involves embedding compatible digital communications to enhance horizontal efforts to acquire, exchange, and exploit timely information in war. The MILSTAR satellite terminal will contribute to this effort by equipping ground forces with lightweight, transportable, beyond the line of sight secure means of communication. As with many new technologies, its effectiveness will depend on how it is employed. For instance, not every armored fighting vehicle may need digitized communications. Ground and air reconnaissance elements, indirect fire, and stand-off weapons need a secure means of digitally bursting vital information to higher headquarters or to adjacent units, but every tank commander clearly does not need to focus his attention on a computerized window displaying digitally transmitted information.[70] The squad leader doesn't need to surf the Internet, but he does need to know what is going on in his respective battlespace. Common, relevant battlespace is the key to implementing the Army's program for digitization.

Of the funds for the Department of Defense's Top 20 Modernization Investment Programs (see Figure 6.2), the Army receives less than 8 percent, yet its inexpensive, broad-based approach to force modernization provides the nation with an enormous range of important future military options. Each of the Navy's top three procurement items—DDG51, FA-18E/F, and the new attack submarine—equals more than two-thirds of the Army's total acquisition budget.[71] The annual procurement budget is less than $5.4 billion a year. By any estimation, American landpower is a bargain. In contrast to the tendency in the other services to invest heavily in silver bullet systems with a potentially fleeting value in the perpetual cycle of measures and countermeasures, America's ground forces are being equipped to confront an enemy with a variety of hedging requirements and dilemmas. The enemy's capacity to defeat one of several systems will be negated by his inability to cope with the synergistic effect of multiple threats. The principal challenge for the Army is reorganization, not expensive recapitalization.

Figure 6.2
Top 20 Investment Program Comparison, FY96

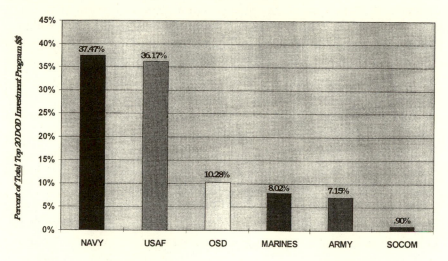

Source - FY96 - 13 DPP

CONCLUSIONS

Many of these points are familiar. The information revolution simply offers opportunities to affect the conduct of war by adopting new operational concepts and new organizational structures. Enabled by new information age organizations and technologies, the U.S. Army can obtain substantial improvements in force effectiveness and adapt to a new strategic environment, no longer relying on the "overwhelming force" paradigm.[72] A precept of U.S. military preparation for combat is that the U.S. Armed Forces should train as they intend to fight. Still, the military continues to view future conflicts and contingencies from distinctly service-based, rather than joint, perspectives.[73] The concepts for assigning, training, and employing Army forces within a new standing JTF headquarters framework presented here are possible guideposts for the development of an information age Army with a warfighting doctrine and organization to fight and win jointly. The concept of deterrence implicit in this JTF-based strategy is the recognition that without American landpower "peace does not keep itself."[74]

Joint simultaneous attack is already enshrined in the context of joint doctrine.[75] However, the importance of infiltration tactics on the operational level is neither widely discussed nor understood. Since the ground campaign during Desert Storm was so short, the possibility of reorganization and retraining to fight differently in the future has been omitted from most doctrinal discussions. In this connection, control of the air in contemporary concepts of future warfare has become synonymous with centralization of control over all land-based and sea-based deep strike assets in the hands of the JFACC. This approach does not admit the possibility that the success of future operations may depend on more than success in the preparatory phase outlined earlier or that aircraft will not "always get through."[76] It ignores the complexity of the close battle and the compression of the close and deep battles into one larger fight as the conflict unfolds. Centralization of control may be the answer at the outset or at the end, but not throughout the conduct of operations in future warfare. The same technology that facilitates centralization must also be flexible enough to facilitate decentralization of command and control over all land, air, and sea forces when necessary.

This point notwithstanding, ground forces are still structured for the type of deliberate conventional warfare that was demonstrated during Desert Storm. As a result, the concept of radical autonomy in organizational and tactical terms set forth here is beyond the capability of the existing Army force structure. During the Gulf War, Army Heavy Divisions attacked in zones of 10–15 kilometers. They are still organized and trained to do so. Yet, very few future enemies are likely to remain as vulnerable to U.S. attack from the air and on the ground as was Iraq. None will indulge the slow, deliberate buildup of combat power and the conservative conduct of operations that characterized the Gulf War.[77] Organizational change within the RMA trendlines outlined earlier will assist with the creation of the capability in the Army's ground forces to cope with more cunning and dangerous enemies in the strategic environment of the future. At the same time, potential adversaries, readiness requirements, and deployability are all factors that must be considered in the course of structuring Army ground forces for future contingencies. The structure described in this work attempts to link these factors in a way that rationalizes the Army's organization for combat.

A joint doctrine for forced entry operations is beyond the compass of this work, but future doctrine in this area of military activity will require innovative thinking, leadership from the CJCS, and time to develop. The proliferation of precision-guided missiles and weapons of mass destruction increases the probability that a future enemy will seek to eliminate an invasion force as it concentrates offshore or in a beachhead. Assuming that the Navy's large industrial age platforms survive the attacks of quiet diesel submarines as well as the barrage of cruise missiles that will be launched from land-based enemy ground and air forces, the troops who go ashore will confront strong defending enemy formations. Joint operations, however, that do not depend primarily on sea-based forces have a much greater chance of success.

The RMA trendlines urge the American military establishment to capitalize on the greatly enhanced capability of American air, ground, and special operations forces to strike inland at points where the enemy's defenses are weak or very vulnerable. Critical port and airfield facilities can then be isolated, attacked, and seized from the land more cheaply, efficiently, and at less risk to American lives than from the sea. This will change the role of sea-based forces and necessitate a reexamination of the way they are structured, trained, and equipped to play their part in future forced entry operations. Ultimately, the realities of the RMA reinforce America's need for regional partners who can provide access without resort to potentially costly forced entry operations. To date, the United States has been both fortunate and wise in this regard. America's alliances with pivotal states in regions of strategic interest have always provided a beachhead for American military power. The United States Armed Forces have not had to conduct forced entry operations from the sea since Inchon in 1950. As always, while the directions are clear and attractive, at least to some, the road ahead is still a rocky one.

The increased demands on human ability to direct complex military operations will not be met, however, through cybernetics and supercomputers. Simply assigning officers to joint staffs for 2 years will not produce "jointness." Experience and equipment will help, but these are not enough. If jointness is equated with effectiveness and efficiency in warfighting, then advancement must be tied more closely to demonstrated proficiency and professional knowledge in the art of war. Leadership in war requires intelligence and character. When war breaks out, the forces with the largest number of people with these capacities in their senior ranks usually win.[78]

A variety of factors enter into the judgment of a military leader's performance in peacetime—all of them in the final analysis, subjective in nature. This is because the only measure of performance is the officer evaluation report (OER). However, an OER's peacetime content is more often than not a reflection of the rated officer's ability to get along with his rater. Thus, the officer with a "perfect file" may simply be someone who "goes along" and never questions his superior's opinions or directives. Elevating such an officer to high command in a peacetime environment may be one way of reassuring his superiors that nothing will happen without their knowledge, but as the Kasserine experience demonstrated, it is a prescription for trouble in wartime.

In his first year as Chief of Staff, because of the need for sweeping and immediate change, General Marshall forcibly retired 500 General Officers and senior Colonels from the Regular Army whose thinking and attitudes obstructed the organizational and doctrinal changes that were necessary to prepare the Army to fight in World War II.[79] Marshall elevated a new generation of professional soldiers without the measured exposure to the authority and responsibility of successive levels of peacetime command. Critics of Marshall's methods at the time admitted later that his decisions brought to prominence a generation of Generals and Colonels whose demonstrated powers of leadership were perhaps unmatched in the history of the United States Armed Forces. In this highly diverse group were men like Ridgway, Patton, Arnold, Wood, Collins, Eichelberger, Gavin, Wedemeyer, Abrams, Quesada, Stillwell, and McAuliffe. In most cases, these men would never have reached high command without Marshall's intervention or support. In the absence of war, the old adage that the subordinate officer must ultimately comply with his superior or resign had become so commonplace in the interwar Army that it obscured the corrollary: the superior officer and the service must provide the opportunities for compromise and change.[80]

In critical situations that cried for solutions to pressing command problems, the burden of responsibility carried by these men made it necessary for them to reach decisions quickly and with minimal guidance. Most of them had taken the time to study their profession and to educate themselves—often to the dismay of their superiors. When war came, they had no time for introspection, patience, or self-doubt. They had to act on the basis of the professional and intellectual capital they had amassed in the years before the conflict began. Of course, in 1941 there was an urgency to the wartime proceedings and a strong desire in Washington to win quickly and decisively.[81]

To offset the features of peacetime military service that exclude officers like Gavin, Patton, and Ridgway from senior rank and command, other sources of information concerning unit and individual performance stemming from objective and dispassionate observers not in the chain of command must be incorporated into the process of selection for battalion-level and higher command. Early and repeated exposure to the broadening experience of civil education is also an important part of the guarantee against professional military insularity and service parochialism. General Sir John Hackett has argued persuasively that the most effective way to arrest the tendency to military insularity is to place officers for 1 or 2 years in the civilian academic community.[82] Yet arresting insularity may be secondary to the more important aspect of breeding generations of officers who will understand that organization to win is more important than interservice competition.

And from time to time, a kind of affirmative action program on the Marshall model is needed to create a diversity of talent and ability in the senior ranks of the U.S. Armed Forces. An example of this process is provided by Admiral Hyman Rickover in the U.S. Navy of the 1950s. Rickover was an unusually intelligent man who had succeeded in irritating the Navy's leadership for years with his passion for nuclear power. When it became apparent that Captain Rickover was about to be passed over for promotion to Rear Admiral for the last time and forced into retirement, congressional pressure was brought to bear on the Navy. Admiral Zumwalt recounts the incident in his memoirs:

> However, there was much sentiment in Congress that, with the new nuclear program in its infancy, Rickover's career should not end that early—a sentiment that many of us middle-grade officers shared, I must add. Evidently, the Secretary of the Navy, Robert B. Anderson, a very competent man, also shared it. Therefore, he included in his instructions to the 1953 selection board the requirement that it select for Rear Admiral one nuclear-qualifed EDO (engineering duty only) Captain. Since there was only one nuclear-qualified EDO Captain in the Navy at that time, and his name was Hyman Rickover, you can safely say that this requirement left little to the board's imagination.[83]

This point simply magnifies the importance of structuring the peacetime training and educational environment to find the future Ridgways and Gavins. History teaches that when officers are advanced solely on the basis of their demonstrated ability to carry out detailed orders and to control their units tightly in peacetime, the selection system frequently advances leaders who, like General George McClellan in the Civil War, have mastered the process but cannot execute it. In one of his finest works, *August 1914*, Alexander Solzhenitsyn begins his chapter concerning Russia's dramatic military defeat in the battle of Tannenberg with an excursion into the politics of the Russian Army. In his timeless observation, however, Solzhenitsyn could just as easily be describing the conditions that confronted Marshall, Patton, Mitchell, Stillwell, Grant, or Sherman:

> There is no innate gift that brings unalloyed reward: it is always a source of affliction too. But for an officer it is particularly galling to be endowed with exceptional talent. The army will gladly pay tribute to a brilliantly gifted man—but only when his hand is already grasping a field marshal's baton.

Till then, while he is still reaching for it, the army's system will subject his outstretched arm to a rain of blows. Discipline, which holds an army together, is inevitably hostile to a man of thrusting ability, and everything that is dynamic and heretical in his talent is bound to be shackled, suppressed, and made to conform. Those in authority find it intolerable to have a subordinate who has a mind of his own; for that reason, an officer of outstanding ability will always be promoted more slowly, not faster, than the mediocrities.[84]

NOTES

1. Christopher Harmon, "On Strategic Thinking: Patterns in Modern History," in *Statecraft and Power: Essays in Honor of Harold W. Rood*, ed. Christopher C. Harmon and David Tucker (New York: University Press of America, 1994), p. 73.

2. Pamela Hess, "Air Force Studies Ability of Air Power to Blunt an Armored Invasion," *Inside the Air Force*, 9 February 1996, p. 11.

3. Steven Metz, "The Army and the Future of the International System," *Parameters* (Summer 1994): 95.

4. Robert S. Chase, Emily B. Hill, and Paul Kennedy, "Pivotal States and U.S. Strategy," *Foreign Affairs* (January/February 1996): 49.

5. Bruce B. G. Clarke, "The Strategic Setting," in *Maneuver Warfare: An Anthology*, ed. Richard D. Hooker, Jr. (Novato Calif.: Presidio Press, 1993), 100.

6. James Blackwell, *The Gulf War: Military Lessons Learned* (Washington, D.C.: Center for Strategic and International Studies, 1991), chapter 6.

7. Dr. Christopher Gabel, "Doctrine: Active Defense," in *Combined Arms in Battle Since 1939* (Fort Leavenworth, Kans.: Command and General Staff College Press, 1992), 91.

8. Christopher Donnelly, "Ground Force," in *Soviet Armed Forces Review Annual*, vol. 3 (Gulf Breeze, Fla.: Academic International Press, 1979), 17.

9. Field Marshal Erwin Rommel, *The Rommel Papers*, ed. B. H. Liddell-Hart (New York: Da Capo Paperback, 1953), 519.

10. Robert Holzer, "Battlefield Vision Stresses Information Speed," *Defense Trends: Future Force* in *Army Times*, 19 February 1996, p. 26. Holzer outlines key aspects of the Chairman of the Joint Chiefs' *Joint Vision 2010*.

11. Major General Jasper Welch, USAF (ret.), "Why the Bomber Question Is So Controversial," *Strategic Review* (Winter 1996): 18.

12. Brendan McNally, "Czechs Ponder 'Stealth Tracker' Sale to Iran; Plan Comes After Government Eases Export Rules," *Defense News*, 12 July 1993, p. 1. This article provides details concerning the truck-mounted Tamara Signal Intelligence System which can reportedly track stealth aircraft at high altitudes.

13. James T. Quinlivan, "Force Requirements in Stability Operations," *Parameters* (Winter 1995): 68–69.

14. FM 100-5 Operations (Fort Monroe, Va.: U.S. Army TRADOC, 1986), 15.

15. Stephen Cambone, "Space Programs and Issues," testimony before the Subcommittee on Strategic Forces of the Senate Armed Services Committee, 104th Congress, May 2, 1995.

16. In the new Unified Command Plan, SOUTCOM has responsibility for the seas around South America and will pick up responsibility for the Caribbean Sea in 1997.

17. Commander Terry J. McKearney, USN (ret.), "Rethinking the Joint Task Force," *Proceedings* (November 1994): 54.

18. General Dennis Reimer, "Leadership for the 21st Century: Empowerment, Environment and the Golden Rule," *Military Review* (January–February 1996): 9.

19. In this scheme, the Army would field three Rocket Artillery Groups. At this writing, there is not enough MLRS in the Army to do this. In view of the reduction in the number of M109 Howitzer Battalions that will occur under this plan, an alternative would involve organizing a Heavy Artillery Group consisting of four M109 battalions until either a follow-on artillery system is developed or enough MLRS is on hand to form a third group. Another alternative could involve fielding three Groups consisting of three MLRS battalions and one M109 battalion each.

20. James F. Dunnigan and Albert A. Nofi, *Shooting Blanks: Warmaking That Doesn't Work* (New York: William Morrow, 1991), 487.

21. Dr. James Burk, "The Army and the People," discussion paper presented to Senior Conference XXXI, *The Army in the 21st Century*, U.S. Military Academy, 2–4 June 1994, p. 5.

22. LTG Frederic J. Brown, USA (ret.), *The U.S. Army in Transition II: Landpower in the Information Age* (New York: Brassey's, 1993), 118.

23. Major Paul Herbert, "Deciding What Has to Be Done: General William E. DePuy and the 1976 Edition of FM 100–5 Operations," *Leavenworth Papers*, No. 16 (Leavenworth, Kans.: Combat Studies Institute, 1988), 105.

24. Martin Blumenson, *Kasserine Pass: An Epic Saga of Desert War* (New York: Berkley, 1983), 303.

25. Martin Blumenson and James L. Stokesbury, *Masters of the Art of Command* (New York: Da Capo Press, 1975), 267.

26. Ibid., 266–67.

27. Major General Ernest Harmon, *Notes on Combat Experience During the Tunisian and African Campaign*, report prepared for the Office of the Army Chief of Staff, April 1943, p. 2.

28. Commander Gerard Roncolato, "Methodical Battle: Didn't Work Then . . . Won't Work Now," *Proceedings* (February 1996): 32.

29. Quoted in Richard Simpkin's *Deep Battle: The Brainchild of Marshal Tukhachevskii* (New York: Brassey's, 1987), 83.

30. These words were suggested in a letter to the author from Dr. Fred Kagan, assistant professor of history in the Department of History at the U.S. Military Academy.

31. Hirsh Goodman and W. Seth Carus, *The Future Battlefield and the Arab–Israeli Conflict* (New Brunswick, N.J.: Transaction Publishers, 1990), 141.

32. Patrick Pexton, "You Will Not Fail: Fear of Mistakes Throttles Initiative in the Ranks," *Army Times*, 12 February 1996, pp. 12–15.

33. Keith Simpson, "Percival," in *Churchill's Generals*, ed. John Keegan (New York: Grove Atlantic, 1991), 259, 269.

34. Ibid., 259.

35. Congressman Ike Skelton, "Inspiring Soldiers to Do Better Than Their Best," *Military Review* (January–February 1996): 71.

36. Colonel G.F.R. Henderson, *The Battle of Spicheren: A Study in Practical Tactics and War Training* (London: Longman, 1909), p. V.

37. "It is essential that leaders develop the initiative of subordinates." Statement by General Dennis Reimer in "Leadership for the 21st Century: Empowerment, Environment and the Golden Rule," *Military Review* (January–February 1996).

38. Leland Joe, John Grossman, Doug Merrill, and Brian Nichiporuk, "High Performance Units for *Force XXI*: Interim Briefing," RAND Report DRR-1052–A (Santa Monica, Calif.: RAND Corporation, April 1995).

39. David Halberstam, *The Best and the Brightest* (New York: Ballantine Books, 1992), 548. Halberstam notes: "Westmoreland was aloof, reserved, a decent man with a high moral tone in the American sense (he would not, as an aide noted, fire a man for incompetence, but he would fire one for the suggestion of immorality)."

40. After all, if any of the nation's top 500 corporations were paying a great deal of money for 2,000 or more of their employess to train nine to twelve times a year in a sophisticated and realistic training environment, corporate leaders would demand to know who turned in the results!

41. James S. Corum, *The Roots of Blitzkrieg: Hans von Seeckt and German Military Reform* (Lawrence, Kans.: University Press of Kansas, 1992), 190.

42. Erwin Rommel, *The Rommel Papers*, ed. B. H. Liddell-Hart (New York: Da Capo Paperback, 1953), 519.

43. John E. Turlington, "Learning Operational Art," *Essays on Strategy IV* (Washington, D.C.: National Defense University Press, 1987), 194.

44. These words are lifted from remarks made by Colonel General Hans von Seeckt in February 1919 that are quoted in Corum, *Roots of Blitzkrieg*, 33.

45. James Gavin, *Airborne Warfare* (Washington, D.C.: Infantry Journal Press, 1947), 140.

46. Jay Parker, "Into the Wind, Against the Tide: Change and the Operational Commander," in *Essays on Strategy, XII* (Washington, D.C.: National Defense University Press, 1994), 401.

47. Everett M. Rogers and F. Floyd Shoemaker, *Communication of Innovations: A Cross Cultural Approach* (New York: The Free Press, 1971), 347–85.

48. Cited by General Paul F. Gorman in "The Secret of Future Victories," *IDA Paper P-2653* (Alexandria, Va.: Institute for Defense Analysis, 1992), I-23.

49. Turlington, "Learning Operational Art," 211–13.

50. Corum, *Roots of Blitzkrieg, 33.*

51. General Pershing's decision to acquire a law degree at his own expense when he was still a Captain profoundly impressed Marshall.

52. Robert O'Neill, "The Vietnam War and the Western Alliance," in *Second Indochina War Symposium: Papers and Commentary*, ed. John Schlacht (Washington, D.C.: Center for Military History, 1984), 234.

53. Halberstam, *Best and the Brightest*, 549.

54. David Mayers, "The Practitioner/Theorist in American Foreign Policy: George Kennan," in *Center-Stage: American Diplomacy Since World War II*, ed. L. Carl Brown (New York: Holmes & Meier, 1990), 326.

55. Matthew Cooper, *The German Army 1933–1945* (Lanham, Md.: Scarborough House, 1978), 401–3.

56. Shelford Bidwell, "Kesselring, Field-Marshal Albert Kesselring," in *Hitler's Generals*, ed. Correlli Barnett (New York: Quill/William Morrow, 1989), 270.

57. Major General F. von Mellenthin, *Panzer Battles*, trans. H. Betzler (New York: Ballantine Books, 1956). See the chapter dealing with the Desert Campaign. The author mentions Kesselring's competence numerous times in connection with land warfare and grand strategy.

58. David Eisenhower, *Eisenhower at War: 1943–1945* (New York: Random House, 1986), 9, 218.

59. Corum, *Roots of Blitzkrieg, 50.*

60. Jeffrey E. Stambaugh, "JFACC: Key to Organizing Your Air Assets for Victory," *Parameters* (Summer 1994): 104.

61. Peter Drucker, *Post-Capitalist Society* (New York: Harper Business Publishers, 1993), 210.

62. At the same time, the Army often funds graduate education for officers who are subsequently passed over for promotion because they have failed as company, battery, or troop commanders. This is a waste of money. The same officer whose performance in company-level command suggests that he should not be promoted to the next rank should not be given a graduate-level educational opportunity at the Army's expense!

63. *Integrating Commercial and Military Technologies for National Strength: An Agenda for Change*, Report of the CSIS Steering Committee on Security and Technology, prepared by Debra van Opstal, project director (Washington, D.C.: The Center for Strategic and International Studies, 1991), p. 5.

64. All of the material presented here can be found in much greater detail in the U.S. Army's Program Objective Memorandum, *POM 97–01: Modernization and Investment* IV (June 19, 1995): A15–A20.

65. Goodman and Carus, *Future Battlefield and the Arab–Israeli Conflict*, 167.

66. David Curtis Skaggs, "Of Hawks, Doves, and Owls: Michael Howard and Strategic Policy," *Armed Forces and Society* 11, no. 4 (Summer 1985): 617.

67. *Integrating Commercial and Military Technologies*, 2. Also see Major General Maggert's comments on future combat vehicles in Greg Caires' "Army Wants Lighter, More Versatile Vehicle to Replace M1 Tanks," *Defense Daily*, 10 July 1996, p. 43.

68. Bill Gertz, "Plea for Missile Defense in Korea Fails: Shalikashvilli Cites Spending Priorities," *Washington Times*, 15 February 1996, p. 4.

69. David A. Fulghum, "New Priorities Refocus Ballistic Missile Defense," *Aviation Week*, 26 February 1996, p. 24.

70. Bryan Bender, "GAO Criticizes Digitization Effort: Army Says It's on the Job," *Defense Daily*, 1 December 1995, p. 291.

71. "DOD Weapons Costs Fall Due to Lower Inflation Rates," *Defense Daily*, 21 January 1996, pp. 60–61.

72. Jeffrey Cooper, "Another View of Information Warfare: Conflict in the Information Age" (August 1995): 24.

73. Bradley Moffett, "Expanding Our Vision of Jointness: Pursuing Joint Force Development Strategies," in *Essays on Strategy XII*, ed. John Petrie (Washington, D.C.: National Defense University Press, 1994), 283.

74. Donald Kagan, *On the Origins of War and the Preservation of Peace* (New York: Doubleday, 1995).

75. *Doctrine for Joint Operations*, Joint Pub. 3–0 (Washington, D.C.: Government Printing Office, 1 February 1995), chapter 4.

76. Stambaugh, "JFACC," 104–5.

77. Jeffrey Record, "Force Projection/Crisis Response," in *Turning Point: The Gulf War and U.S. Military Strategy*, ed. L. Benjamin Ederington and Michael J. Mazarr (Boulder, Colo.: Westview Press, 1994), 145.

78. MG F. W. von Mellenthin, *Panzer Battles*, trans. H. Betzler (New York: Ballantine Books, 1956), 28–30.

79. Gen. Paul F. Gorman, USA (ret.), *The Secret of Future Victories*, IDA Paper P-2653 (February 1992): I-33–II-25.

80. Major Paul Herbert, "Deciding What Has to Be Done," 105.

81. Blumenson and Stokesbury, *Masters of the Art of Command*, 372–73.

82. General Sir John Hackett, *The Profession of Arms* (London: Sidgwick & Jackson, 1983), 201.

83. Admiral Elmo Zumwalt, *On Watch: A Memoir* (New York: Quadrangle Books, 1974), 98.

84. Alexander Solzhenitsyn, *August 1914*, trans. Michael Glenny (New York: Farrar, Straus & Giroux, 1971), 214.

7

Streamlining Defense to Pay for Strategic Dominance

Congressional leaders know that there are potential savings in the Pentagon's budget. Depending on where and what cuts in defense spending are made, the Congressional leadership is right. For leaders on the Senate and the House Armed Services committees, then, the key questions are, What kind of defense spending should lawmakers scale back and how do they invest the funds that are left over? To find answers to these questions that will also serve the national interest, short-term political factors such as jobs tied to unneeded weapon systems must retreat before clear-eyed strategic assessments.[1]

Military strategies should be considered first and foremost in terms of their performance and promise in safeguarding the nation's interests from external threats. In this regard, the previous chapter's conclusions raise important questions about the need to reorganize Army Ground Forces. To recognize that air and maritime forces cannot control events on land in areas of pivotal strategic interest without landpower is also to raise questions about means, effectiveness, and consequences. These involve contentious issues that will inexorably move defense spending to the center of political debate in 1997.

In view of the material presented to this point, it should be possible to answer some of these questions. In a perfect world, a sober strategic assessment would throw the answers into sharp relief. Sadly, the task is not so easy. As mentioned earlier, elected representatives of both parties have come to equate the widely salted military manufacturing appropriations with local jobs, "from the vast aerospace plants of vote-rich California to the boatworks of Maine."[2] Of the nearly $8 billion in unrequested spending on weapons programs contained in the 1996 defense authorization bill, over 80 percent went to states represented by lawmakers who sit on the Armed Services and National Security committees or the Appropriations Defense subcommittees. The two states that gained the most from the unrequested funds were shipyard-dependent Louisiana and Mississippi.[3]

And the Armed Services have been thoughtful and imaginative in the ways that defense contracts are spread across enough states to ensure political support for defense spending on the hill. For example, the success of the Air Force's new F-22 fighter program rests solidly on a foundation that spreads research and development (R&D) subcontracts to 1,150 companies, employing 15,000 people in forty-three states and Puerto Rico.[4] This strategic approach to defense spending results in frequent decisions to buy many weapons that do not make much military sense, but do make a great deal of domestic political sense.[5] Furthermore, military attempts to keep up with the commercial state of the art are frustrated by failures in acquisition reform.

None of these points makes explaining the value of landpower to Congress any easier for the Army's senior leaders. All Army officers esteem the value of American air superiority in warfare and want to preserve it. There is not a single officer, noncommissioned officer, or enlisted soldier in the Army who favors any policy that would degrade or undermine American control of the seas. Army officers are disinclined on the grounds of Army service culture to argue that the current level of defense expenditures on maritime forces or air forces is disproportionate to the nation's strategic needs. The fact that a similar attitude is seldom exhibited by Air Force, Navy, or Marine officers changes nothing in the Army's cultural attitudes toward the defense debate.

Yet, the Army must join this debate if the nation is to have the armed forces it will need in the 21st century. The sharp increases in the number of operations involving Army forces and the rapid and simultaneous drawdown of those same Army forces make public debate imperative. Defense spending has already fallen 35 percent, in real dollars, since 1985. The only question is how much further the defense budget will be reduced and what kind of force structure will emerge at the end of the process. For the Army, this means (1) illustrating the value of a new, reorganized information age Army in the context of the nation's evolving military strategy and the nation's need for economy and (2) urging a new strategic focus for defense spending.

The central conclusion of this chapter is that reorganizing the Army's ten division force into twenty-six Combat Groups would produce savings exceeding $1 billion a year in operating and maintenance costs alone. However, reorganizing the Army along the lines suggested in this work may not make much difference if the capital intensive search for single-service silver bullets denudes the Army's capability to fulfill its critical national security role in the turbulent days ahead.

CHANGE ON A STRATEGIC LEVEL

If a long-term military strategy to preserve American strategic dominance is to be realized, it seems prudent to accompany any recommendations for change in the warfighting structure with some recommendation for change in the command structure. This is because, in theory, the pursuit of strategic dominance not only guides domestic economic policies as they relate to defense spending, it also shapes the American military force structure.[6] The Goldwater–Nichols Act was the first dramatic step in this direction since the codification of World War II experience in the National Security Act of 1947. The National Security Act of 1947 formalized the National Security Council and the Joint Chiefs of Staff.

Goldwater–Nichols was fundamentally about rearranging power on the strategic level among institutions within the Department of Defense— namely, the Chairman of the Joint Chiefs of Staff, the Services, and the unified commands.[7] It was intended to reduce the influence of the Service Chiefs and to increase the power of the Chairman and the Unified Commanders-in-Chief. In fact, the combatant commanders were given explicit authority over the employment of U.S. forces in their respective areas of responsibility. In the midst of these changes, the services set out for institutional reasons to highlight the contribution of their respective forces to the national military strategy. In the context of the Bottom-Up Review, these parochial, service-led efforts resulted in what turned out to be an underfunded, overstretched U.S. defense establishment[8] that did not look significantly different from its Cold War ancestor.[9]

In judging the results of the Goldwater–Nichols system, however, it is important to note the pressures of international and domestic change after 1989 which altered the climate for strategic decision making. Few periods in American history present such a dramatic series of events or illustrate so well the problems of developing a coherent framework for strategic thinking as the interval between the disintegration of Russian power in Eastern Europe and the American military intervention in Haiti. Emerging missions obliged the national command authorities to reexamine America's military role in international order, to create a balance of military forces to discourage future aggression, and to wrest out of the chaos of international order some organizing principles which would ensure security.

Today, the challenge is no less daunting. In a world where new threats to American national security are emerging, it is more important than ever to rationalize the allocation of scarce economic resources to America's military establishment without putting American national security at serious risk. Because this effort involves the painful process of developing a national military strategy that does not emphasize types of armed forces independently of the criteria by which the potential warfighting utility of military power should be judged, the success of the process depends on extending the process of reform begun in Goldwater–Nichols. This process requires the same type of organizational thinking prevalent in the private sector that was addressed earlier in this work. This also means a return to the frontier of interservice rivalry on a strategic level.

On the surface, the concept and practice of jointness appear to be irrevocably established. But each service still writes its own budget and promotes its own officers. Fearing possible reductions in its force structure, each service strives to impart its unique perspectives to every joint military endeavor. An example is provided by the additional funding offered for antimissile defense, which is widely recognized as the top joint military priority for operational success in any future conflict. But theater missile defense means both financial resources and power to the services. Although the Army has developed and fielded the first antimissile defense system in the form of the Patriot missile, the Air Force has responsibility for developing a joint system. At the same time, the Navy quickly marketed its Aegis-equipped destroyers and cruisers as a central component part of the antimissile defense effort.[10] This rivalry mirrors the U.S. Armed Forces' efforts in the mid-1950s when the Army's Nike Zeus missile systems competed with Air Force and Navy missile systems for the same role.

The interest in antimissile defense is justified. All of the services have a stake in it and each will play a critical role. But decisions to allocate funds should not become the object of interservice competition. Attempts of the Joint Staff to assess the immediate and long-term military value of weapons and forces dispassionately in the context of national military strategy are consistently obstructed through a complex system of checks and balances that strongly favor the services. When attempts were made by the Joint Staff in January 1996 to examine the $214 billion in costs over the next decade for recapitalization of tactical aircraft, the Navy, Marine Corps, and Air Force were able to stop them.[11]

On the basis of these observations, it would seem that the Chairman is hardly more capable today of forcefully advancing a unified strategic position on purely military matters than he was before Goldwater–Nichols! While this may strike some as an exaggeration, it is still true that the chiefs of service exert a degree of influence over national strategic decisions which may be disproportionate to what was envisioned in the original Goldwater–Nichols reforms.[12] What, then, is to be done?

Successful strategy thrives on perpetual creation and on constant redefinition of strategic goals. Today, USTRANSCOM consolidates the Navy's sealift, the Air Force's transport aircraft, and the Army's trucks under central management.[13] Each service continues to maintain its own transportation assets, but all of the services work in tandem to organize and move military personnel and materiel under the leadership and control of USTRANSCOM. By establishing a unified commander with responsibility for supporting the regional CINCs with these multiservice assets, the interservice fight for control over these assets was contained and moderated.[14]

As mentioned in the last chapter, organizational change cannot occur in isolation from doctrinal change. Indeed, the potentially unifying influence of joint warfighting doctrine on the services should not be underestimated. Exhorting soldiers, sailors, airmen, and Marines to fight jointly is an empty slogan as long as the services rigidly resist the development of strategic and operational doctrine that unifies them. Varying single-service institutional structures for doctrinal formulation actually exacerbate the natural tensions that pull the services in opposite directions. While the current Joint Warfighting Center and the Chairman's personal emphasis on removing this impediment to "jointness" have resulted in enormous improvement in this area, the need for an independent institution for the development of operational and strategic doctrine under joint command and control is still acute. In most ways, the U.S. Army's Training and Doctrine Command (TRADOC) headquarters is an excellent model for such a unified command. More important, establishing this institution should not be a major problem.

Founded in 1973 to develop virtually all of the Army's doctrine from the capstone manual, FM 100–5 *Operations*, to the lowest tactical publication, the U.S. Army's TRADOC established a powerful integrating agency that made doctrine the engine that drove the Army. Until recently, doctrinal development in the Air Force, Navy, and Marine Corps was more diffuse because it tended to be a more tangential concern in these services.[15] This is no longer the case. The Air Force theme of "Victory Through Airpower" and the Navy's "From the Sea" are really examples of the cross-currents in the context of interservice rivalry.[16] Since the services tend to fight in dissimilar environments, single-service doctrine becomes an instrument of self-preservation that often accelerates the centrifugal forces that pull the services apart. *What real jointness requires is an engine on the joint level to drive the formulation of military doctrine in support of the national military strategy.* Debates about theater missile defense, the fire support coordination line (FSCL), or close air support planning and execution may be easier to conduct and resolve on the joint level.

Why not consolidate these organizations under joint leaders within the broad framework of the Joint Requirements Oversight Council? The United States Army's Training and Doctrine Command is located across the river from Norfolk at Fort Monroe, Virginia. The Naval Doctrine Command is in Norfolk and the Air Force Doctrine Center is at nearby Langley Air Force Base. Not only is it easier and cheaper to link one unified Joint Training and Doctrine Command to the recently established Joint Warfighting Center at Fort Monroe, Virginia, electronically; it is also the only way to change the shape of America's ground, air, and maritime forces fundamentally. Tactical doctrine will properly remain firmly in service hands. Service expertise will continue to play a key role in the debate about operational doctrine, but this organizational change will supplant the doctrinal interaction among the services, which frequently resembles a dialogue of the deaf.[17]

What would the savings amount to? The costs of campaigns are always greater than originally forecast and the savings from reform are always less than anticipated. *From the vantage point of the American taxpayer, however, reform always pays off in the form of greater efficiency.* Further, the reorganization of the nation's fighting forces should also include the reorganization of their senior command structure to leverage greater agility in military decision making. It seems reasonable to insist that many of the various major headquarters internal to the services be reformed, reorganized, or eliminated before a single combat soldier, sailor, airman, or marine is removed from the U.S. Armed Forces. It is in the context of reorienting defense spending on the strategic level that the reader should view the majority of proposed changes in the ground, air, and maritime forces detailed in the sections that follow.

GROUND FORCES

The Army Chief of Staff states that further reductions in the size and striking power of the Army would be antithetical to the national security interest and to the viability of the Army force structure. Today's 495,000 man force is smaller than the hollow army with which the United States began the Korean War.[18] Before more soldiers are ejected from the Active Army in another round of salami slicing the existing force, a plan to reorganize in ways that preserve and enhance the Army's fighting power is essential. Any discussion about reductions in defense spending for Army ground forces must include the Army National Guard (ARNG). This is because the current ARNG structure contains more combat division equivalents than the active Army and because the Guard has an enormously important role inside the United States.[19]

The history and origins of the Army National Guard are too well known to recount here, but its principal raison d'être can be traced to the Guard's Divisions. These divisions saw extensive service in both wars and the casualties sustained by these units were very high.[20] The high casualties in Guard units during World War II prompted a deliberate effort in Washington after the war to keep the National Guard out of the fighting. The fighting in Korea and Vietnam did not involve the mobilization of the Guard Divisions. After the experience of fighting an unpopular war in Vietnam the situation changed. In 1973, the Total Force Policy was adopted to ensure that at least a portion of the American public would be involved in any future war by mobilizing the Army National Guard when needed from its thousands of locations throughout the United States.[21] During the run-up to the 1991 Persian Gulf War, the Army mobilized three National Guard Roundout Brigades, but they were never deployed to the Middle East because they were seen as not ready for combat, an allegation that still rankles many reservists.[22]

In retrospect, the "Regulars" have underestimated the contribution that Guard elements can make to wartime operations, and the Army National Guard, for its part, tends to overestimate its ability to conduct operations early and independently of Active Component command and control.[23] Military success in the new strategic environment requires a high level of military preparedness in the training, coordination, command, control, and integration of enabling joint capabilities with ground forces. It is not reasonable to expect most Reserve Component elements to be capable of achieving adequate readiness levels in the very limited training time available to them. New pressures for reductions in the strength of the National

Guard,[24] however, simply infuse the old Army–National Guard rivalry with new strength. Edward J. Philbin, executive director of the National Guard Association of the United States, reminded Defense Secretary William Perry in a recent letter that the ARNG divisions slated for cutbacks in the Department of the Army's plans are located in twenty-five states and that a "precipitous restructuring could very well affect the 1996 elections."[25]

There is room for compromise, however. The solution to rationalizing the Guard and Reserve issue is to disestablish the division structures in the Guard and to integrate that portion of the ARNG to which the active Army needs access early and often. The Air Force has had considerable success with their efforts to integrate the force and there is no reason why an integrative approach with ground forces could not also succeed.[26] The potential for astronomical equipment consumption rates and catastrophic losses from weapons of mass destruction in the new strategic environment makes early access to the Reserve Component essential. The Active Army has conducted plenty of research to determine what it needs from the Guard.[27] The Guard also has a pretty good idea of what it needs to survive on the domestic level. Between the two, an agreement could be reached that resulted in a three tiered ground force consisting of tier 1, the active Army; tier 2, the portion of the Guard integrated with the active Army; and tier 3, the remaining Guard Force.

Tier 2 would comprise the Strategic Reserve Corps and tier 3 would consist of units with important domestic utility that would only be mobilized for defense missions in a national emergency. In this light, the formation of an Active Component Strategic Reserve Corps structure to integrate, command, control, train, and deploy reserve and Army National Guard combat, combat support, and combat service support formations is even more sensible and attractive and should be considered as a significant element in any calculation of American military power. An example of what elements could be included in the Strategic Reserve Corps is shown in Figure 7.1.

This proposal retains some combat elements on the assumption that under Active Component command and control, these elements could achieve a much higher state of readiness for deployment than under independent ARNG control. By converting to a Group-based structure, the Army can also reorganize the Guard on the same model. The structure depicted in Figure 7.2 includes an ARNG Chief of Staff. In fact, the personnel and logistics officers could also be ARNG officers. At the corps level, some number of the General Officers in the corps staff could also be ARNG officers.

Figure 7.1
Possible Strategic Reserve Corps Elements

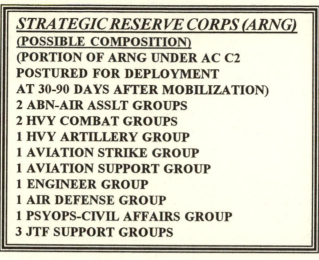

> ### *STRATEGIC RESERVE CORPS (ARNG)*
> **(POSSIBLE COMPOSITION)**
> **(PORTION OF ARNG UNDER AC C2**
> **POSTURED FOR DEPLOYMENT**
> **AT 30-90 DAYS AFTER MOBILIZATION)**
> **2 ABN-AIR ASSLT GROUPS**
> **2 HVY COMBAT GROUPS**
> **1 HVY ARTILLERY GROUP**
> **1 AVIATION STRIKE GROUP**
> **1 AVIATION SUPPORT GROUP**
> **1 ENGINEER GROUP**
> **1 AIR DEFENSE GROUP**
> **1 PSYOPS-CIVIL AFFAIRS GROUP**
> **3 JTF SUPPORT GROUPS**

NOTE: *DECISIVE FORCE CORPS AND STRATEGIC RESERVE CORPS HEADQUARTERS ARE NOT* DESIGNED TO OPERATE AS RAPIDLY DEPLOYABLE JTFS. STRATEGIC RESERVE CORPS DOES NOT INCLUDE ALL ARNG ELEMENTS; ONLY THOSE FOR EARLY MOBILIZATION AND DEPLOYMENT.

Figure 7.2
Structure of Tier II Arng

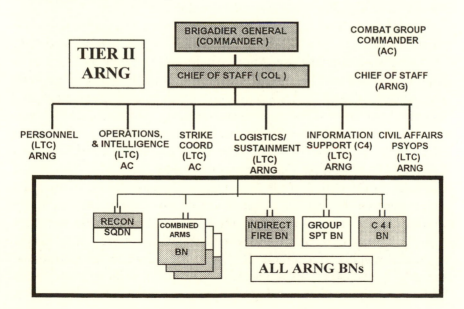

As far as the Army National Guard elements not in the Strategic Reserve Corps are concerned, the nation's governors should have much more say concerning how these organizations are equipped and prepared for employment in their respective states. How much of this force should be federally funded is another matter for discussion between the governors and their legislative representatives in Congress. Much of the modernized combat equipment could be reallocated from these ARNG units to prepositioned sets afloat or ashore in the unified commands. In the new strategic environment, however, civil defense, border security, and related internal security missions should not be overlooked in the context of missions for future tier 3 ARNG forces.

The potential in this conceptual approach for the more efficient preparation of Army National Guard elements to cooperate closely and deploy with the active Army calls to mind related programs in Israel, where higher levels of combat readiness and proficiency exist in the reserve ground forces.[28] Again, those elements not in the Strategic Reserve Corps *would remain under independent Guard control*. The savings from such an approach would probably be considerable. The Army's current proposal to convert the twelve ARNG combat brigades to combat support and combat service support is projected to cost roughly $3 billion. Estimates will vary, but this much more modest approach to integrating only that portion of the Guard needed for future contingencies outside the United States would save at least $2 billion.[29] And these savings could be achieved without jeopardizing the long-term viability of the Army National Guard.

This leaves the first tier or the Active Component Army. Estimating the long-term cost of a given military force structure is a complicated task. Producing cost estimates for Army, Air Force, Navy, or Marine forces requires care and remains a somewhat inexact science.[30] Still, even in an approximate form, estimates are useful analytical tools. To this point, the focus in Army Ground Forces has been on change within the RMA trendlines. Nevertheless, change in the direction recommended here is also a change in the direction of economy and efficiency. Using the U.S. Army's *Force and Organization Cost Estimation System* (version FY96) that is employed in the Office of the Secretary of Defense, Office of Program Assessment and Evaluation, to estimate the cost of the twenty-six Army Combat Groups suggests that replacing the Army's ten division structures with twenty-six Combat Groups would result in a steady-state annual savings of roughly $1.1 billion. The analysis assumes an unchanged end strength of 495,000 troops in the Active Army. All units were created at ALO 1 and C-1 readiness ratings for the purpose of this estimate. This means full manning at 100–105 percent for all units. Personnel saved from the elimination of the division overhead are used to fill out the units.

It is important to put these numbers into perspective. First, unit costs were computed by using the *Army Forces model* with FY95 cost factors.[31] These factors are used in the 1996 version of the model. Units were created by using existing tables of organization and equipment (TOE) that closely match the description of the Combat Groups in Chapter 4. In particular, the C4I units were created by using company and detachment size units from existing Army Signal, Military Intelligence, Air Defense, Military Police, and other units (see Figure 7.3). The equipment in the C4I units does not exactly match all of the items described in Chapter 4, but it does provide a good analogy for cost estimating purposes. The estimates for the Group Support Battalion were created from assets in the current division support commands.

Second, all costs include military and civilian personnel. Personnel costs range from 52 percent of the total for aviation units to 62 percent of the cost for armor and mechanized units. The civilian personnel cost is minor compared to that of military personnel, but the civilian cost is an actual savings because the civilians go away with the elimination of the division structure. Third, the infrastructure costs and the cost of keeping Major Generals as post commanders except where corps/JTF Commanders are permanently stationed have been held constant. At those installations where division staffs are completely eliminated, those personnel spaces have been utilized elsewhere to fill out the fighting force. Fourth, at peak strength, this structure encompasses 130,000 (+) troops. The current ten division structure, which is manned at a level below 100 percent contains 140,000 (+) troops.

Finally, this is only a macrolevel estimate and many details are not addressed. Efficiencies will be gained through ongoing modernization. But far greater economies will be gained through the efficiency with which this alternative structure can be strategically deployed to meet contingencies in the new international security environment. For example, this proposed structure can deploy more than the combat capability associated with the Mobility Requirements Study Bottom-Up Review Update (MRS-BURU), three division equivalents in fewer than 30 days and a full corps in 75 days with at least 10 percent less strategic air and sealift. This capability is achieved by creating more combat power from existing assets at lower levels in a warfighting configuration that supports rapid deployment.

The transition costs associated with disestablishing division structures are also not included in this analysis. However, in terms of recent experi-

Figure 7.3
Examples of How Individual Unit Costs Were Used to Establish Group Operating and Maintenance Costs

COMBAT GROUPS

(15) HEAVY COMBAT GROUPS	4833.0
(7) AIRBORNE-AIR ASSAULT GROUPS	2142.0
(2) HEAVY RECON-STRIKE GROUPS	879.6
(2) LIGHT RECON-STRIKE GROUPS	290.2
TOTAL	8144.8

10 DIVISION FORCE

(6) HEAVY DIVISIONS	6458.7
(1) AIRBORNE DIVISION	706.7
(1) AIR ASSAULT DIVISION	919.0
(2) LIGHT INFANTRY DIVISIONS	1186.6
TOTAL	9271.0

HVY CBT GROUP COST ESTIMATES
(in FY95 $ in Millions):

Element	Annual Operating Costs
Recon SQDN	49.842
Combined Arms BNs	147.219
Indirect Fire BN	47.998
C4I BN	55.278
Support BN	21.822
TOTAL	322.159

ABN-AIR ASSLT GROUP COST ESTIMATES
(in FY95 $ in Millions):

Element	Annual Operating Costs
Recon SQDN	37.067
Parachute Inf BNs	100.006
Indirect Fire BN	29.239
C4I BN	29.261
Support BN	12.502
UH60 BNs (Avn Lift)	97.945
TOTAL	306.020

ence, division deactivation costs generally do not exceed the annual operating cost for an existing division. Thus, the Army should be able to
disestablish two or three divisions a year without jeopardizing the overall
readiness of the total force. This does not mean ending the association of
the Combat Groups with the Army's historic division organizations. For
instance, two Heavy Combat Groups stationed at Fort Riley would continue
to wear the Big Red One patch and could even be designated Combat
Command A and Combat Command B, 1st Infantry Division (Mechanized).
However, when these Combat Groups deploy in peace or war, they deploy
and operate under the command and control of standing JTF Headquarters
in one of the Unified Commands, as outlined in Chapter 6.

Other Group structures at echelons above the Combat Groups referred
to in Chapter 4 were not considered in this economic analysis. It seems
reasonable to assume, however, that the process of reorganization and
consolidation (see Figures 7.4 and 7.5) applied to the ten divisions could be
applied at the corps and theater/field army levels with similar results.
Experience with consolidation and reorganization in the private sector
would lend support to this view.[32] The Army has begun to add more MLRS
to its inventory and plans to place one battalion of MLRS in each division.
Under the proposed redesign, the Army's indirect fire capability expands to
fifty-five MLRS batteries. Currently, the Army maintains the equivalent of
fourteen MLRS battalions or forty-two MLRS battery equivalents in the
Active Component. Since the proposed force structure calls for fifty-five
MLRS batteries, with the elimination of the towed 105 millimeter artillery
battalions, one towed 155 millimeter artillery battalion, and four battalions
of M109 Howitzers, the savings in manpower and operating funds could be
rolled into the fielding of thirteen additional MLRS batteries.

The Army's attack aviation community provides opportunities for similar change. In the proposed reorganization, the number of AH64-equipped
battalions increases from eighteen to twenty-one. With the elimination of
all Cobra AH1F airframes from the current inventory a process similar to
that described for the artillery could also begin within the Army's aviation
community. In addition to the introduction of the RAH66, this analysis does
not address the procurement of additional communications equipment,
UAVs, and Crusader (formerly the advanced field artillery system). In this
connection, the proposal to compress the current corps support command
from 22,000 troops to 15,000 troops is a function of reorganizing tactical
logistics to confer greater independence on the Combat Group structure.

In sum, warfare evolves, technologies improve, and exactly as with the
post-Napoleonic armies and the prewar German Army of World War II,

Figure 7.4
Headquarters Realignment/Reorganization

10 Division and 40+ Brigade ———→   26 Combat Group
Command and Staff Structures   Command and Staff Structures

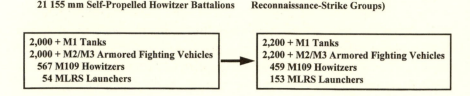

Results of Consolidation and Reorganization
(Heavy Combat Forces)

DIVISION UNITS (Ground)	COMBAT GROUP UNITS (Ground)
30 Tank Battalions	45 Combined Arms Battalions
25 Mechanized Infantry Battalions	21 Heavy Reconnaissance Squadrons
6 Division Cavalry Squadrons (armored)	17 Hybrid Artillery Battalions
3 Regimental Cavalry Squadrons (armored)	(Includes Heavy Combat Groups and Heavy
21 155 mm Self-Propelled Howitzer Battalions	Reconnaissance-Strike Groups)

2,000 + M1 Tanks	2,200 + M1 Tanks
2,000 + M2/M3 Armored Fighting Vehicles	2,200 + M2/M3 Armored Fighting Vehicles
567 M109 Howitzers	459 M109 Howitzers
54 MLRS Launchers	153 MLRS Launchers

Figure 7.5
Results of Consolidation and Reorganization

Results of Consolidation and Reorganization in Army Light Forces

DIVISION UNITS (Ground)	COMBAT GROUP UNITS (Ground)
39 Light Infantry Bns	21 Airborne Air Assault Infantry Bns
3 Light Cavalry Squadrons	6 Light Reconnaissance Sqdns
8 155 mm Towed Howitzer Bns	7 155 mm Towed Artillery Bns
12 105 mm Towed Howitzer Bns	252 AGS, 252 LAV (PI) and 18 MLRS
36 MLRS launchers	launchers (HIMARS added in future)

RESULTS OF REORGANIZATION AND CONSOLIDATION IN SUPPORT STRUCTURE

DIVISION UNITS	COMBAT GROUP UNITS
Combat Support and Combat Service Support:	**Combat Support and Combat Service Support:**
10 Air Defense Bns	26 C4I Battalions (*ADA, MI, CHEM* assets)
10 Military Intelligence Bns	26 Support Battalions
22 Combat Engineer Bns	45 Engineer Mobility Companies
30 Support Bns	(2) Light Armored Engineer Bns in the
Additional elements including Chemical and	Light Recon-Strike Groups
Military Police units.	

SOME ELEMENTS WILL BE CONSOLIDATED WITH CORPS/JTF LEVEL CS/CSS GROUPS steps can be taken to overcome human and technical limitations in order to adapt organizations for combat to the forces of change in military affairs.[33] As noted in the preceding chapters, the thrust of change is toward strengthening C4I and exploiting new human and technological capabilities in a strategic environment where knowledge-based military operations and the necessity for dispersion require greater operational and tactical autonomy at increasingly lower levels.

The proposed structure also provides at least the same level of combat platforms as the existing divisional structure. The suggested mix of Combat Groups outlined in this work is only one option. Other mixes, including more Recon-Strike and fewer Heavy Combat Groups, are also possible. This is a matter that needs to be hammered out within the broader framework of the national military strategy before reorganization begins. In the current environment, the addition of another Airborne-Air Assault Group and the reduction of the Heavy Combat Groups in the United States from twelve to eleven would seem to be viable alternatives. Another alternative would involve adding another parachute infantry battalion to the Airborne-Air Assault Group Structure. This would raise the number of Airborne-Air Assault Infantry battalions to twenty-eight.

However, defense planners should expect even greater combat power and capability to accrue within this new structure as a result of the enhanced integration of information technology, direct and indirect fire systems, and more robust and flexible C2. Because of its smaller size and modular character, the structure will probably also be easier and less expensive to modernize and modify in the years ahead as new technological capabilities enter the force. Although experience in the private sector suggests that organizational change produces monetary savings, the fact that organizational change in the Army will also save money is really a bonus.

AIR FORCES

American airpower is the nation's most responsive and flexible military capability.[34] When the Air Force has access to usable bases, land-based fighters can quickly deploy from the United States and assemble a large amount of firepower. A fighter squadron that makes its morning sortie against a close air support target can fly an afternoon sortie against strategic targets hundreds of miles inside the enemy's territory. Dramatic contemporary improvements in surveillance, communications, and computation that promise to find, track, and support missile and precision strikes on all manner of military targets are unprecedented. There is also stealth technology, which not only assists in reducing aircraft losses, but also allows for the use of direct attack munitions that often cost less than many stand-off systems.[35]

Air warfare is also that form of warfare most dependent on technology and the extraordinary costs of future high-tech systems place a tremendous fiscal burden on the Department of Defense (see Figure 7.6). Procurement spending for new Air Force and Navy aircraft in the President's proposed 1997 budget accounts for more than 40 percent of the total budget for the Top 20 defense modernization programs budgeted from 1997 to 2001. The Air Force proposes to spend a total of $58.9 billion on aircraft modernization in the 97–01 Future Years Defense Plan (FYDP).[36] Much of this expense is a function of the technology involved. For instance, stealth technology allows an Air Force bomber to drop 16 tons of ordnance on sixteen different targets. Of course, at well over $1 billion per plane, this is an awfully expensive way to move ordnance, even if, in theory, the plane can go it alone with only a two-man crew.[37]

In no area of defense spending is the cost explosion more evident than in the Air Force's plan to spend $86 billion (in constant FY 96 dollars) between 1996 and 2013 to buy 982 F-22 and Joint Aircraft Strike Technology (JAST) fighter aircraft. On average, the new fighters will cost $88 million per copy, or 280 percent more than the $23 million per copy

Figure 7.6
DoD Investment Programs

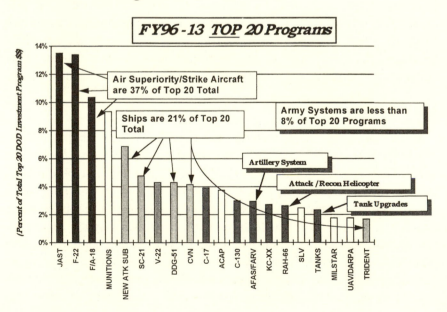

averaged between 1973 and 1990. As a result, total expenditures for new tactical fighters (F-22, Joint Strike Fighter, F/A 18-E/F) over the next 18 years will equal $169 billion, or only $9 billion less (in constant dollars) than the $160 billion spent from 1973 to 1990. Total "buy-out" of all planned tactical aircraft will exceed $200 billion.[38]

The question for defense planners is how to preserve U.S. air supremacy in the years ahead without investing the entire national treasury in manned aircraft. There is no easy answer to the question. With falling budgets, designing aircraft has become much more problematic. Before aircraft can be designed for future use in contingencies, key questions must be answered up front. Should air-to-ground sensors and systems be carried internally or in pods? The fighter that must spend time within range of ground-based threats will need built-in defense systems to reduce the plane's radar signature and to automate countermeasures against infrared and radar-guided missiles.[39] Is the primary threat to American airpower new air defense technology or will the U.S. Air Force encounter a robust air-to-air combat challenge in the near future?

The F-22 was designed in the last years of the Cold War to achieve air superiority against a robust Soviet fighter threat. Today, most analysts discount the possibility that future adversaries will seek to match American airpower in the context of air-to-air combat. Michael O'Hanlon, a Brookings Institution analyst, suggests that although the Eurofighter, Rafale, and advanced Russian programs could put improved aircraft into the hands of certain potential adversaries in the future, they are unlikely to exceed the capabilities of the U.S. Air Force F-15.[40] For that matter, the platform is now much less important, while the quality of what it carries—sensors, munitions, and electronics of all kinds—has become critical. "A modernized 30 year-old aircraft armed with the latest long-range air-to-air missile, cued by an airborne warning plane, can defeat a craft a third its age but not so equipped or guided."[41]

On the other hand, as illustrated in the 2003 scenario, widely exported Russian air defense systems are already being upgraded with West European microcircuitry and communications.[42] Thus, all future aircraft—long-range bombers and fighters—will have to cope with much more serious air defense measures than was the case during the Gulf War.[43] According to this line of thinking, the real balance of importance seems likely to be U.S. attack aircraft capability versus the air defenses of potential regional adversaries,[44] given that it is through airpower that the United States hopes to compensate for the reduction of American ground forces from 781,000 in 1989 to 495,000 today.[45]

To exploit airpower's potential, however, the United States needs to ensure its ability to control the air, which allows it to conduct more effective attacks against enemy forces and strategic assets.[46] Whether it is prudent to dismiss the possibility that an air threat to U.S. air and ground forces will exist in the future that justifies the acquisition of the F-22 is open to debate. What is certain is that if the enemy's air defenses cannot be neutralized, or better yet, destroyed, long-range fighters carrying a mix of precision-guided munitions and heavy bomb loads like the F-15e are unlikely to strike their targets.

The suppression or neutralization of enemy air defenses will require more effort from all of the services in the future. The experience with air defense suppression in the Gulf demonstrated that above 15,000 feet, every aircraft can become stealthy when the enemy's sophisticated antiaircraft systems are put out of action. Because the electronic warfare tactics that worked so well against a rather unimaginative Iraqi enemy may not work as well in the future against more capable air defense technologies and more resourceful and intelligent enemies, the Army has a stake in these operations and can play a critical role. Army ground forces can strike enemy air defense targets with great certainty and precision with ATACMs. More important, the cost of ATACMs is relatively modest compared with that of most precision-guided munitions. This is because the level of certainty associated with reaching and destroying the target with ATACMs is also much higher.[47]

Unlike land-based fighters, the B-2 bomber currently enjoys a degree of survivability against most of the contemporary air defense capabilities that is likely to endure into the first few years of the next century. The problem with the B-2 is cost. The twenty existing B-2 bombers cost $44 billion to develop and build. Adding another B-2 will rescue jobs in California, but it will also cost nearly $1 billion to produce.[48] A more viable long-term solution may be to begin work on unmanned platforms that can perform many of the B-2 missions with equal success.[49] As the on-board responses to air defense systems become more and more automated and aircraft operate at increasingly high altitudes, UAVs armed and equipped like the B-2 can be remotely operated. For instance, a critical role for future unmanned B-2s will entail locating and attacking theater ballistic missiles from altitudes of 50,000 feet. In this role, a UAV like the Loral/Frontier System W570 air vehicle, which can carry payloads weighing more than 4,500 kilograms and supply 200–300 kilowatts of power will accommodate a variety of sensors and weapons carried by both fighters and bombers. Without the requirement to man the equipment, the price of the B-2 UAV variant could be reduced by as much as a third.[50] This is an approach which must be seriously examined before constructing any more manned bombers.

Hedging against future threats requires the United States to maintain selected, critical elements of combat power.[51] In reduced numbers, the F-22 may qualify in this category if the USAF is to maintain its current edge into the first part of the next century. Though "fewer" usually means more expensive, a life-cycle cost analysis of the F-22 may reveal that fewer, more capable F-22s which require less support by escorts and tankers and fewer people to operate them are not prohibitively expensive. When combined with a plan to buy new F-16s and to double the service life of the Air Force's older F-16s from 4,000 to 8,000 hours with a midlife upgrade program, this approach may work.[52] In the meantime, scarce capital can be directed toward the development of the Joint Strike Fighter, which does not depend on stealth technology for long-term survival and which can be utilized by the air forces in the USAF, the USN, and the USMC.

MARITIME FORCES

Almost all naval battles, throughout the history of war at sea, have been fought in close proximity to land. Even in the vastness of the Pacific in the Second World War, most encounters between fleets, or between fleets and maritime aircraft, took place close to the mainland, to large islands, or to archipelagos. The deep oceanic encounters—the Battles of Midway and the Philippine Sea—stand alone in terms of their distance from any considerable landmass at which they were fought.[53] None of this is really news to the U.S. Navy, however. American fleets have always fought for control of the sea as part of the broader effort to control events on land. What is new since the recent decline of Soviet power is the absence of any threat on the high seas to the U.S. Navy. In fact, since 1991 there has been no threat to the movement of American commerce or troops on the high seas. To paraphrase the former USACOM Commander, Admiral Paul David Miller, an ocean without challengers forced the Navy after 1991 to confront a big change in operational culture.[54]

Sensing that in the new strategic environment classic sea control need no longer be the Navy's first priority, the Department of the Navy published a White Paper in 1992 to address the need for what was termed "doctrinal adjustment." This Navy White Paper recognized that for the foreseeable future control of the seas would not be challenged and called for U.S. Naval Forces to be part of the nation's effort directly to control events ashore.[55] The Navy defines its area of operations as encompassing any territory lying within the 650 nautical mile range of American naval strike capabilities. The real question is to what extent the American taxpayer should invest in the Navy and Marine Corps to perform missions on land that are already performed by the U.S. Air Force and the U.S. Army.

Having watched plenty of World War II films and read some military history, most Americans understand that sea-based air forces were vital to America's offensive to gain control of the sea when the radius of attack for a fighter plane was a couple of hundred miles and the range of bombers was perhaps one or two thousand. These were the conditions in the Pacific during World War II when carriers operated as mobile airstrips. Today, conditions are different. Land-based air forces can now dominate large bodies of water. Coastal mines, cruise missiles, land-based fighters, and quiet diesel submarines can severely limit the ability of American naval forces to operate close to shore. During Britain's war with Argentina in the Falkland Islands, the vulnerability of surface combatants in littoral waters to these new technologies was demonstrated when three Exocet missiles sank two British warships and damaged a third.[56] These systems are proliferating and will profoundly influence future operations in littoral waters.

For reasons that have nothing to do with the superb fighting qualities of the forces involved, the results of forced entry operations from the sea with Marine amphibious forces in the Straits of Hormuz, in the Straits of Taiwan, or on the Korean coastline, could be disastrous. Other than the Royal Navy's experience with the Exocet missile during the Falklands War, there are few historical analogies for the possible impact of cruise missile technology on future attempts at forced entry from the sea. However, the Navy's experience with Japanese kamikaze assaults provides a glimpse of what could happen. In nine separate Japanese attacks (3,000 suicidal sorties) on U.S. Marine Amphibious Forces and U.S. Navy aircraft carriers between 12 and 13 April 1945, Japanese manned "cruise missiles" netted a total of twenty-one U.S. ships sunk, forty-three additional ships permanently out of action, and twenty-three more ships out of action for a month or more.[57] It is not hard to imagine large numbers of cruise missiles, at a future price of $100,000 apiece, having a similar effect on today's large industrial age billion dollar aircraft and amphibious carriers. Rear Admiral Henry Griffin, commander of an eight ship Navy battlegroup in the Adriatic during December 1995, no doubt had these weapons in mind when he told a reporter aboard the U.S.S. *George Washington*, a 97,000 ton Nimitz-class carrier, "This ship will not go to a place where 6,000 people are put at risk."[58] Directed energy weapons used in conjunction with greatly improved radars that can track sea-skimming missiles may offer better point defense of large sea-based platforms in the future, but these are concepts and ideas, not existing defense systems.

The current problem with mines in coastal waters is no less daunting. Forty-five years ago, during the Korean conflict, a planned amphibious landing at Wonson was stalled when it was discovered that the port had been heavily mined by North Korean fishing boats. The Navy's Fleet Admiral observed later: "We lost control of the seas to an enemy without a navy using World War I weapons employed from vessels that were built before the time of Christ." As the Navy found out in 1990 when an amphibious assault ship and a guided missile cruiser struck sea mines and retired with serious damage, not a heck of a lot had changed. Discussing the vulnerability of amphibious forces to mines, Marine Major General James L. Jones stated, "All it takes to panic a battlegroup is seeing somebody dropping a couple of 50 gallon drums into the water."[59] Even the staunchest supporters of the Navy's new littoral warfare doctrine, those who insist that sea-based air and missile power can always protect and support Marine landing forces, quail at saying clearly that they could actually project Marine Forces more than a few kilometers inland in any military environment—low, middle, or high intensity.[60]

The performance of sea-based aircraft during Desert Storm suggests that naval aviation is far less efficient than land-based aviation and that carriers have much lower sortie rates.[61] Further, no amount of additional investment in carrier aviation technology seems to overcome the deck cycle limitations and engineering constraints inherent in sea-based aviation. The Navy's new F/A-18E/F fighter aircraft is no exception. At a cost of over $100 million each, the F/A-18E/F costs about $35 million more apiece than the C/D, although the Navy data show both aircraft are expected to hit the same ground targets with the same munitions.[62] In addition, the A-6E, which was procured in the 1960s, has a greater operating range and carries a heavier bomb load than the F/A-18E/F.[63] None of this diminishes the criticality of sea-based aviation to the protection and control of sea lines of communication as well as the movement of American forces over the seas, but the trendlines in military affairs suggest that the long-term contribution of carrier-based aviation to a major land campaign is likely to be marginal.

In the time it takes to deploy one carrier to waters in the vicinity of a potential regional conflict, the U.S. Air Force can deploy 2.2 fighter wing equivalents (FWEs) to the same conflict. Within a week, the Air Force can move 8.8 FWEs into the same region. It is no wonder that Admiral Spane, former Commander of the U.S. Pacific Fleet's Naval Air Force, acknowledged in a recent report on close air support for the Marine Corps that the

Navy's interest in reorienting carrier-based aviation to the traditional Marine close air support mission is aimed at maintaining the relevance of aircraft carriers![64] In addition, insensitive munitions capable of being launched by both land-based and sea-based fighter aircraft are more expensive to produce. Special flashpoint and stability requirements associated with storage on board carriers add to the cost of munitions.

The premise that sea-based operations are conducted independently is also misleading. During the Gulf War, the CVBG in the Red Sea depended heavily on the port cities of Jedda, Alexandria, Haifa, and Augusta Bay for fuel, ordnance, and supplies. In the Indian Ocean, U.S. Naval Forces depended on ports and airfields in Diego Garcia, Manama, and Dhahran. Without in-flight refueling from Air Force tankers, the CVBGs would have been unable to launch air strikes against any deep targets. In a more recent example, the U.S.S. *Normandy* (Aegis cruiser, Ticonderoga class) had to reposition from the Adriatic to Western Italy in order to reload missiles after launching strikes against targets in Bosnia. As a result, the ship was out of action for several days because a commercial port facility was required to reload missiles in the ship's vertical launch system tubes. All of these points suggest that if offensive and air strike operations can be carried out more cheaply and effectively by land-based airpower than sea-based airpower, reductions in spending for modernized sea-based aircraft should be considered before cutting funds for land-based airpower and tactical missile systems.

Finally, the most dramatic evidence for the unpromising military character of littoral warfare is found in the Navy's current argument for the construction of arsenal ships. Recognizing that surface combatants are unlikely to survive against the array of threats to Navy and Marine forces in littoral waters, the Navy proposes that the nation should fund the construction of "arsenal ships." In a proposal that contradicts some of the basic tenets of littoral warfare, the Navy insists that 25,000 ton arsenal ships should be built that can carry as many as 1,000 precision guided missiles. This, the Navy argues, would allow arsenal ships to operate 500 to 1,000 miles from shore.[65]

Beyond littoral warfare, the Navy's claim to the mission of forward presence must be reexamined. The requirement to adopt tactics which entail projecting sea-based combat power from outside the reach of enemy weapon systems such as cruise missiles and sea mines in strategically critical areas will raise questions in the minds of U.S. allies concerning American commitment, relevance, and timely response to regional crises. Even the presence of large naval forces off the coast of Haiti failed to impress the Haitian military leadership. It was not until an airborne assault by the 82nd Airborne Division was imminent that the Haitian leaders agreed to give up power and permit the return of exiled President Jean Aristide. Historical experience suggests that deterrence is in the eye of the beholder, and that offshore naval forces usually fail to impress an opponent who is ashore.[66] Future adversaries can be expected to move fast in an attempt to present U.S. forces with a fait accompli and confront the United States with a protracted war of attrition in order to defeat the United States politically by eroding national will forcibly to restore the status quo ante. Only Army ground forces already ashore and on the scene can deter or defeat these attacks in regions of pivotal strategic importance to the United States. Perhaps these are some of the reasons why General Sheehan, CINC, USACOM, has questioned the Navy's need for twelve CVBGs and has urged the NCA to scale back the Navy's forward presence deployments.[67]

But maritime superiority in the new strategic environment does not have to mean that American sea-based forces must be omnipresent on every ocean or always within reach of the enemy's land-based or littoral weapons. In the early phases of military operations on land near the open sea, naval forces in regions of pivotal strategic interest will continue to represent a critical mass of firepower and C4I. From the vantage point of defense planners, then, the key implications of the new strategic environment and new emerging technological capabilities within that environment suggest the following points:

- First, American control of the seas, though not currently challenged, must be maintained. Without control of the sea, no serious military operation to assist or support allies on the Eurasian landmass in areas of pivotal strategic interest is possible. Thus, funding for the maintenance of American sea control is not an option; it is a necessity.

- Second, the expense of insulating current and future U.S. naval forces from future enemy reconnaissance and strike capabilities as well as ensuring surface combatant survivability in the face of expanding shallow water threats—sea mines, cruise missiles, and diesel attack submarines—is cost effective only if the commensurate advantage in sea-based offensive capability against land forces is attained. In other words, do not spend on sea-based platforms if land-based aviation and ground forces can accomplish the same purspose more cheaply and efficiently. In fact, mission and burden allocation based on the idea of comparative advantage suggests a better solution to the problem of air–land–sea cooperation than that currently offered in "From the Sea."[68]

On the one hand, the Navy should capitalize on its ability to launch cruise missiles like the Tomahawk against deep enemy targets that pose a serious threat to the security and survivability of air and ground forces ashore in a lodgment area. Conversely, deep enemy targets whose control may be critical to the overall war effort, but that do not threaten early entry forces in a lodgment area close to the sea should be left to land-based aviation and strike systems.[69] In addition, the Navy will want to expand its contribution to theater missile defense insofar as it can afford protection to early entry ground forces. Clearly, the arsenal ship may be part of the answer to deep strike needs, although the Navy will want to avoid single-use craft that can not make a contribution to sea control in the years ahead. The DDG 51 Arleigh Burke Aegis class destroyers are well positioned both to augment theater missile defense and to contribute to the land attack cruise missile arsenal. However, in the long run, submarines and smaller, faster surface combatants will still enjoy greater freedom of action in the new strategic environment and should be considered for a dual role in the context of sea control and landpower augmentation.

On the other hand, the Congress should halt further investment in large-deck carriers or sophisticated sea-based aviation. By 1998, the United States Navy and Marine Corps will operate twenty-three world-class carriers. These will consist of twelve large-deck (larger than 60,000 tons displacement) and eleven midsize carriers (30,000–60,000 tons displacement). Each large deck carrier will be able to carry between eighty and ninety aircraft. There are currently nine Marine Corps midsize carriers capable of fixed wing operations. Four Wasp class carriers will be comissioned by the end of FY98. Five Tarawa class carriers can carry approximately six AV-8Bs or twenty-one amphibious assault helicopters. There are four foreign midsize carriers, one operated by Russia and three by France. This would suggest that no other state in the world sees the investment in carrier-based aviation as an essential feature of power projection capability.

Operating large deck carriers without an air wing or accompanying battlegroup to protect the carrier costs roughly $330 million per year. Furthermore, periodic refueling of nuclear carriers represents a $3 billion deferred operations and maintenance bill. Over the future years defense program (FYDP), the bill for operating a single large deck carrier approaches $2 billion! When the host of ships and aircraft that are designed to protect the carrier are added to the cost, the sum rises geometrically.[70] One defense analyst has estimated that the total cost, direct and indirect, of keeping one CVBG on station is roughly $10 billion per year.[71]

If the RMA trendlines are taken seriously, the majority of future crises in which naval air and amphibious forces will have a significant role will also not require large amphibious forces. For example, amphibious readiness groups (ARGs) led by Marine carriers deployed for potential noncombatant evacuation operations off the coast of Lebanon in 1989 and Burma in 1988. In Liberia during 1990, the Saipan ARG accomplished the largest NEO (Noncombatant evacuation operation) since the fall of Saigon in 1975. In Somalia, U.S. Marines went ashore unopposed and were able to overpower the Somali opposition with little difficulty. More recently in Liberia, the Air Force and Army Special Forces were the first on the scene and played the critical role in securing and evacuating American citizens and U.S. Embassy personnel.[72] Still, none of these operations required the application of military force against a robust and dangerous opponent.

These points suggest that the amphibious capability to support numerous "OOTWs from the sea" by Marines in peripheral areas where the threat to sea-based forces is low should be considerably less than what the Navy and Marine Corps want. By 2010, the Marine Corps goal is twelve amphibious readiness groups consisting of thirty-six ships based around twelve "big deck" amphibious assault ships: five Tarawa class LHAs and seven Wasp class LHDs.[73] The procurement and system integration bill for the V-22 could easily approach $50 billion. At $140 million per aircraft, this is an awfully expensive way to move eighteen Marines from ship to shore. Further, what level of combat potential can eighteen Marines provide? USSOCOM could handle the V-22 mission far more efficiently by employing a joint approach. Is the expenditure of $58 billion really necessary for embassy evacuations, civil assistance operations, and limited special operations raids from the sea?[74] More important, can the nation afford these expensive forces?

When these points are considered in the context of delivering a Light Recon-Strike Force from the air to cope with a regional crisis or developing conflict, the potential savings in money and human lives is clear. For the projected $1.2 billion required to build the Marine Corps' new LPD-17 (LX), the U.S. defense establishment could operate and maintain seven Light Recon-Strike Groups. This point should not be overlooked in the context of forward-stationed ground forces. When combined with their inherent deterrent value, forward stationed ground forces in strategically important regions are a bargain. For the cost of the Navy's new attack submarine, $2.7 billion, the Air Force could add more than 100 F-16s to the existing inventory, not to mention the F-22. Or the Army could procure 80–100 RAH66s and 100 ATACMs!

For defense planners, these points suggest opting whenever possible
for less expensive alternatives that are much more likely to succeed.
Admiral Owens, former Vice Chairman of the Joint Chiefs, has presented
the Mobile Offshore Base as one alternative to investing in another round
of large-deck carriers. It is more survivable than the Navy's carriers and
its size and structure will accommodate large numbers of U.S. Air Force
fighters, Army combat forces, Army theater air defense forces, and even
the C17 Globemaster. Relative to what the shipyard-dependent states are
now planning to procure for national defense at sea, this option is worth
examining (Figure 7.7).

Other prudent actions include scaling back the procurement of more
ships until new designs that are more useful in the new strategic environment can be developed. At the same time, the retirement of some of the large
deck carriers in order to reduce the numbers of aircraft carriers to nine or
seven should be planned and executed as soon as possible. This will also
ease the burden of aircraft modernization, which threatens to absorb most
of the Navy' resources.[75] Reductions in the carrier force along with the

Figure 7.7
Combat Equipment Estimated Costs

MARINE EXPEDITIONARY UNIT (SOC) (smallest Marine Force afloat)	Command Element (165 men) Battalion Landing Tm (1200 Men) (6) 155mm Howtizers (17) Nortars (81mm and 60mm) (10 Tow Anti-Tank Weapons) (17) LAVs, (4) M1A1 Tanks (15) AAVs, trucks, small arms Composite Helicopter/Vstol Squadron (416 men) (23) Helicopters (all types), (6) AV-8B Fighters (5) Stinger Tm Service Support Group (252 Men) 3 Ships Approx Total: 2050 men	**208**
LT RECON-STRIKE GROUP	(126) AGS, (160) LAV(PI) (include (27) 120mm Mortars), (9) MLRS, (30) RAH66, 25 (UH60) + engineer mobility equipment and wheeled vehicles. Total 5,000 troops.	**145.1**
US Navy CVBG	Includes all O&M and MILPERS for an aircraft carrier and support ships.	**488**
USAF F-16 Wing	Includes only O&M and MILPERS for a PAA of 54. Ammo and basing costs not included	**124**

Cost estimates in FY 95 $ in millions provided by Office of the Secretary
of Defense, Program Assessment and Evaluation.

cancellation of the F/A-18 E/F and a reduction in the number of V-22 aircraft proposed by the Marine Corps (458) would save billions of dollars in defense spending and put contractors on notice that they must produce technology that increases performance while reducing costs. Then, instead of developing and launching Seawolf submarines or single-use arsenal ships or building vulnerable, industrial age "big deck" amphibious carriers for the Marines, the Navy could shift its attention to designs for modified Trident D submarines, which can surface close to shore and support Marine special operations. Not only would these actions reduce some of the parts and training problems which needless Army–Marine redundancy creates, they would actually support the Marine Commandant's *Sea Dragon* initiative for reorganizing the Marine Corps into smaller, more mobile units.[76]

Conducting amphibious assaults is the primary mission of the Marine Corps. Yet it is time to reconsider the narrowness of this orientation as it relates to future warfare. Space-based surveillance, microcircuitry, and the diffusion of new knowledge will change this orientation one way or the other.[77] While the requirement for OOTW from the sea in peripheral regions necessitates the retention of an amphibious capability, the existing capability is more than adequate and can be retained at significantly lower cost. The Marine role in operations from the sea to find and destroy enemy weapons of mass destruction as well as to neutralize coastal air and cruise missile defenses in regions of pivotal interest could also be shifted to USSOCOM.[78]

CONCLUSIONS

This chapter began with two questions: Where can congressional leaders cut the defense budget? and What should Congress do with the funds that remain? When the principle of economy is applied to the development and use of military power for the future, the answer to the first question is a new mix of air-, land-, and seapower. This mix is primarily an air-land structure with fewer sea-based air and sea-based landpower assets. The appropriate strategy, then, is neither purely continental nor purely maritime, but rather one of integrated air-, land-, and seapower directed toward preserving sufficient landpower at home and in regions of pivotal strategic importance to exert influence and to deter or win regional conflicts quickly.

The answer to the second question is part of the larger question concerning whether a $60 billion procurement account will buy the forces necessary to recapitalize the Bottom-Up Review Force of ten active Army Divisions, eleven active CVBGs, and thirteen active Air Force wings.[79] The answer is probably no. Redundancies were a luxury of the Cold War. Fiscal realities require elimination of duplications across all of the services just as combat requires the joint integration of all the services' warfighting capabilities.[80] With these points in mind, the following areas offer enormous potential savings:[81]

PROGRAM	TOTAL PROGRAM COST	POTENTIAL SAVINGS
UAV for Satellite/Manned Reconnaissance Substitution	**Classified**	**$3 billion +**

Note: UAVs can increasingly serve as satellite surrogates. High altitude endurance UAVs such as the Global Hawk UAV can also eventually assume the U2 manned reconnaissance mission.[82] The national intelligence board budget is approaching $30 billion, but specific program costs are classified. Several billions in savings could be obtained from the effective integration of UAVs. This approach could be the catalyst for reengineering the structure of America's satellite program.

USMC 4BN & 4BW	**<$2 billion +**	**Modest if any**

Note: Cancel USMC plans to reengineer UH1 Huey and AH1W Cobra helicopters to extend their utility until 2020. It makes no sense to attempt to fly 50 year old airframes well into the 21st century when modern technology exists on the shelf. There may never be a TOW II air-to-ground missile follow-on for AH1W. Reengineering this Vietnam era airframe would cost another $1 billion. Marine modernization accounts should be augmented to procure lift and attack variants of UH60 aircraft, provided that the USMC is going to retain aviation mission.

ARNG Force	**$8 billion**	**$3–$4 billion**

Note: Disestablish ARNG divisions and reorganize fifteen enhanced readiness brigades into Combat and Combat Support Groups. Terminate AC–RC equipment transfers until reductions and conversions of AC and RC force structure are completed.

Crusader Artillery System	**$3–$5 billion**	**$3 billion**

Note: Postpone the Crusader 155 millimeter advanced artillery system until the liquid propellant works effectively. Also, the system weighs nearly 70 tons, which unnecessarily stresses strategic mobility requirements and battlefield evacuation.

| **F/A-18 E/F** | **$90 billion** | **$90 billion** |

Note: Cancel F/A-18 E/F.[83] Navy should support the transition direct to Joint Strike Fighter and F-22 variant if required from a joint perspective.[84]

| **F-22** | **$75 billion** | **$20 billion** |

Note: Reduce F22 buy to approximately 300. Replace F-15s on a capability basis (for example, two F-22s replace three F-15s, rather than a one-for-one platform exchange).

| **Carrier Fleet** | **$6 billion per Carrier** | **$12 billion** |
| | **$3 billion for refuel** | |

Note: Cancel carrier planned for 2002 new-starts. Proceed with CVX new carrier design to start construction in approximately 2007. Also cancel next two refuels on oldest carriers and retire them.[85]

| **DDG51** | **$58 billion** | **$5+ billion** |

Note: Reduce the DDG51 by 10 percent. DDG51s are approximately $1 billion per copy with nearly sixty planned. The Navy is building roughly three per year for the next several years.

| **V-22** | **$52 billion** | **$5 billion** |

Note: Reduce the number of V-22 aircraft that the USMC plans to buy (nearly 459) in favor of focusing on the special operations version of the airframe. At $140 million per copy, V-22 is too expensive for troop medium lift and logistical support. Employ less expensive aviation options. Reducing purchase to 360 V-22 airframes will still support USMC *Sea Dragon* initiative.

| **AAAV** | **>$6 billion +** | **$6 billion +** |

Note: Cancel the Armored Amphibious Assault Vehicle. Given the trendlines in military affairs, why should U.S. forces ever attempt an opposed amphibious landing? The USMC is proposing to procure over 1,000 AAAVs. The Inchon paradigm is bankrupt given precision weapons and safer, alternative means of delivering Marines to the battlefield. The AAAV is early 1980 technology being considered for fielding in 2007. Clearly, the United States can do better with newer information age technology. It makes more sense to employ the V-22. Also, the USMC can employ LCACs to carry LAVs, AGS, and other systems ashore much faster and in much higher sea states.

Assuming that the present trend toward regional strategies for the employment of conventional American military power within a joint frame-

work continues, streamlining defense to cope with the alteration of traditional service missions and new technology seems unavoidable. The total
savings from adopting the approach outlined here is nearly $150 billion. In
a fiscally constrained environment, Congress will have to contemplate a
much more efficient military capability with more emphasis placed on
land-based air and ground forces. Judging from the U.S. Navy's unchallenged position on the world's oceans, this reallocation of economic resources can also be achieved without jeopardizing American control of the
seas. The nation does not need and cannot afford to maintain two more air
forces as well as an amphibious army at sea. Salami slicing must end in
favor of reform, reorganization, and jointness.

Just as economic growth can be attempted in many different ways, armed
conflict can be conducted in different ways. A U.S. defense strategy in
which land-based aircraft and other non-carrier-based resources are efficiently utilized would allow the Navy to secure the sea lanes with as few as
nine or seven carriers. Carrier-based fleets and large amphibious forces are
no bargain in a strategic environment where their orientation is anachronistic.[86] The enormous expense of replacing industrial age naval platforms and
amphibious forces with a new generation of similar structures is one the
Congress should avoid.[87] This recognition makes it tough for representatives to prevent the public accusation that recapitalizing an industrial
age amphibious warfare structure is simply more pork barrel spending as
well as evidence for needless "imperial overreach."[88] With current and
future economic growth depending heavily on private and public investment, these savings could be rolled into the modernization programs for the
armed forces, deficit reduction, and other productive uses.

Savings from the cancellation of programs to recapitalize old structures
and privatization programs can also be applied to more pressing and
strategically critical programs like theater ballistic missile defense.[89] If the
United States had even a limited defense against long-range missiles, it
would be in a more secure position in the event that the NCA decided to
become more directly involved in a possible conflict between China and
Taiwan.[90] At the same time, the services can roll some of these savings into
more fruitful areas. For the U.S. Army, this means focusing funding to
support the RAH66, AGS, and programs to modularize and improve tactical
logistics. On the national level, consideration should be given to prepositioning more Army equipment afloat and ashore in pivotal states. The
expense of adding to the existing APA is modest compared with that of
building another aircraft carrier the nation does not need.

Although the United States is still the richest nation per capita in the world, Americans are not accustomed to making the changes in national defense appropriate to the nation's strategic needs and reduced economic means. A doctrinal engine on the joint level empowered to develop a unified warfighting doctrine at the strategic and operational levels of war is an important step in the direction of rationalizing the types and sizes of armed forces the nation needs in the 21st century. However, for any of these changes to occur, Congress will have to enact them. It is unrealistic to expect the large and powerful service institutions to do the work themselves. Part of this process will involve a high-level review of national military strategy. But the most important feature of change will be legislation to reorganize the structure of the armed forces to compel creation of smarter, smaller, faster, and more technologically advanced warfighting organizations. This will not eliminate the requirement for soldiers to slog through the mud in Bosnia or Korea. This will not end periodic cruises by U.S. Naval Task Forces through troubled waters in Southwest Asia or the Pacific. But it will reduce defense spending on unnecessarily redundant capabilities and the intensity of interservice rivalry.[91]

Militarily, a vast number of forces have been built and will continue to be built which fit poorly within the strategic environment. This is because it is easier to build new weapons than it is to place them within a strategic–doctrinal framework.[92] On a grand scale, the increasing complexity of foreign affairs and diminished economic resources will probably not prevent the building of more large-deck aircraft carriers, additional manned bombers, new sea-based fighters, and more amphibious ships. However, the closer America comes to a dispassionate appraisal of the new strategic environment, the more Americans will realize that the prosperity of the American economy combined with new challenges to American security interests demand basic changes in the composition and structure of the U.S. defense establishment.[93]

Reorganizing the Army along the lines suggested in this work is but one important feature of this broader process. However, before further cuts are made in the size of the Army, a plan for reorganization must be adopted and implemented. Otherwise, the Army will simply lose more capability as its best soldiers leave its ranks and seek opportunity in other professions. To preserve the seed corn of future victories and to enhance and modernize American landpower, reorganization must begin before additional reductions in end strength further erode the Army's warfighting capability.

NOTES

1. "The Pentagon's Reprieve," *Christian Science Monitor*, 2 February 1996, p. 20.

2. Jackie Calmes, "Both Parties Keep Pentagon from Budget Saw, but Some on Capitol Hill Are Growing Restless," *Wall Street Journal*, 17 January 1996, p. 8

3. James Kitfield, "Ships Galore," *National Journal*, 10 February 1996, p. 298.

4. Franklin C. Spinney, "Defense Time Bomb: The Case of Tactical Aviation in the Air Force," unpublished manuscript, p. 8.

5. Jeffrey Madrick, *The End of Affluence* (New York: Random House, 1995), 34.

6. David Abshire, "U.S. Global Policy: Toward an Agile Strategy," *Washington Quarterly* (Spring 1996): 61.

7. Representative Ike Skelton [Congressman from Missouri], "Taking Stock of the New Joint Era," *Joint Force Quarterly* (Winter 1993–94): p. 17.

8. Ibid., 19.

9. James Kitfield, "Pentagon Power Shift," *Government Executive* (April 1994): p. 72.

10. Phillip Gold, "The New Frontier of Inter-Service Rivalry," *Washington Times*, 31 August 1994, p. 17.

11. Robert Holzer, "Navy, Air Force Stymie JCS Study of Aircraft Costs," *Defense News*, 5–11 February 1996, p. 4.

12. "Marine Corps Moves into Pentagon, Learns Lesson About Change," *Inside the Navy*, 29 January 1996, p. 2.

13. U.S. Transportation Command (TRANSCOM) was formed in April 1987 as a result of the Goldwater–Nichols Act to ensure the availability and readiness of the nation's military air, sea, and land transportation capabilities.

14. Lisa Burgess, "Pentagon Tackles Logistics Challenges: Planners Working on Better System to Track Materials," *The Journal of Commerce*, 1 December 1995, p. 1.

15. Harold Winton, "Partnership and Tension: The Army and Air Force Between Vietnam and Desert Shield," *Parameters* (Spring 1996): 102.

16. John Robinson, "Navy Vision Sees Greater Role in Conventional Deterrence," *Defense Daily*, 28 February 1996, p. 295.

17. Winton, "Partnership and Tension," 117.

18. Col. Harry Summers, USA (ret.), *Air Force Times*, 12 February 1996, 54.

19. An example of the Guard's domestic importance is provided in a statement by MG Robert C. Brandt, AUS, Assistant Adjutant General, California National Guard, before the House Committee on Government Reform and Oversight Subcommittee on Government Management, Information and Technology field hearing, California State University at Northridge, California, on the California National Guard's response to the 1994 Northridge earthquake: "The National Guard is a unique organization and the only *military service* with three missions:

National Defense, State Public Safety, and Community Support. . . . Each year the California National Guard is called to help civil authorities protect life and property during state emergencies. California averages 33 percent of our nation's military support to civil authority missions. In 1994, year of the Northridge Earthquake, the California National Guard responded to 51 percent of the nation's military support to civil authority missions. . . . Our third mission is Community Support. Youth Programs and community service projects are the principle focus of our Community mission. Our programs target inner-city youth, providing education and training in various formats that build self-esteem, discipline, and leadership skills. National Guard units also support recreation activities and public service events that benefit all members of the community."

20. LTC Thomas Christianson, "Morale: The Destruction of the 28th Infantry Division in the Huertgen Forest, November 1944," in *Combined Arms in Battle Since 1939*, ed. by Roger Spiller (Fort Leavenworth, Kans.: U.S. Army Command and General Staff College Press, 1992), 188–89.

21. *Statement Before the Subcommittee on Personnel*, House Committee on National Security, by MG John R. D'Araujo, Jr., Director Army National Guard, United States Army, 23 March 1995, p. A-3.

22. Sean Naylor, "Guard Eyed for New Combat Role: Would Run Air Defense, Field Artillery to Ensure Best Use of Resources," *Army Times*, 19 February 1996, p. 14.

23. Allan R. Millett and Williamson Murray, eds., *Military Effectiveness*, vol. 2 *The Interwar Period* (Boston: Allen & Unwin, 1988), 92–93.

24. "National Guard Needs a Dose of Downsizing, Guarded Too Well," *The Virginian–Pilot* (Norfolk), 31 December 1995, p. J4. The spokesman said: "What's clear is the cost of keeping the Guard at its present strength of more than a third of a million men—more than $1 billion a year. It's estimated that cutting the Army National Guard roughly in half could save hundreds of millions in training and equipment costs. A Pentagon spokesman, quoted in a *New York Times* report, says the Guard is irrelevant to military strategy in the '90s and represents 'a kind of welfare program for weekend warriors.' . . . That's blunt, but at this point the country can't afford euphemism or equivocation. The Army is in the middle of a decade-long downsizing that will shrink it by 36 percent. By contrast, Congress has restricted cuts in the Guard to only 20 percent. That makes no sense."

25. *Sacramento Bee*, 30 December 1995, p. 63.

26. General Meyer, former Army Chief of Staff, quoted by John Tirpak in "Hollow Pockets: The Meyer Panel Advises the Pentagon to Head-off Readiness Problems Before They Get Out of Hand," *Air Force Magazine* (December 1994): 52.

27. Naylor, "Guard Eyed for New Combat Role," p. 14.

28. Dan Horowitz, "The Israeli Concept of National Security," *National Security and Democracy in Israel*, ed. Avner Yaniv (Boulder, Colo.: Lynne Rienner Publishers, 1993), 15–19.

29. "National Guard Needs A Dose of Downsizing," J4.

30. Michael E. O'Hanlon, *The Art of War in the Age of Peace: U.S. Military Posture for the Post–Cold War World* (Westport, Conn.: Praeger Publishers, 1991), 91.

31. *Force and Organization Cost Estimating System*, FORCES 96.0, Resident SRCS, December 1995 (Falls Church, Va.: Department of the Army, U.S. Army Cost and Economic Analysis Center, 1995). The FORCES models are tools for providing quick and reasonable cost estimates to meet a wide variety of analytical needs. The FORCES family of models bring together into one application numerous sources of cost data, cost factors, and personnel and equipment densities, for over 1,000 TOE units. To keep this compilation of data usable on a personal computer, many of the actual cost data are precomputed and aggregated into cost factors. Additionally, FORCES is updated annually on the basis of the most current data available at that time from the definitive data source (MTMC for transportation, BLTM for OPTEMPO, etc.). As such FORCES data provide a current snapshot in time. Because of possible delays in updating data, all data in FORCES are not the model used by Headquarters, Department of the Army, in the development of the OPTEMPO requirement in the budget or POM (Program Objective Memorandum). However, FORCES is ideally suited for providing reasonable estimates for time-sensitive "what if" comparative analysis.

32. W. Edward Deming, *The New Economics* (Cambridge, Mass.: MIT Center for Advanced Engineering Studies, 1994), 92–106.

33. Alvin Toffler and Heidi Toffler, *War and Anti-War* (New York: Warner Books, 1993), 213.

34. "Air Expeditionary Force Demonstrates Responsiveness, Flexibility of Air Power," *Policy Letter Digest: Policies, Issues and News from the Office of the Secretary of the Air Force* (March 1996): 5.

35. MG Jasper Welch, USAF (ret.), "Why the Bomber Question Is So Controversial," *Strategic Review* (Winter 1996): 18.

36. Theresa Hitchens, "Weapon Funds Dip in DoD '97 Budget: $242.6 Billion Plan Favors Tactical Aircraft," *Defense News*, 4–10 March 1996, p. 1.

37. Phillip Gold, "Why We Don't Need More B-2s," *The Washington Times*, 14 November 1995, OP-ED page.

38. Franklin C. Spinney, "Defense Time Bomb: The Case of Tactical Aviation in the Air Force," unpublished manuscript, p. 8. Also see Tony Capaccio's "Air Force to Pay $442 Million in F-22 Cost Growth," *Defense Week*, 6 May 1996, p. 1.

39. Bill Sweetman, "Designing a 21st Century Fighter," *International Defense Review* (June 1995): 34.

40. Michael O'Hanlon, *Defense Planning for the Late 1990s: Beyond the Desert Storm Framework* (Washington, D.C.: The Brookings Institution, 1994), 54.

41. Eliot Cohen, "A Revolution in Warfare," *Foreign Affairs* (March/April 1996: 45.

42. Robert Holzer and Frank Oliveri, *Defense News*, 12–18 February 1996, p. 1.

43. MG Jasper Welch, USAF (ret.), "Why the Bomber Question Is So Controversial," 18.

44. O'Hanlon, *Defense Planning for the Late 1990s*, 54.

45. Stephen T. Hosmer, *Effects of the Coalition Air Campaign Against Iraqi Ground Forces in the Gulf War*, MR-305-AF (Santa Monica, Calif.: RAND Corporation, 1994), 58. The Gulf War Air Power Study noted that of 163 Iraqi tanks examined by battlefield analysis groups, between 10 percent and 20 percent had been struck by air-delivered munitions. According to Stephen T. Hosmer, the three Republican Guard Divisions in the Kuwait Theater of Operations as of 1 March 1991 left behind in their prewar deployment areas 166 tanks, 203 armored personnel carriers (APCs), and 99 artillery pieces. As percentages of prewar deployment totals, these amounted to losses of 21 percent tanks ($n = 786$), 28 percent APCs (736), and 32 prcent artillery (308).

46. C. Bowie, F. Frostic, K. Lewis, J. Lund, D. Ochmanek, and P. Propper, *The New Calculus: Analyzing Airpower's Changing Role in Joint Theater Campaigns* (Project Air Force), (Santa Monica, Calif.: RAND Corporation, 1993), excerpted from the summary on p. 20.

47. "Naval Overseas Presence: Issue Can a Mix of Large and Mid-Size Carriers Meet Our Naval Presence Requirements?" *Air Force Staff Paper* presented to Commission on Roles and Missions, 16 November 1994.

48. "B-2 Be Gone," *San Francisco Examiner*, 12 February 1996, OP-ED page.

49. Dan Gouré suggested to the author that in many ways contemporary UAVs are in the same position as manned aircraft were at the outset of World War I. We have only begun to explore their utility, particularly at high altitudes.

50. Mark Hewish, "Scudkillers: Tough Choices for Boost-Phase Intercept," *International Defense Review* (January 1996): 30.

51. Statement before the Senate Armed Services Committee in connection with the FY 1997 budget by Dr. William J. Perry, Secretary of Defense, 5 March 1996.

52. "Aviation Spending to Exceed Cold War Levels: Perry Sends Controversial Aircraft Modernization Charts to Congress," *Inside the Pentagon*, 4 April 1996, p. 1.

53. John Keegan, *The Price of Admiralty: The Evolution of Naval Warfare* (New York: Penguin Books, 1988), 325.

54. Jan S. Breemer, "The End of Naval Strategy: Revolutionary Change and the Future of American Naval Power," *Strategic Review* (Spring 1994): 48.

55. Vice Admiral Owens, "The Quest for Consensus," *Proceedings* (May 1994): 69.

56. O'Hanlon, *Art of War in the Age of Peace*, 119.

57. R. E. Dupuy and T. N. Dupuy, *The Encyclopedia of Military History from 3500 B.C. to the Present* (New York: Harper & Row, 1970), p. 1195.

58. Peter G. Chronis, "Carrier Destined for Bosnia, Ready for War," *The Denver Post*, 27 December 1995, p. 1.

59. Quoted by David Wood in "Navy Tries to Handle Mines," *The Plain Dealer*, 23 September 1995, p. B–11.

60. Naval Studies Board, *The Implications of Advancing Technology for Naval Aviation* (Washington, D.C.: National Academy Press, 1982), 13, 23. The report concluded: "In any but the most minor conflict, 30–40 attack airplanes per carrier, using the simple ballistic weapons that currently constitute the bulk of our air-delivered weapon inventory, can do little damage to the opposing target complex unless they revisit it many times, with cumulative attrition that could be fatal in the case of adequate enemy defenses. In present circumstances, the carrier is therefore at risk for periods that are too long, the attack aircraft are likely to be lost to target area defenses before their mission is completed, and the political consequences of long war and collateral non-tactical damage are likely to be severe."

61. Before embracing the cause of aircraft recapitalization avoidance, the distinctions between land-based aviation and sea-based aviation should not be ignored. For example, 36 F-117s attacked more targets on day 1 of the Gulf War than the entire 6 aircraft carrier force and TLAMs combined. During the first 2 weeks of the conflict the U.S. Air Force provided over eight times as many strike sorties with just over twice the number of combat assets as carrier forces. In fact, whereas the Navy's aircraft carriers provided 79 strike sorties per day (13.2 per carrier), the U.S. Air Force provided 653 strike sorties per day. On average, the Air Force launched more air strikes in 2 days than the carriers launched in 2 weeks! Using all USAF deployed manpower (fighters, bombers, tankers, airlift), roughly 90 men are required to generate 1 strike sortie per day. Estimates of the numbers of men required to support 1 strike sortie from a carrier range from 400 to 800, depending on whether the CBVG is partially or completely deployed. See the *Gulf War Air Power Study*.

62. "Draft GAO Report Disputes Military's Need For F/A-18E/F, B1B Upgrades Saying Services Have Too Much Interdiction Capability," *Inside the Pentagon*, 25 January 1996, p. 1.

63. Steven Uehling, "The Case for the F/A-18E/F Just Doesn't Fly," *Navy Times* (September 1995): p. 39.

64. "Naval Air Commander Wants Carrier Air to Better Support Marine Corps," *Inside the Pentagon*, 25 January 1996, p. 1.

65. Robert Holzer, "Warships May Use Leaner Crews: Report Recommends Additional Firepower for U.S. Navy Vessels," in *Defense News*, 29 January–4 February 1996, p. 4. Larry Lynn, Director of the Department of Defense's Advanced Research Projects Agency (ARPA), stated: "Doing the Arsenal Ship is a pretty expensive proposition that ARPA can't afford to put a lot of money into. We're trying to see how we can help without mortgaging our children."

66. Quoted by David Isenberg, "The Illusion of Power: Aircraft Carriers and U.S. Military Strategy," *Cato Institute Policy Analysis*, no. 134, 8 June 1990: p. 5.

Isenberg quotes Luttwak as saying: "Presidents unwilling to use force, but equally unwilling to admit impotence, have developed the habit of sending aircraft-carrier task forces to regions in crisis where American interests are in danger. The carriers go off, and the mighty armada is duly filmed in distant waters for the benefit of the nightly television news. The President, it seems, has acted. But the crisis continues to unfold just as before, and the natives do as they want with our interests in need of protection, quite unafraid of those 34 attack aircraft. Nothing of value is therefore achieved: but the aircraft carriers and all of their escorts are kept on station day after day, for weeks or months."

67. Phillip Gold, "The Birth of a U.S. General Staff," *The Washington Times*, 30 November 1994, p. 23.

68. Breemer, "The End of Naval Strategy," 47.

69. Ibid., 48.

70. "Naval Overseas Presence: Issue Can a Mix of Large and Mid-Size Carriers Meet Our Naval Presence Requirements?" *Air Force Staff Paper* presented to Commission on Roles and Missions, 16 November 1994.

71. Attributed by Phillip Gold in "The Military Frets Over the Absence of 'Presence,' " *Washington Times*, 25 October 1994, p. A21.

72. Phillip van Niekerk, "U.S. Flies Citizens out of a Liberia Torn by Civil War," *New York Times*, 10 April 1996, p. 1. Also reported by UPI in Washington, April 10, 1996. MH53J helicopters and 60 Army Special Forces troops went in immediately to provide security and to rescue American citizens. Aircraft included MC130 combat Talon I's, three HC130 P Hercules Shadow refueling planes, five MH53J transport helicopters, two C130s, two AC130 Spectre Gunships: all USAF and U.S. Army.

73. Lieutenant Colonel Arthur Brill, USMC (ret.), "Can the New Commandant Ensure That His Marines Always Have a Decisive Edge with Their Tools of War?" *Seapower* (January 1996): 12.

74. U.S. General Accounting Office, *Marine Corps: Improving Amphibious Capability Would Require Larger Share of Budget than Previously Provided* (Washington, D.C.: General Accounting Office, February 1996), 3–7. Also see Peter Chronis's article "Carrier Destined for Bosnia, Ready for War," *The Denver Post*, 27 December 1995, p. 1. Navy sources quoted in this article indicate that the U.S.S. *John C. Stennis*, commissioned on 8 December 1995, cost the taxpayer $3.49 billion. The ship's crew consists of 3,200 sailors and the air wing on board the vessel includes 2,480 more men and 80 aircraft.

75. Kerry Gildea, "Admiral Sees End of Large Deck Carriers After CVN-76," *Defense Daily*, 13 April 1995, p. 59.

76. Robert Holzer, "Sea Dragon Calls for Lethal, Mobile U.S. Marine Units," *Defense News*, 27 November–3 December 1995, pp. 4, 28. Also see Major David A. Anderson, USMC, "Stretched Too Thin," *Proceedings*, July 1996, pp. 48–50.

77. Toffler and Toffler, *War and Anti-War*, 240.

78. O'Hanlon, *Art of War in the Age of Peace*, 50.

79. James L. George, "'97 Defense Budget: More Weapon Procurement Myths," *The Virginian–Pilot & Ledger–Star*, 1 April 1996, p. 4.

80. William T. Pendley, "Mortgaging the Future to the Present in Defense Policy: A Commentary on the Bottom-up Review," *Strategic Review* (Spring 1994): 36–39.

81. Cost estimates are derived from the following sources: "DOD Weapons Costs Fall Due to Lower Inflation Rates," *Defense Daily*, 10 April 1996, pp. 60–62, and Thersa Hitchens, "Weapon Funds Dip in DOD's 97 Budget: $242.6 Billion Plan Favors Tactical Aircraft," *Defense News*, 4–10 March 1996, p. 1.

82. David A. Fulghum, "Global Hawk UAV May Fly Early," *Aviation Week & Space Technology*, 29 April 1996, p. 24.

83. Jack Dorsey, "Navy Hustles with 'Air Ships' and Air Shipping: F-14 Tomcats to Arrive at Oceana This Thursday," *The Virginian–Pilot & Ledger–Star*, 1 April 1996, p. 1.

84. "Air Force, Navy Prepare for Capitol Hill Showdown Between F-22, F/A-18–EF," *Inside the Air Force*, 3 May 1996, p. 1. Air Force sources indicate that "The FA18E/F may be able to establish air superiority over his carrier, but he can't do it over the enemy's territory." Despite an overwhelmingly negative draft report on this aircraft by the GAO, the McDonnell Douglas–built aircraft continues to enjoy strong support in Congress.

85. Steve Glain, "For U.S. Carrier in Troubled Waters, Technology of the 1950s Will Have to Do," *Wall Street Journal*, 22 March 1996, p. 1/8. Also see Ramon Lopez, "Future Flat-Top: Can the U.S. Navy Afford to Develop a New Aircraft Carrier?" *Flight: International*, 20–26 March 20 1996, p. 35.

86. Breemer, "End of Naval Strategy," 47.

87. See James Kitfield's "Ships Galore! Federal Dollars Are Scarce. Belts Everywhere Are Being Tightened. But Thanks to Their Friends in Washington, Half a Dozen Yards That Build Ships for the Navy Are Doing Just Fine." *National Journal*, 10 February 1996, p. 298.

88. In an article on page 1 by Michael D. Towle, "Bell's Outlook Is Healthy with Osprey, Study Says," that appeared in the *Fort Worth Star–Telegram*, the following statement makes clear why the American taxpayer is being forced to fund the V-22: "The Osprey's future is crucial to Bell's success."

89. "Pentagon Plan Boosts $15 Billion in Savings," *Washington Times*, 5 April 1996, p. 6. DoD request for funds for new weapons included no new money for the Nautilus Tactical High Energy Laser although the Israelis are prepared to invest $20 million of their own in the system. In February 1996, the Army research teams at White Sands were able to shoot down two Katyusha rockets. The laser, beamed at a rocket for only a second or two, disables it by melting its surface, causing it to explode and crash to earth. See "Israelis Eye U.S. Laser as Anti-Rocket Defense," *Washington Post*, 25 April 1996, p. 12.

90. Bill Gertz, "Legislators Push Missile Defense System: Beijing's Threats Not Seen As Remote," *Washington Times*, 11 March 1996, p. 10.

91. "Defense Spending, Defense Goals," *Washington Post*, 22 March 1996, p. 24.

92. Steven R. Mann, "Classical Theory and Strategic Thought," *Parameters* (Autumn 1992): 56.

93. Jim Hoagland, "Ready for What?" *Washington Post*, 28 March 1996, p. 27.

8

Final Thoughts and Future Prospects

For the American people, the future challenge in foreign policy will be to create an international order in which change can be brought about through a sense of obligation and justice, instead of an assertion of power.[1] Regardless of which political party gains the presidency in 1996, the broad intent of American foreign policy will be to lead the world away from old concepts of international relations as an arena for ideological contest or as a rich field for exploitation by nations, classes, or multinational corporations. Instead, America will strive to replace these old frameworks with a new concept of the world as a community to which Americans and the citizens of all nations have responsibilities. The success of this effort will require a change in American thinking not only about the structure of its military power, but about its uses as well. Priority in this respect belongs to a deeper understanding of landpower in the context of American military strategy.

Comprehending the role of landpower in future American military strategy demands an understanding of what airpower and seapower cannot achieve on their own. In the turbulent years that lie ahead, the United States cannot afford to repeat Britain's historic mistake of always fielding an army too late to deter war, but just in time to prevent defeat.[2] The only sure deterrent to any potential adversary (who is not insane) in regions of strategic importance to the United States is the certainty of the presence on land, soon after the beginning of any crisis or conflict, of an American ground force large enough to make a quick victory impossible. In the event

of a conflict with the United States, any power, great or small, should have
to reckon with the arrival on its soil of U.S. Ground Forces that can exert
absolute power and influence over whatever portion of strategic territory
the United States' leaders deem essential until the conflict or crisis is
resolved.[3]

Because the essence of strategy consists primarily of neither words nor
deeds, but of intentions, this work has also argued that the supreme decision
in military strategy is defining principles and designating interests important enough to fight for. In order to deter future aggression where the
strategic stakes justify the risks, the United States must be willing and able
to respond vigorously with American landpower.[4] In Europe, the Middle
East, Southwest Asia, and Northeast Asia, future adversaries will move fast
in an attempt to present the United States with a fait accompli. They will
want to confront U.S. forces with a protracted war of attrition designed to
erode domestic political will.[5] Future adversaries will invest heavily in
sophisticated military technology that will aim at nullifying traditional
American strengths—airpower and seapower. They will pursue an approach
that is designed to allow them to fight the U.S. Armed Forces on an equal
footing within their region.

Combat is still the coin of war. It is, as Clausewitz observed, "what cash
payment is to commerce."[6] It may be rare in day-to-day transaction, but
confidence in its resort is the foundation of all calculations. Demonstrable
combat capability, like bank cash reserves, gives confidence to others that
should the resort to "coin" be required, America will redeem its pledge. For
this reason, deterrence will continue to be in the eye of the beholder.
Forward-stationed U.S. Army Ground Forces will have to provide both the
link to America's strategic offensive military power and the foundation for
American-led alliances. The good news is that fewer forces will be needed
to deter armed aggression provided that an adequate mix of prepositioned
equipment ashore and afloat is on hand in areas of strategic importance.
However, only combat forces-in-being on hand at the beginning of a crisis
are likely to have much deterrent effect on future adversaries. In fact, when
U.S. Army Ground Forces are already positioned in a region, it may not be
necessary to fight at all because signaling the intention to fight is frequently
enough to so weaken the opponent's resolve that he may never strike.[7] As
Americans learned during the Cold War, the acme of military skill resides
in the strategist who maintains the positional dominance which secures his
ends without fighting.[8]

As mentioned in the Introduction, the inspiration for this strategic vision
of reorganized American landpower is the Roman Legion—a self-con-

tained, mobile armed force that can deploy on a phone call to defend American interests. The supremacy of the Roman military system—and thus the continued existence of the empire—was in large part due to the continued pragmatic, logical approach of the Romans to practical problems. They respected tradition, but they were not slaves to it, and the Romans were extremely flexible in adapting themselves to change in military affairs. Through organizational skill and economy, a relatively small number of Legions was able to deter, defeat, or suppress numerically superior enemies on Rome's frontiers for several hundred years.

Exploiting the value of landpower on the Roman model in contemporary American military strategy involves understanding change in military affairs. Recognizing the degree to which the conquest of time and space by revolutionary technology has already changed the way the United States Army must organize, train, and prepare to fight is part of this understanding. This is what is meant by "breaking the phalanx." Trained and organized for a style of war that has changed very little since World War II, current Army organizational structures will limit the control and exploitation of superior military technology and human potential in future operations. Attempts to graft large-scale technological change onto old thinking and old structures can only be a temporary expedient; new capabilities demand their own organizations and operational culture. Along the way, new organizations— not just technology—will revolutionize warfighting.

After almost two centuries, the age of mass mobilization armies manned by short-service conscripts or part-time volunteers is truly at an end.[9] In an international security environment characterized by sudden, violent, and, above all, unpredictable change, the complexity of joint military operations places the skilled, experienced, and educated military professional at the center of events. The predominance of warfare on land for limited strategic aims combined with the requirement in conflict or crisis quickly to coordinate and exploit the vast array of multiservice capabilities will not completely eliminate reliance on reserve mobilization structures, but it must result in the reorganization of remaining reserve mobilization elements within a new, integrated framework.

These views are based on the assumption that future combat operations involving American ground forces will, of necessity, be rapid and intense, that they will take place over extended frontages and depths; and that ground combat formations smaller than the contemporary Army division will have to operate independently for long periods. Under these conditions, the potential advantages of revolutionary change in warfare must be exploited at lower levels of command than in either World War II or the years since 1945. Rapid deployability and reduced demand for elaborate logistic support combined with the need to link multiservice capabilities to Army ground forces position joint command, control, communications, computers, intelligence, surveillance, and reconnaissance at the heart of this organizational effort. In this connection, the real promise of information age warfare is not that it will allow the centralization of decision making and the exercise of increased control, but rather that it will liberate the initiative of junior officers and noncommissioned officers to perform independently and synergystically within the limits of operational and strategic commanders' intents.

History is filled with military victories not of resources, but of strategic doctrine, based on the ability to "break the framework which had come to be taken for granted and to make victory all the more complete by confronting the antagonist with contingencies which he had never even considered."[10] The basic problem with the theory that the commitment of air and missile resources in war or peace will destroy an enemy's will and capability to fight is that it assumes that one can always guage and understand one's enemy and that future adversaries will remain as vulnerable to air and missile strikes as Iraq was. Today's argument that things have now changed—that precision strike and smart munitions have finally come into their own (aside from ringing with the same false hope as the last 70 years of promises from airpower enthusiasts)—is based on data of very questionable reliability.[11] While many of the new information age technologies may or may not yield an enduring advantage in warfare, as Navy Rear Admiral J. C. Wylie noted, "The ultimate determinant in war is the man on the scene with the gun."[12] Typically, this is why seapower and airpower tend to play enabling, rather than concluding executive roles in warfare; the human being is still a land animal.

These points notwithstanding, when the critics of defense spending assert that today's armed forces and military institutions were built for threats that no longer exist, *they are half right*! The threat of a massive Soviet juggernaut rolling across Western Europe has indeed withered. Today, however, more than two dozen nations possess tactical ballistic missiles and a number of these states will soon have missiles capable of reaching the continental United States.[13] Roughly the same number are developing the capability to construct ground-launched cruise missiles. All have large standing armies, substantial air defenses, and modern air forces. None has a large naval or marine force.[14]

Unfortunately, the implications of these facts seem lost in public policy debates, which define current choices and agendas in terms that ignore opportunities to reallocate scarce defense dollars.[15] Expensive Cold War capabilities like carrier battle groups, B-2 bombers, and large amphibious forces continue to incur huge opportunity costs when developments in military affairs make it clear that they will be at most secondary elements in future conflict. The notion that the technology of warfare has already altered the relative importance of land, air, and naval power is seldom discussed.[16] To break this "phalanx," defense dollars must be apportioned primarily according to one criterion: How will funding programs and forces today affect the overall outcome of future conflicts?

There is no denying that the chances of streamlining defense spending in the near term along the lines suggested in the last chapter are not great. In American politics, the overwhelming weight of local and special interests in the policymaking process, the continual temptation to focus on issues with high impact on local constituencies and to postpone dealing with the long-term consequences of today's decisions are well known.[17] Yet the obstacles to change in large military establishments are just as formidable— and painfully familiar to students of military affairs.[18]

Change in military affairs can be evolutionary or revolutionary. For it to be implemented quickly, however, the direction of organizational change must be more revolutionary than evolutionary.[19] This is because most of the arguments against change are not based on disputes about warfighting; opposition is usually rooted in established, peacetime, bureaucratic interests. When the United States Congress introduced a bill in 1902 designed to transform the U.S. Army from the large, unwieldy bureaucracy it had become after the Spanish–American War into a body capable of making the country ready for war against other great powers, the bill met with almost universal opposition from senior leaders inside the military, all of whose positions the proposed legislation weakened. Perhaps this is why one analyst of contemporary military affairs argues that modifications to the current force structure will be incremental and marginal unless change is pushed by assertive elected leaders who wish to see substantial change.[20] In other words, changing the organizational structure and strategic focus of the U.S. Armed Forces will require not only pressure and influence from above and outside the services, but also anticipation of how the prior experiences and cultural norms of the rank-and-file professional military resistant to change will lead them to slow or otherwise misdirected change.[21]

Perceiving the factor of American military dominance to be a permanent feature of the future strategic environment, critics inside and outside the Army will contend that the argument for change in this book devotes insufficient time to the subject of organizing and preparing the active Army for operations other than war. These critics insist that "low-intensity conflict" is the wave of the future. Although there is something to be said for the low-intensity warfare school of thought, its development to date seems to betray a readiness in some Army circles to be overimpressed by recent trends in civil disturbance.[22] It is, however, one thing to employ the Army in areas of peripheral strategic importance in order to secure the ideals and habits of democracy; it is quite another to organize and shape the Army's warfighting capability to perform such missions. Believing World War I to have been the last major conflict of the 20th century, the interwar British, French, and American armies failed to address the demands of future battle in the context of training and organization and, thus, forfeited the strategic initiative to the Germans, Japanese, and Russians in the early years of World War II.

Other Army critics of the changes proposed in this work will argue for the retention of branch-pure combat units—tank battalions, artillery brigades, aviation brigades, signal brigades—on the grounds that these organizations can be task-organized, broken up or combined with each other as necessary, before deploying to combat. But this approach ignores the need to reduce unneeded headquarters as well as to create higher levels of battlegroup cohesion and training readiness in future joint warfighting. The strategic value of American landpower rests on tactical proficiency at the "point of the spear." Soldiers and organizations will do in war what they do in peace. Tactical organizations that have not lived and trained together before they deploy cannot be transformed overnight on the basis of a single exercise into a fighting force that will stand up to future adversaries that are potentially much more capable than the Iraqis.[23]

These comments apply with equal force to logistics. "Just in time logistics," "velocity management," and "total asset visibility" are initiatives that must move rapidly from slogans to plans. Moreover, these initiatives address only half of the logistics problem. With equal or greater vigor, ground forces must work to reduce the demand that combat forces place on the logistics system. This demand reduction covers an entire spectrum of issues from the culture of leanness and privatization to the importance attached to fuel efficiency and maintainability in ground force modernization plans. The high fuel consumption rates of Army Heavy Forces in the Gulf War are well known. Accepting this experience as a premise for future conflict has imbued Army thinking, structures, and systems with a demand for logistic support undeliverable except through an extensive build-up such as that afforded by Desert Shield. Fighting on short notice at the end of a long supply line and assuming the operational offensive without pause from the time ground forces arrive in a warfighting theater impose many requirements on the future U.S. Army. The most important of these will be to reduce the demand for extensive material support through training, organization, privatization, and modernization coupled with speeding of supply through the many ongoing initiatives named.

The proposals set forth in this work to posture the Army to execute dominating maneuver in the 21st century may require the modest reallocation of funds within the defense budget. This will not be an easy task given the propensity to allocate funds on the basis of historical precedent instead of holistically validated requirements. Power, it is said, is a zero sum game and as this statement relates to defense spending nobody in the Pentagon wants to lose anything. Paul Nitze's 1979 observation still applies: "Ship types which have, by virtue of long existence, a substantial constituency behind them continue to appear in budgets, even when their continued utility is openly doubted both outside and within the service. New threats which promise to render cherished practices or systems unviable are ignored."[24] Even the Commandant of the Marine Corps, who questions the wisdom of investing in the newest Navy/Marine fighter-attack jet, the F/A-18E/F Hornet, has been unable to persuade either Congress or the Navy to opt for less expensive alternatives.[25] The U.S. Navy and the U.S. Marine Corps continue to maintain the world's third largest air force at sea in a maritime environment dominated by land-based aircraft and missiles. Apparently, nothing in national defense is doomed to extinction merely because we don't need it or it costs too much!

This point is important because too many Americans are inclined to think that military history came to a standstill with the coalition victory in the Gulf War, and that "today's holders of apparently limitless military resources and unchallengeable power cannot fail to enjoy this power tomorrow and the day after."[26] It is also one of the paradoxes of our times that greater American military mobility and potential access to new regions of the world and their inhabitants do not seem to have broadened or deepened the American appreciation for American landpower's decisive strategic role in peace and war.

Like some of their predecessors, today's policymakers still embrace grand objectives in the world, but overlook the need for landpower to achieve them. Expanding the NATO alliance to include Poland is a case in point. The real question is not whether Poland should be admitted to NATO, but how NATO will defend Poland. Unless large U.S. and allied ground forces can be committed quickly to Poland's eastern frontier in a future regional crisis, any NATO security guarantee to Poland based on U.S. and allied airpower means little more than that the United States and NATO will have to fight to restore Poland's independence after the Russian Army overruns it! Yet, has the U.S. Congress seriously examined the requirement to increase the striking power of the U.S. Army in Europe to cope with this possibility?[27] Moscow may not be able to stop Poland's incorporation into the West today, but this does not mean that Moscow will not seek to reverse it in the future.[28]

It is unnecessary for America's potential opponents to surpass the United States in military power. It is enough to make the cost of an American military victory so high in material and human terms that an American military victory would still dangerously weaken the United States' strategic position in the world. This too is not new thinking. In the years leading up to the outbreak of World War I, Germany's leading naval theorists advanced the famous "risk theory": Because Great Britain could not as a rule concentrate all of its striking forces in Europe, it was thought that smaller, concentrated German forces would have an excellent chance of a quick and decisive victory in Western Europe. In any event, the cost of defeating the Germans would so substantially weaken the British Empire that, in spite of the victory Britain might achieve, Great Britain's position in the world would no longer be secure.[29] When combined with American ignorance and illusion about other societies, this thinking by potential adversaries can have dire consequences for U.S. national security that may not be noticed by the average citizen for years.

With fewer troops and more missions than ever, today's U.S. Army is compelled to demand more of its smaller forces with the result that soldiers and their equipment are being worn out. Because landpower is the glue that holds alliances together, Army forces are engaged in peace support operations as well as enlargement and engagement activities at a much higher rate than the USAF, USN, and USMC forces. At this writing, 40 percent of the Army's combat troops are forward deployed. At the same time, less than 12 percent of the contemporary defense funds allocated to research and development are for Army programs. While operations and maintenance accounts are robbed to pay for contingency operations, modernization is slowing.[30] A decline in the retention of the nation's most skilled and capable soldiers resulting in higher work loads for the soldiers who remain is accompanying the declining defense budget.

In spite of these points, Americans remain convinced with considerable justification that their armed forces are the best in the world. Victory in the fight with Iraq continues to provide more than adequate justification for preserving the American military status quo, which, with its few faults, still performs brilliantly even under the adverse conditions of Somalia, Haiti, and Bosnia. But this static and uncritical view of military affairs is deceptive and potentially dangerous. Constrained defense budgets, technological change, and emerging centers of power cannot be ignored in the context of either national military strategy or force development. When they are, the results are tragic.

In his book *The Franco–Prussian War* Michael Howard explores the reasons for the disastrous defeat of the French Army, widely considered the best in the world in 1870, in France's war with Prussia. By the standards of its past campaigns, the French Army was ready for war in 1870. By 1860, the French military establishment had been victorious in battle against two of its chief European adversaries, Russia and Austria. Inadequate as French military logistics, administration, leadership, training, and organization may have been, that of the Russians and the Austrians was demonstrably worse. Consequently, the French Army of 1870 was ready to fight success-fully, but only against armies constituted and trained like it or against ill-equipped, second-rate military opponents like the Mexicans or the Berbers. It was the tragedy of the French Army and of the French people that they did not realize in time that military affairs had entered into a new age. "The lines of French military organization had to be drawn within the narrow limits of what was politically possible for a people which grudged every penny spent on the Army, distrusted its own rulers and was deeply divided in itself."[31]

Fortunately, contemporary America differs from 19th-century France in a very important way. American society holds people of many opinions, but a majority are aware of the importance of military power to the life of the United States. They learned from their experiences in Vietnam as well as Southwest Asia that there is no more important principle of military strategy than retention of the initiative—the ability to influence the circumstances, nature, and duration of one's military efforts.[32] In contrast to the French of the last century, Americans of all classes, races, and political opinions have a keen interest in the maintenance of American military strength. The upheaval of the 1960s could have produced a generation of Americans who equated military weakness with either moral or political strength. It did not. Americans believe that deterrence necessitates having a ready and effective warfighting capacity.[33]

Still, defense spending competes with other national priorities. An American Congress that is trying to balance reductions in deficit spending against the American public's insatiable appetite for government services must not fall victim to the delusion that a pattern of military success was revealed in the Gulf War which, if only faithfully pursued, will assure even a distant future.[34] Advocates of reliance in the future on an isolationist strategy based primarily on American air and naval power are adhering to strategic principles which are impractical in the complex environment of information age conflict.[35] If new technologies are to confer a true advantage on the United States in using war and its threat to secure U.S. national interests, Americans must truly "break the phalanx."

Clearly, the United States and its military approach this task at a certain disadvantage. Typically, the vanguard elements of RMAs have been armed forces unfettered by the legacy of recent victory. Defeated armies find their way into the future more easily because for them the past holds no allure. Recent victors are always hostage to their successes, revering and holding tenaciously to what they know. These thoughts were probably on the mind of LTG James Gavin (World War II 82nd Airborne Commander) when he wrote the following words about the U.S. Army's Korean War experience:

> If we had had the vision to see, and the courage to venture in our research and development programs, we could have had a tactical mobility in Korea that would have enabled us to run circles around our opponents. . . . Neither our imagination nor vision in the years since World War II had given us a combat capability that would provide the technical margin of advantage that we needed in land warfare to win decisively and quickly.[36]

Although intended to advance the defense debate, this monograph has not been able to address all of the challenges that confront America's military leaders. The politics of economic stringency created by years of unconstrained deficit spending will not be remedied by simple exhortations to reduce the defense budget. Disharmony in the Department of Defense, stemming from competition among the services and regional combatant commanders for fewer and fewer military resources, is likely to ebb and flow without relief for the rest of the decade. In the years ahead, however, beleaguered American political and military leaders will need to examine the proposed design for the use and organization of American landpower presented in this work if they are not to be driven to short-sighted solutions by external forces over which they have little control. This, after all, is what the late Sir Winston Churchill probably meant when he said: "There are very grave dangers—that is all I am going to say today—in letting everything run on and pile up until something happens, and it passes, all of a sudden, out of your control."[37]

NOTES

1. Henry Kissinger, *A World Restored: Metternich, Castlereagh and the Problems of Peace 1812–1822* (Boston, Mass.: Houghton Mifflin, 1988), 125.

2. Donald Kagan, *On The Origins of War and the Preservation of Peace* (New York: Anchor/Doubleday, 1995), 211.

3. Trading intercontinental ballistic missile strikes with an adversary like China is unlikely to result in an outcome of strategic value for the United States. Blockading a continental power like China from the sea would be futile. Seizing and controlling key centers of Chinese industrial and political power, however, could secure a strategic advantage for the United States and place the survival of the opposing regime in real jeopardy.

4. Floyd D. Spence, "What to Fight For? American Interests and the Use of Force in the Post–Cold War World," *The Brown Journal of World Affairs* (Winter/Spring 1996): 281–82.

5. Steven Butler, Susan V. Lawrence, Bruce Auster, and Gloria Borger, "Refocusing in Asia: Stability Depends on Mending Frayed U.S.–Japanese Security Ties," *U.S. News and World Report*, 22 April 1996, p. 49.

6. Carl von Clausewitz, *On War*, ed. and trans. Michael Howard and Peter Paret (Princeton, N.J.: Princeton University Press, 1976), p. 97.

7. Paul Seabury and Angelo Codevilla, *War: Ends and Means* (New York: Basic Books, 1991), 161.

8. Sun Tzu, *The Art of War* (Oxford: Oxford University Press, 1963).

9. Eliot A. Cohen, "A Revolution in Warfare," *Foreign Affairs* (March/April 1996): 47.

10. Henry Kissinger quoted in Russell F. Weigley's *The American Way of War: A History of United States Military Strategy and Policy* (Bloomington: Indiana University Press, 1977), 417.

11. Robert P. Haffa, Jr., "A 'New Look' at the Bottom-up Review: Planning U.S. General Purpose Forces for a New Century," *Strategic Review* (Winter 1996): 21–25. Also see Gary W. Anderson and Terry C. Pierce, "Leaving the Technocratic Tunnel," *Joint Forces Quarterly* (Winter 1995–1996): 69.

12. Quoted by Colin S. Gray in "The Changing Nature of Warfare?" *Naval War College Review* (Spring 1996): 9.

13. "The ABM Treaty's Threat," *The Wall Street Journal*, 2 January 1996, p. 1/8.

14. Iran maintains robust littoral warfare naval and marine forces. These are structured for coastal rather than ocean operations, however. From 1977 on, the Soviets viewed U.S. attack carriers and amphibious forces as secondary threats. See Jacob Kipp's essay "Naval Air Forces," *Soviet Armed Forces Review Annual*, vol. I, ed. David R. Jones (Gulf Breeze, Fla.: Academic International Press, 1977), 77–79. In view of this observation, it is interesting to recall the vast quantities of money spent on the 600 ship navy which, with the exception of the U.S. submarine fleet, the Soviet military largely disregarded as a serious threat.

15. "Trim Some Defense Pork," *Boston Herald*, 22 December 1995, p. 32.

16. Jeff Erlich, "IG Audit Finds Navy Overstates Weapon Needs," *Defense News*, 22–28 April 1996, p. 3. A step in the right direction is suggested in an article

by Major David Anderson, USMC, "Stretched Too Thin," *Proceedings*, July 1996, pp. 48–50.

17. Harvey Brooks, "U.S. Defense: Is Reform Possible?" *International Security*, 14, no. 3 (Winter 1989/90): 173–74.

18. "Desert Storm: The USN's War," *Jane's Defence Weekly*, 30 March 1991, p. 471.

19. Dr. James J. Tritten, "Revolutions in Military Affairs, Paradigm Shifts and Doctrine," *Naval Doctrine Command*, Norfolk, Virginia, February 1995, p. 15. Large military establishments often risk obsolescence, rather than risk change. The experiences of Spanish Vice Admiral Jose de Mazarredo Salazar strongly suggest that just having a good idea is not enough. De Mazarredo authored many excellent doctrinal works and offered good recommendations for improving the readiness of the Spanish fleet prior to its defeat together with the French fleet at Trafalgar in 1805. Although de Mazarredo never lost a battle at sea, his outspoken criticism of the state of the Spanish fleet and its lack of preparedness doomed all of his good work to the history books.

20. Eliot A. Cohen, "Defense and Technology: Come the Revolution," *National Review*, 31 July 1995, p. 25.

21. Jeffrey I. Sands, *On His Watch: Admiral Zumwalt's Efforts to Institutionalize Strategic Change* (Alexandria, Va: Center for Naval Analyses, July 1993), 79. Admiral Zumwalt discovered that if the directions of future change in the reorganization of American armed forces are vague or ambiguous, the precise tasks associated with change will ultimately be shaped by the incentives of those tasked rather than by the preferences of those doing the tasking.

22. Gray, "Changing Nature of Warfare?" p. 9

23. Martin Blumenson and James L. Stokesbury, *Masters of the Art of Command* (New York: Da Capo Press, 1975), 217.

24. Paul Nitze, *Securing the Seas: The Soviet Naval Challenge and Western Alliance Options* (Boulder, Colo.: Westview Press, 1979), 448.

25. Gidget Fuentes, "Krulak Takes to the Adriatic," *Navy Times*, 8 January 1996, p. 10.

26. Hans J. Morgenthau, *Politics Among Nations: The Struggle for Power and Peace*, 5th ed. (New York: Alfred A. Knopf, 1973), 163.

27. See John Hillen's essay "Getting NATO Back to Basics," *Backgrounder*, no. 1067 published by the Heritage Foundation during February 1996, p. 4.

28. Alan Philips, "Dr. Strangelove Puts Peace in Doubt: Russia Sees NATO as Potential Enemy," *Daily Telegraph*, 13 February 1996, p. 18.

29. Robert K. Massie, *Dreadnought: Britain, Germany, and the Coming of the Great War* (New York: Random House, 1991), 181.

30. John P. Cann, "These Defense Plans Are No Plans at All," *Washington Times*, 8 May 1996, p. 17.

31. Michael Howard, *The Franco–Prussian War* (New York: Methuen, 1981), 31.

32. Walter LaFeber, "Commentary," in *Second Indochina War Symposium: Papers and Commentary*, ed. John Schlacht (Washington, D.C.: Center of Military History, U.S. Army, 1986), p. 95.

33. David B. H. Denoon, ed., *Constraints on Strategy: The Economics of Western Security* (Washington, D.C.: Pergamon-Brassey's International Defense Publishers, 1986), 210.

34. Robert W. Tucker and David C. Hendrickson, *The Imperial Temptation: The New World Order and America's Purpose* (New York: Council on Foreign Relations Press, 1992), 154.

35. See Senator John McCain's paper *Ready Tomorrow: Defending American Interests in the 21st Century*, paper prepared for the U.S. Senate Committee on Armed Services, March 1996.

36. Weigley, *American Way of War*, 423.

37. Sir Winston Churchill, *Parliamentary Debates* (London: Hansard Publishing, 1951), House of Commons, vol. 446, no. 48, 562–63.

Appendix A:
Glossary of Military Terms

Capability	Ability of a properly organized, trained, and equipped force effectively to accomplish a particular mission or function.
Chairman	Unless otherwise stated, refers to the Chairman, Joint Chiefs of Staff.
Close Air Support (CAS)	Air action by fixed- and rotary-wing aircraft against targets in close proximity to friendly forces that, in order to prevent fratricide, requires detailed integration of each air mission with the fire and movement of those forces.
Close combat	Combat in which opposing forces are in close proximity.
Coalition operation	Operation conducted by military elements of a group of nations that have joined for some specific purpose.
Combatant command	See **Unified command**.
Combating proliferation	Full range of actions by the U.S. government to deter, delay, halt, or roll back the proliferation of weapons of mass destruction (WMD) and their delivery systems; includes waging war against WMD-armed adversaries.
Commander in Chief	President of the United States. Also, the Commander of one of the unified combatant commands established by the President.

Contingency   Situation or emergency. Military plans are often pre-
                                pared for the most likely contingencies that could re-
                                quire the employment of forces.

Deep attack   Application of force beyond the area of close combat
                                (see **Close combat**), includes interdiction, strike, stra-
                                tegic air warfare, deep supporting fires, and conven-
                                tional counterforce operations.

Defense agency   Organization designated by the Secretary of Defense to
                                provide a service or supplies common to more than one
                                department (e.g., Defense Information Systems
                                Agency, Defense Intelligence Agency, and Defense Lo-
                                gistics Agency).

DoD components   Major organizational elements of the Department of
                                Defense, such as services, agencies, and unified com-
                                mands.

DoD Directive 5100.1   Document that promulgates the responsibilities and
                                functions of the Department of Defense.

Electronic warfare   Military action involving use of electromagnetic and
                                directed energy to control the electromagnetic spectrum
                                or attack the enemy.

Executive Agent   Authority delegated (normally to a military department
                                or combatant commander) by the Secretary of Defense
                                to act on his behalf with respect to certain activities
                                and/or resources.

Field activity   Organization designated by the Secretary of Defense to
                                provide a service or supplies that are common to more
                                than one department (e.g., Defense POW/MIA Office,
                                Washington Headquarters Services).

Force package   Grouping of forces from one or more services, gener-
                                ally formed into joint task forces before they are em-
                                ployed.

Forward presence   See **Presence**.

Functional CINC   Unified Commander in Chief who is assigned a specific
                                worldwide support function. Currently, these are Spe-
                                cial Operations Command (SOCOM), Headquarters at
                                MacDill Air Force Base, Florida; Strategic Command
                                (STRATCOM), Headquarters at Offutt Air Force Base,
                                Nebraska; Transportation Command (TRANSCOM),
                                Headquarters at Scott Air Force Base, Illinois; and
                                Space Command (SPACECOM), Headquarters in Pe-
                                terson AFB, Colorado.

Functions	Specific responsibilities assigned by Congress, by the President, or by the Secretary of Defense to enable DOD components to fulfill the purposes for which they were established.
Geographic CINC	Unified Commander in Chief who is assigned a regional/geographic area of responsibility (AOR). Currently, these are Atlantic Command (ACOM), Headquarters in Norfolk, Virginia; Central Command (CENTCOM), Headquarters at MacDill AFB, Florida; Pacific Command (PACOM), Headquarters in Camp Smith, Hawaii; European Command (EUCOM), Headquarters in Stuttgart, Germany; and Southern Command (SOUTHCOM), Headquarters in Rodman, Panama.
Goldwater–Nichols Act	The Department of Defense Reorganization Act of 1986. The original bill was (10 U.S.C. 164[c]) sponsored by Senator Goldwater and Congressman Nichols.
Information warfare	Offensive and defensive measures aimed at controlling, disrupting, or destroying an adversary's information flow while protecting one's own.
Interservice	Between services, for example, interservice training (training provided by one service to members of another).
Interagency working group (IWG)	Group formed by the National Security Council to deal with specific issues, composed of representatives from various U.S. government departments and agencies.
Joint Mission Essential Task List	List of the primary tasks that joint forces must be prepared to execute to accomplish missions they are most likely to be assigned, used for training and evaluation purposes.
Marine Expeditionary Force	The Principal Marine Corps warfighting organization, particularly for a larger crisis or contingency, it can range in size from less than one division to multiple divisions and aircraft wings, together with one or more force service support groups.
Military Departments	Departments of the Army, Navy, and Air Force.
Military Services	Army, Navy, Air Force, Marine Corps, and Coast Guard.
Missions	Tasks assigned by the President or Secretary of Defense to the combatant commanders.

Mobile Subscriber Equipment (MSE)	Modern, secure communications system for ground forces.
National Command Authority (NCA)	President and the Secretary of Defense or their alternates or successors.
National Military Strategy (NMS)	Produced by the Chairman of the Joint Chiefs of Staff, articulates the military component of the National Security Strategy.
National Reconnaissane Office (NRO)	Agency that buys and operates satellites for intelligence purposes.
National Security Strategy	Document published by the President that articulates the security strategy of the nation.
Operational control	Authority to organize, employ, assign tasks, designate objectives, and give authoritative direction over subordinate forces engaged in operations or joint training; does not automatically include authoritative direction for logistics, administration, discipline, internal organization, or unit training.
Operational Support Airlift (OSA)	All airlift transportation in support of command, installation, or management function using DoD-owned or -controlled aircraft.
Operations and Maintenance (O&M)	Funds programmed for routine activities such as training and maintenance of equipment.
Operations Other Than War (OOTW)	Military activities during peacetime and conflict that do not necessarily involve armed clashes between organized forces or sustained combat.
Orginal Equipment Manufacturer (OEM)	Company or corporation that originally produces a weapon system or item of equipment.
Outyears	Used in programming, the fiscal years beyond the current 6-year plan.
Peace operations	Umbrella term that encompasses the full range of military and diplomatic activities to prevent, halt, or contain conflicts.
Preposition	To place military units, equipment, or supplies at or near the point of planned use or at a designated location to reduce reaction time, and to ensure timely support of a specific force during inital phases of an operation.
Presence	Ability of U.S. military forces to exert influence abroad during peacetime resulting from their proximity, capability to get to the scene quickly, or engagement activities with foreign nations.
Proliferation	Spread of WMD and associated military technologies.

Roles	Broad and enduring purposes specified by Congress in law for the services and selected DoD components.
Secretariat	Staff of the Secretary of a military department, currently separate from the staff of the Service Chief of Staff.
Secretary	Unless otherwise stated, refers to the Secretary of Defense.
Service Chief	Senior military person in service: Chief of Staff of the Army, Chief of Naval Operations, Commandant of the Marine Corps, Chief of Staff of the Air Force, and Commandant of the Coast Guard.
Theater	As used in this report, refers to the area of operation of a geographic CINC.
Title 10, T.S.C.	Title 10, United States Code (Armed Forces), law establishing the broad responsibilities of the Department of Defense and its components.
Total Force	Combined capabilities of all components of all services—active, reserve, and National Guard.
Unified command	Functional or geographic command composed of forces provided by two or more Military Departments.
Weapons of Mass Destruction (WMD)	Nuclear, chemical, or biological weapons that can be used for large-scale and indiscriminate attack on populations.

Appendix B:
Military Abbreviations and Acronyms

A-10	USAF close air support fighter
A-76	Office of Management and Budget Circular A-76
aaslt	air assault
AAV	assault amphibian vehicle
abn	airborne
ACE	air combat element
ACOM	U.S. Atlantic Command
ADA	air defense artillery
ADEA	Army Development and Employment Agency
admin	administration
ADS	Advanced Distributed Simulation
AEF	American Expeditionary Forces
AF	numbered air force, or U.S. Air Force, depending on context
AFB	Air Force Base
AFFOR	U.S. Air Force component of a joint force
AFLant	U.S. Air Force component of U.S. Atlantic Command
AGS	armor gun system (i.e., light tank) under development
AI	air interdiction
air def	air defense
ALFA	Air/Land Force Application (Agency)

alft	airlift
ALO	air liaison officer
amphib	amphibious or amphibians, depending on context
ANG	Air National Guard
AOR	Area of responsibility
Apache	AH-64 attack helicopter
ARG	Marine amphibious ready group
ARFOR	U.S. Army component of a joint force
armd	armored
ARNG	Army National Guard
arty	artillery
ASD	Assistant Secretary of Defense
ASOC	air support operations center
AT	antitank
ATACMS	Army Tactical Missile System
ATF	amphibious task force
ATO	air tasking order
ATS	Army Transport Service
AV-8B	Marine short/vertical takeoff and landing attack aircraft
avn	aviation
AWACS	airborne warning and control system
B-2	USAF Stealth Bomber
B-52	USAF Bomber aircraft
BAI	battlefield air interdiction
BCE	battlefield coordination element
bde	brigade
BLT	battalion landing team
bn	battalion
BRAC	Base Realignment and Closure
BSSG	brigade service support group
btry	battery
C^2	command and control
C^3	command, control, and communications
C^3I	command, control, communications, and intelligence
C^4I	command, control, communications, computers, and intelligence

C-5A	USAF large heavy airlift aircraft
C-17	USAF heavy airlift aircraft
C-130	medium airlift aircraft
C-133	medium/heavy airlift aircraft (obsolete)
C-141	medium/heavy airlift aircraft
CAS	close air support
CASF	composite air strike force
CAT	crisis action team, or common air tasking, depending on context
CATF	commander amphibious task force
cbt	combat
cbt engr	combat engineer
cdr	commander
CENTAF	U.S. Air Force component of U.S. Central Command
CENTCOM	U.S. Central Command
CG	commanding general
CH-46	medium cargo helicopter (USMC)
CH-47	medium cargo helicopter (U.S. Army)
CH-53	heavy lift helicopter
CINC	Commander in Chief (of one of the unified commands)
CINCCENT	Commander in Chief, U.S. Central Command
CINCSOC	Commander in Chief, U.S. Special Operations Command
CINCSOUTH	Commander in Chief, U.S. Southern Command
CJCS	Chairman, Joint Chiefs of Staff
CLF	commander landing force
CMC	Commandant of the Marine Corps.
CNO	Chief of Naval Operations
co	company
CONUS	Continental United States
COSCOM	corps support command
CRAF	Civil Reserve Air Fleet
CSAR	Combat Search and Rescue
CSSE	combat service support element
CTF	commander task force
CTG	commander task group
CVBG	USN Carrier Battlegroup

DAB	Defense Acquisition Board
DARPA	Defense Advanced Research Projects Agency
DCAA	Defense Contract Audit Agency
DCI	Director of Central Intelligence
DCMC	Defense Contract Management Command
det	detachment
DIA	Defense Intelligence Agency
DISA	Defense Information Systems Agency
div	division
DoD	Department of Defense
DS	direct support
DSO	Defense Support Organization
EAC	electronic warfare aircraft
elm	element
engr	engineer
ENWGS	enhanced naval wargame system
EuCom	(U.S.) European Command
EW	electronic warfare
F-15	USAF fighter aircraft
F-16	USAF fighter aircraft
F-117	USAF stealth fighter aircraft
FA	field artillery
F/A-18	USN fighter/attack aircraft
FMFLant	Fleet Marine Force, Atlantic
FORSCOM	Forces Command (JCS specified command), or the U.S. Army
	Forces Command (Army major command using same headquarters), depending on context
FYDP	Future Years Defense Program
GAO	General Accounting Office
GCE	ground combat element
GHQ	General Headquarters
GME	Graduate Medical Education
GOCO	Government owned, contractor operated
gp	group
grd	ground

HMA	USMC attack helicopter squadron
HMH	USMC heavy lift helicopter squadron
HML	USMC utility helicopter squadron
HMM	USMC medium lift helicopter squadron
HMO	Health Maintenance Organization
HQTRS	headquarters
Inf	infantry
intel	intelligence
IWG	Interagency Working Group
J-3	staff officer for operations on a joint staff
J-4	staff officer for logistics on a joint staff
J-6	staff officer for communications–electronics on a joint staff; Command, Control, and Communications Directorate of the Joint Staff, depending on context
J-7	Operational Plans and Interoperability Directorate of the Joint Staff
J-8	Force Structure, Resource, and Assessment Directorate of the Joint Staff
JAST	Joint Advanced Strike Technology
JCS	Joint Chiefs of Staff
JDA	Joint Deployment Agency
JDS	Joint Deployment System
JESS	Joint Exercise Support System
JFACC	Joint Force air component commander
JFDG	Joint Force Development Group
Joint Pub	Chairman, JCS, Publication (formerly JCS Pub)
JOPES	Joint Operations Planning and Execution System
JOPS	Joint Operations and Planning System
JSOTF	Joint Special Operations Task Force
JSTARS	joint surveillance target attack radar system aircraft
JTC3A	Joint Tactical Command, Control, and Communications Agency
KC-130	tanker aircraft
LAAD Bn (Stgr)	USMC air defense battalion, Stinger equipped
LAAM Bn (Hawk)	USMC air defense battalion, Hawk equipped
LAV	light armored vehicle

LantCom	(U.S.) Atlantic Command
LantFlt	Atlantic Fleet (U.S. Navy component of Atlantic Command)
LCAC	landing craft air cushion
LHA	amphibious assault ship (Tarawa class)
LHD	amphibious assault ship (Wasp class)
LPH	amphibious assault ship (Iwo Jima class)
log	logistics
lt	light
M-1A1/A2	U.S. Army 70 ton main battle tank
MAG	Marine Aircraft Group
MAGTF	Marine Air–Ground Task Force
maint	maintenance
MarCent	U.S. Marine Corps component of U.S. Central Command
MARFOR	U.S. Marine Corps component of a joint force
MATS	Military Air Transport Service
MEB	Marine Expeditionary Brigade
mech	mechanized
med	medical or medium, depending on context
MEF	Marine Expeditionary Force
MEU	Marine Expeditionary Unit
MEU (SOC)	Marine Expeditionary Unit (Special Operations Capable)
Ml	military intelligence
MLRS	Multiple Launch Rocket System
MPF	maritime prepositioning force
MSC	Military Sealift Command
MSE	Mobile Subscriber Equipment
MSTS	Military Sea Transport Service
MTMA	Military Traffic Management Agency
mtr	motor
mtr trans (MT)	motor transport
NATO	North Atlantic Treaty Organization
NavCent	U.S. Navy component of U.S. Central Command
NAVFORUS	Navy component of a joint force
NavLant	U.S. Navy component of U.S. Atlantic Command
NCA	National Command Authority

NMS	National Military Strategy
NPR	National Performance Review
NRO	National Reconnaissance Office
NSC	National Security Council
NTS	Navy Transport Service
OA-4A	high speed observation aircraft
OEM	Original Equipment Manufacturer
OMB	Office of Management and Budget
OOTW	Operations Other Than War
opcon	operational control
OPFOR	opposing force
opnl	operational
opns	operations
OSA	Operational Support Airlift
OSD	Office of the Secretary of Defense
OV-10	slow flying observation aircraft
PaCom	Pacific Command
PEO	Program Executive Officer
plat	platoon
PM	Program Manager
PPBS	Planning, Programming, and Budgeting System
pub	publication
QSR	Quadrennial Strategy Review
RC	Reserve Components
RCT	regimental combat team
RDT&E	Research, Development, Testing and Evaluation
recon	reconnaissance
regt	regiment
rein (reinf)	reinforced
RF-4B	photo reconnaissance aircraft
SACEUR	Supreme Allied Commander Europe
SAMS	School of Advanced Military Studies
SEAL(s)	sea–air–land team (U.S. Navy special operations forces)
SecDef	Secretary of Defense
SF	special forces

sig	signal
SME	Single Managemnt Element
SOC	special operations capable
SOCOM	(U.S.) Special Operations Command
SOF	special operations forces
SOUTHCOMUS	Southern Command
SPACECOMUS	Space Command
spt	support
sqdn	squadron
SSM	surface-to-surface missile
SSN	attack submarine, nuclear powered
STRATCOM	U.S. Strategic Command
svc	service
TAC	Tactical Air Command
tacAL	tactical airlift
TACC	tactical air control center (USAF and USN); tactical air command center (USMC)
tac ftr	tactical fighter
TACP	tactical air control party (USAF and USMC)
TADC	tactical air direction center (USMC and USN)
TAMD	Theater Air and Missile Defense
TAOC	tactical air operations center (USMC)
TASS	tactical air support squadron (USAF)
TF	task force
TFS	tactical fighter squadron
TFX	Tactical Fighter, Experimental
Title 10, USC	Title 10, United States Code (Armed Forces)
TNK	tank
TOW/LAV	antitank missile mounted on light armored vehicle
TQM	Total Quality Management
TRADOC	(U.S. Army) Training and Doctrine Command
TRANSCOM	U.S. Transportation Command
UCP	Unified Command Plan
UH-1	Huey Army utility helicopter
UH-60	Blackhawk Army utility helicopter
UN	United Nations

US	United States
USA	United States of America, or United States Army, depending on context
USAF	United States Air Force
USD(A&T)	Undersecretary of Defense for Acquisiton and Technology
USEUCOM	U.S. European Command
USMC	United States Marine Corps
USN	United States Navy
V-22	vertical takeoff and landing aircraft (Osprey), under development
VMA	USMC attack squadron
VMFA	USMC fighter/attack squadron
wg	wing
WMD	weapons of mass destruction

Appendix C:
Notional Corps Support Command (COSCOM)

Unit Name	SRC	Mult	Personnel Strength	SQ FT	STON	MTON	Self-Propelled	Towed
HHC, CORPS SPT CMD	6343lL000	1	347	7259	283	1248	40	13
MMC, CORPS SPT CMD	6343 3L000	1	378	8427	284	1395	31	31
DATA PROCESSING UNIT	1145OL000	2	7	1797	77	402	5	5
EOD CONTROL TEAM	09527LA00	7	12	692	18	106	5	1
EOD DETACHMENT	09527LB00	7	23	2577	76	371	14	8
HHD, PETRL SUP BN	10426L000	1	56	2071	70	336	10	7
QM PETROLEUM SUPPLY CO	10427L000	8	197	37600	1326	4898	53	53
T MDM TRK CO 5000 GAL	55727L200	2	172	31217	1099	7613	71	66
QM PETRL PL & TML OP	10417L000	1	168	19920	877	3088	39	39
QM HHD WTR SUP BN	10466L000	1	40	1756	56	276	12	3
WATER SUPPLY COMPANY	10468L000	5	141	14239	651	2644	26	26
WATER PURIF DETACHMENT	10469L000	1	50	7379	429	1752	11	11
QM TAC WTR DISTR	10570LG00	2	19	3677	161	689	5	5
HHC, SUPPORT GROUP (CORPS)	63342L000	2	114	4545	146	695	25	11
HHD, CORPS SUPPORT BN	63426L000	9	56	3568	116	546	19	12
HHD, S AND S BN	42446L000	1	52	1650	62	223	10	4
MAINT CO NON-DIV DS	43209L000	9	195	23334	1075	5005	62	59
QM SUPPLY CO	42247L000	9	118	14973	677	2811	33	33
QM FLD SVC CO DS/AOE	42414L000	6	106	6042	283	1046	19	19
ORD CO, AMMO (MOADS) DS	09483L000	9	212	2444	1293	4444	56	44
T MDM TRK CO 20 FT CNR/CGO	55728L100	2	183	49469	1899	10491	70	70
TRANS LIGHT-MDM TRUCK	55719L100	9	164	19805	1254	4081	72	32
MP SECURITY COMPANY	19698L000	2	152	6667	207	1010	39	22
CORPS RAOC	62413L000	4	23	1208	41	195	8	1
AVN MAINT CO,III CORPS-AC	01947L100	2	269	31814	1258	6565	58	58
QM HVY MS CO GS CORPS/AOE	42427L100	1	156	11336	512	1953	17	17
QM REP PARTS SUPPLY CO	42419L000	2	182	23582	963	4519	38	38
QM LIGHT AIRDROP SUPPLY CO	10443L000	1	173	13454	430	1723	21	21
QM AD EQ REP&SUP CO(CORPS)	10449L100	1	96	8585	197	795	7	7

Unit	SRC							
HHD, ORD BN (AMMO) DS	09666L000	1	53	2512	78	387	15	5
ORD CO, AMMO, CONV, GS	09149L000	2	227	29188	1271	4811	30	20
MP CO (HVY SECURITY)	19497L000	2	209	10599	359	1644	65	28
MED CO, AIR AMBL (UH-60A)	08447L200	5	129	21428	637	4189	24	15
MEDICAL AMBULANCE COM	08449L000	6	122	7751	276	1483	52	8
HHD, TRANS MOTOR BN	55716L000	1	45	1817	65	291	10	5
TRANS HEAVY TRUCK COM	55729L000	2	159	34378	1780	8542	47	41
T TML SVC CO (CNTNR/BB)	55827L000	1	357	45524	1873	6798	35	35
TRANS CARGO TRANSFER	55817L100	1	90	11804	470	1740	9	9
HHC, MEDICAL BRIGADE	08422L100	1	89	3512	110	556	18	10
HHD, MED BN, (DEN SVC)	08476L000	1	10	343	9	51	2	1
MED CO, DENTAL, SVC	08478L000	2	60	3729	135	591	14	14
MED DET, DENTAL SVCS	08479L000	2	28	2407	95	395	9	9
HHD, MEDICAL BN, LOG(FWD)	08486L000	1	46	1221	42	180	5	4
MED BN, AREA SUPPORT	08455L000	1	338	24313	959	4147	125	82
LOG SPT CO, MED BN, LOG(FWD)	08487L000	1	119	11739	485	2052	22	22
MEDICAL CO (AREA SPT)	08457L000	3	64	4956	197	846	26	17
MED CO, CMBT STRESS CONTL	08467L000	1	84	3591	139	572	17	15
MED DET, PM (SANITATION)	08498L000	2	11	610	14	85	3	3
HOSPITAL UNIT, HOLDING	08739L000	1	64	4221	166	824	2	1
HHD, MEDICAL GOUP	08432L000	2	62	2143	67	330	11	5
COMBAT SUPPORT HOSPITAL	08823L000	8	295	17945	550	3000	9	9
MEDICAL DET (SURG)	08407L100	5	9	201	5	23	1	1
HHD, MED EVAC BN	08446L000	2	45	2461	78	371	11	11
MOBILE ARMY SURGICAL	0P8765L000	2	128	5520	319	981	21	15
HHD ORD(MNT)BN DS/GS	43436L000	1	48	1986	69	320	13	3
QM SUPPLY CO, GS	42418L000	4	137	10299	410	1450	10	10
AVN MAINT CO, XVIII CORPS	01947L.500	2	318	28302	1131	5843	51	51
AVN MAINT CO (AVUM/AVIM)	01839L000	2	226	16267	716	3012	37	37
CORPS SUPPORT COMMAND			2210	233258	98717	424318	5299	4403

NOTE: COSCOM SRC data totals include unit multipliers--UNIT SRC data is for one unit.

Appendix D:
Army Prepositioning Afloat

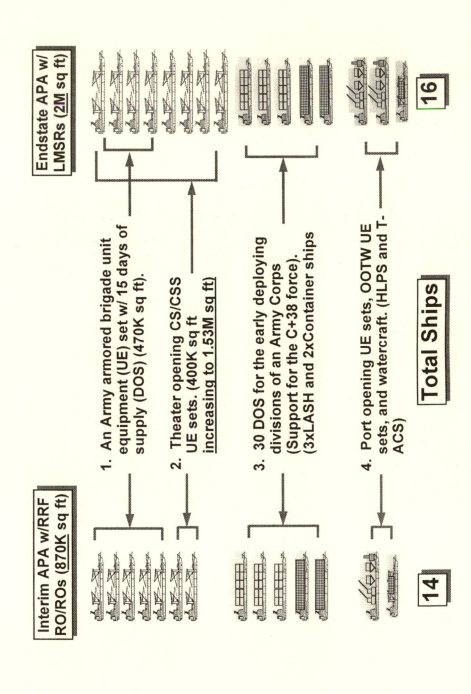

Interim APA w/RRF RO/ROs (870K sq ft)

Endstate APA w/ LMSRs (2M sq ft)

1. An Army armored brigade unit equipment (UE) set w/ 15 days of supply (DOS) (470K sq ft).

2. Theater opening CS/CSS UE sets. (400K sq ft increasing to 1.53M sq ft)

3. 30 DOS for the early deploying divisions of an Army Corps (Support for the C+38 force). (3xLASH and 2xContainer ships

4. Port opening UE sets, OOTW UE sets, and watercraft. (HLPS and T-ACS)

14

16

Total Ships

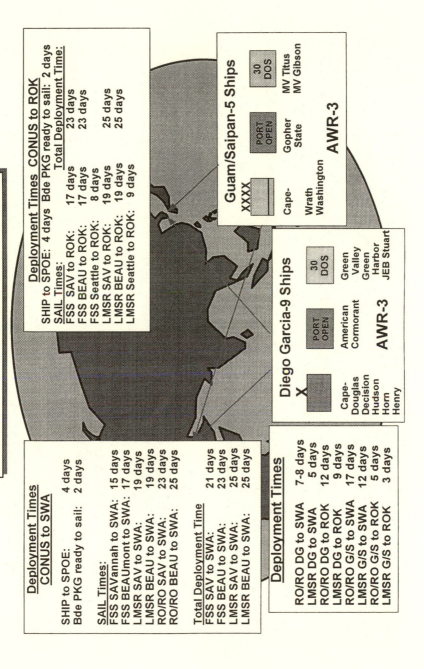

Sealift Planning Factors

Deployment Times CONUS to SWA

SHIP to SPOE: 4 days
Bde PKG ready to sail: 2 days

SAIL Times:
FSS SAVannah to SWA: 15 days
FSS BEAUmont to SWA: 17 days
LMSR SAV to SWA: 19 days
LMSR BEAU to SWA: 19 days
RO/RO SAV to SWA: 23 days
RO/RO BEAU to SWA: 25 days

Total Deployment Time
FSS SAV to SWA: 21 days
FSS BEAU to SWA: 23 days
LMSR SAV to SWA: 25 days
LMSR BEAU to SWA: 25 days

Deployment Times CONUS to ROK

SHIP to SPOE: 4 days   Bde PKG ready to sail: 2 days

	Total Deployment Time:
SAIL Times:	
FSS SAV to ROK:	17 days	23 days
FSS BEAU to ROK:	17 days	23 days
FSS Seattle to ROK:	8 days	
LMSR SAV to ROK:	19 days	25 days
LMSR BEAU to ROK:	19 days	25 days
LMSR Seattle to ROK:	9 days	

Deployment Times

RO/RO DG to SWA: 7-8 days
LMSR DG to SWA: 5 days
RO/RO DG to ROK: 12 days
LMSR DG to ROK: 9 days
RO/RO G/S to SWA: 17 days
LMSR G/S to SWA: 12 days
RO/RO G/S to ROK: 5 days
LMSR G/S to ROK: 3 days

Diego Garcia-9 Ships

X   PORT OPEN   30 DOS

Cape-Douglas
Decision
Hudson
Horn
Henry

American Cormorant

Green Valley
Green Harbor
JEB Stuart

AWR-3

Guam/Saipan-5 Ships

XXXX   PORT OPEN   30 DOS

Cape-Wrath
Washington

Gopher State

MV Titus
MV Gibson

AWR-3

APA CS/CSS Theater Infrastructure

46% of the Interim APA -- 77% of the Endstate APA

Initiates execution of Army Wartime Executive Agent Responsibility (WEAR) for line haul and sustainment and inland support of the armored brigade.

Interim APA Daily Line Haul Capability

CLASS I (W) - 490K GAL

CLASS III (B) - 531K GAL

CLASS II/IV - 2400 STONs

Hvy Equipment - 102 Vehs

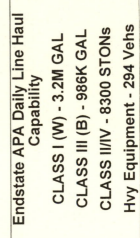

Cbt Bde 23%

CSI CSS 77%

An increase of 385% in EAD/EAC CS/CSS theater infrastructure

CSI CSS 46%

Cbt Bde 54%

Endstate APA Daily Line Haul Capability

CLASS I (W) - 3.2M GAL

CLASS III (B) - 986K GAL

CLASS II/IV - 8300 STONs

Hvy Equipment - 294 Vehs

Endstate theater infrastructure capabilities meet early WEAR requirements and maximize APOD/SPOD thruput of surging forces from CONUS.

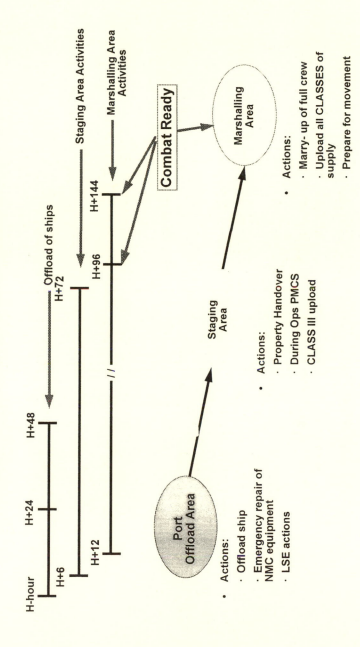

Combat ready times for afloat prepo.
-- parallel, not sequential actions --

Selected Bibliography

Adler, Selig. *The Isolationist Impulse: Its Twentieth Century Reaction*. New York: Free Press, 1957.

Aldinger, Charles. "Russian Defense Chief Warns NATO Not to Expand." *Washington Times*, 5 January 1996.

Allard, Kenneth C. "The Future of Command and Control: Toward a Paradigm of Information Warfare." In L. Benjamin Ederington and Michael J. Mazarr, editors, *Turning Point: The Gulf War and U.S. Military Strategy*. Boulder Colo.: Westview Press, 1995.

Anderson, David A., Major, USMC. "Stretched Too Thin." *Proceedings* (July 1996).

Atkinson, Rick. *Crusade: The Untold Story of the Persian Gulf War*. Boston, Mass.: Houghton Mifflin, 1993.

Attarin, Amir. "Soviet Nuclear Droppings Get Hotter." *Wall Street Journal* 23 January 1996.

Bartlett, Henry, G. Paul Holman, Timothy Stone. "The Art of Strategy and Force Planning." *Naval War College Review* (Spring 1995).

Bermudez, Joseph S., Jr. "Iraqi Missile Operations During Desert Storm." *Janes Soviet Intelligence Review* (March 1991).

Blackwell, James. *The Gulf War: Military Lessons Learned*. Washington, D.C., Center for Strategic and International Studies, 1991.

Blinken, Donald. "America's Stake in NATO Expansion." *Wall Street Journal* 5 July 1996.

Blumenson, Martin. *Kasserine Pass: An Epic Saga of Desert War*. Berkeley, Calif.: Berkeley Publishing, 1983.

Blumenson, Martin. *The Battle of the Generals: The Untold Story of the Falaise Pocket—the Campaign That Should Have Won World War II*. New York: William Morrow, 1993.

Blumenson, Martin. *The Patton Papers 1885–1940*. Vol. I and II. Boston: Houghton Mifflin, 1972.

Blumenson, Martin, and James L. Stokesbury. *Masters of the Art of Command*. New York: Da Capo Paperback, 1975.

Blumenthal, Sidney. "The Return of the Repressed: Anti-Internationalism and the American Right." *World Policy Journal* (Fall 1995).

Bonin, John A., Col. "Brigades: Building Blocks for FORCE XXI." *USAWC Research Project* (Academic Year 1994–95).

Bowie, C., F. Frostic, K. Lewis, D. Ochmanek, and P. Propper. *The New Calculus: Analyzing Airpower's Changing Role in Joint Theater Campaigns* (Project Air Force). Santa Monica, Calif.: RAND Corporation, 1993.

Boyd, John R. "A Discourse on Winning and Losing." Unpublished manuscript, pp. 175–189.

Breemer, Jan S. "The End of Naval Strategy: Revolutionary Change and the Future of American Naval Power." *Strategic Review* (Spring 1994).

Brinkerhoff, John. "The American Strategy of Unpreparedness." *Strategic Review* (Winter 1994).

Brungess, James R. *Setting the Context: Suppression of Enemy Air Defenses and Joint War Fighting in an Uncertain World*. Maxwell AFB, Ala.: Air University Press, June 1994.

Burk, James. "The Army and the People." Discussion paper presented to Senior Conference XXXI, *The Army in the 21st Century*. U.S. Military Academy, 2–4 June 1995.

Chase, Robert S., Emily Hill, and Paul Kennedy. "Pivotal States and U.S. Strategy." *Foreign Affairs* (January–February 1996).

Churchill, Winston. *The World Crisis, 1911–1918*. Vol. I. London: Odhams Press, 1938.

Cohen, Eliot. *Gulf War Air Power Survey*. Washington, D.C.: U.S. Government Printing Office, Department of the U.S. Air Force, 1993.

Cohen, Eliot and John Gooch. *Military Misfortunes: The Anatomy of Failure in War*. New York: The Free Press, 1990.

Collins, John M. "Prepositioned Weapons, Equipment and Supplies: Overview and Evaluations." *CRS Report for Congress* Washington, D.C.: Congressional Research Service, Library of Congress, 27 October 1995.

Congressional Budget Office. *An Analysis of U.S. Army Helicopter Programs*. Washington, D.C.: U.S. Government Printing Office, December 1995.

Conrad, Scott W. "Moving the Force: Desert Storm and Beyond." *McNair Paper 32* Washington, D.C.: National Defense University Press, 1993.

Cooper, Jeffrey R. "Implementing Coherent Operations: An Action Plan for the Deputy Chief of Staff, Operations and Plans, U.S. Army." Paper prepared under contract to the Department of the Army by SRS Technologies, June 1994.

Cooper, Matthew. *The German Army, 1933–1945: Its Political and Military Failure*. Lanham, Md.: Scarborough House, 1978.

Cordesman, Anthony, and Ahmed Hashim. *Iran and "Dual Containment": A Net Assessment*. Washington, D.C.: Center for Strategic and International Studies, 1995.

Corum, James S. *The Roots of Blitzkrieg: Hans von Seeckt and German Military Reform*. Lawrence, Kans.: University Press of Kansas, 1992.

"Crises and Constraints." Paper prepared for the Air Force Chief of Staff, December 1995.

Cushman, John H. *Command and Control of Theater Forces: The Future of Force Projection*. Cambridge, Mass.: Harvard University Center for Information Policy Research, March 1995.

Cushman, John J. "Make It Joint Force XXI." Unpublished manuscript.

Dandeker, Christopher. "Bureaucracy Planning and War: The Royal Navy, 1880 to 1918." *Armed Forces and Society* 11, no. 1 (Fall 1984).

Davis, Paul K., and Donald Blumenthal. "The Base of Sand Problem: A White Paper on the State of Military Combat Modeling." *A Rand Note*, N-3148-OSD/DARPA, Santa Monica, Calif.: RAND Corporation, 1991.

Deighton, Len. *Blitzkrieg: The Rise and Fall of Hitler to the Fall of Dunkirk*. New York: Ballantine Books, 1980.

Depres, John. "The Timely Lessons of History: The Manchurian Model for Soviet Strategy." *RAND Report R-1825-NA*, Santa Monica, Calif.: RAND Corporation, 1976.

Directions for Defense. Report of the Commission on Roles and Missions of the Armed Forces, Washington, D.C.: U.S. Government Printing Office, 24 May 1995.

Douglass, Joseph D., Jr. "Critical Questions Loom in Assessing the Gulf War." *Armed Forces Journal International* (April 1991).

Drucker, Peter F. *Post-Capitalist Society*, New York: HarperCollins, 1993.

Dunn, Richard, III. "From Gettysburg to the Gulf and Beyond." *McNair Paper No. 13*, Washington, D.C.: Institute for National Strategic Studies, 1991.

Dunnigan, James F., and Albert A. Nofi. *Shooting Blanks: War Making That Doesn't Work*. New York: William Morrow, 1991.

Dupuy, R. E., and T. N. Dupuy. *The Encyclopedia of Military History from 3500 B.C. to the Present*. New York: Harper & Row, 1970.

Dykes, David A. "Does Longbow Apache Really Make a Difference?" *Army Aviation*, 29 February 1996.

Elting, John R. *Swords Around a Throne: Napoleon's Grande Armeé*. New York: Macmillan, 1988.

Erlich, Jeff, and Teresa Hitchens. "Counterproliferation Efforts Await Requirement Review." *Defense News*, 6–12 November 1995.

Evans, Michael. "Yes, It Really Was a Famous Victory: Michael Evans, in Kuwait, Argues That Tactical Brilliance, Not Just Force of Arms, Won the Gulf War." *The Times*, 14 March 1991.

Fehrenbach, T. R. *This Kind of War: The Classic Korean War History*. London: Brassey's, 1988.

Fialka, John J. *Hotel Warriors: Covering the Gulf War*. Washington, D.C.: The Woodrow Wilson Center Press, 1991.

Fitchett, Joseph. "Germany Moves to Shoulder Europe's Post-2000 Military Burden." *Herald Tribune*, 7 December 1995.

Friedman, Norman. *Desert Victory: The War for Kuwait*. Annapolis, Md.: Naval Institute Press, 1991.

Friedman, Thomas L. "The No-Dead War." *The New York Times*, 23 August 1995.

Fulghum, David A. "Glosson: U.S. Gulf War Shortfalls Linger." *Aviation Week & Space Technology*, 29 January 1996.

Gabel, Christopher. *The 4th Armored Division in the Encirclement of Nancy*. Fort Leavenworth, Kans.: Combat Studies Institute, 1986.

Gaddis, John Lewis. "Risks, Costs and Strategies of Containment." In Carl Brown, editor, *Centerstage: American Diplomacy Since World War II*. New York: Homes & Meier, 1990.

Gavin, James. *Airborne Warfare*. Washington, D.C.: Infantry Journal Press, 1947.

Gelb, Norman. *Ike and Monty: Generals at War*. New York: William Morrow, 1994.

Gellman, Barton. "Study on Gulf War Points Out Limits of Air Power." *The Washington Post*, 13 May 1993.

Gellman, Irwin F. *Secret Affairs: Franklin Roosevelt, Cordell Hull and Sumner Wells*. Baltimore, Md.: Johns Hopkins University Press, 1995.

General Accounting Office. *Marine Corps: Improving Amphibious Capability Would Require Larger Share of Budget than Previously Provided*. Washington, D.C.: U.S. Government Printing Office, February 1996.

General Accounting Office Report to Congress: *Navy Carrier Battle Groups: The Structure and the Affordability of the Future Force*. Washington, D.C.: U.S. Government Printing Office, February 1993.

General Accounting Office Report to Congress: *Operation Desert Storm—Evaluation of the Air War*. Washington, D.C.: U.S. Government Printing Office, July 1996.

George, James L. "97 Defense Budget: More Weapon Procurement Myths." *The Virginian–Pilot & Ledger–Star*, 1 April 1996.

Gertz, Bill. "N. Korean Missile Could Reach U.S., Intelligence Warns." *The Washington Times*, 29 September 1995.

Gertz, Bill. "Plea for Missile Defense in Korea Fails." *The Washington Times*, 15 February 1996.

Gilpin, Robert. *War and Change in World Politics*. London: Cambridge University Press, 1981.

Glynn, Patrick. *Closing Pandora's Box: Arms Races, Arms Control, and the History of the Cold War*. New York: A New Republic Book, 1989.

Goodman, Hirsh, and W. Seth Carus. *The Future Battlefield and the Arab–Israeli Conflict*. London: Transaction Publishers, 1990.

Gordon, Michael R., and Bernard E. Trainor. *The Generals' War*. Boston: Little, Brown, 1993.

Gorman, Paul F. "The Secret of Future Victories." *IDA Paper P-2653*, Alexandria, Va.: Institute for Defense Analysis, 1992.

Gouré, Daniel. "Is There a Military–Technical Revolution in America's Future?" *The Washington Quarterly* (Autumn 1993).

Gray, Colin S. "The Changing Nature of War?" *Naval War College Review* (Spring 1996).

Guderian, Heinz. *Guderian: Erinnerungen eines Soldaten,* 13th ed. Stuttgart, Germany: Motorbuch Verlag, 1994.

Hackett, James. "Missile Menace Lurking in China." *The Washington Times*, 14 January 1996.

Halberstam, David. *The Best and the Brightest*. New York: Ballantine Books, 1992.

Harmon, Christopher, and David Tucker, eds. *Statecraft and Power: Essays in Honor of Harold W. Wood*. New York: University Press of America, 1994.

Harmon, Ernest, "Notes on Combat Experience During the Tunisian and African Campaign." Report prepared for the Office of the Army Chief of Staff, April 1943.

Helprin, Mark. "For a New Concert of Europe." *Commentary* (January 1996).

Henderson, G.F.R. *Stonewall Jackson and the American Civil War*. New York: Da Capo Press, 1988.

Herbert, Paul. "Deciding What Has to Be Done: General William E. DePuy and the 1976 Edition of FM 100-5 Operations." *Leavenworth Papers*, No. 16, Fort Leavenworth, Kans.: Combat Studies Institute, 1988.

Herman, Paul F., Jr. "The Revolution in 'Military' Affairs." *Strategic Review* (Spring 1996).

Hess, Pamela. "Air Force Studies Ability of Air Power to Blunt an Armored Invasion." *Inside the Air Force*, 9 February 1996.

Hochevar, Albert, James Robards, John Schafer, and James Zepka. "Deep Strike: The Evolving Face of War." *Joint Forces Quarterly* (Autumn 1995).

Holz, Robert F., Jack H. Hiller, and Howard H. McFann. *Determinants of Effective Unit Performance: Research on Measuring and Managing Unit Training Readiness*. Alexandria, Va.: U.S. Army Research Institute for Behavioral and Social Sciences, July 1994.

Hosmer, Stephen T. *Effects of the Coalition Air Campaign Against Iraqi Ground Forces in the Gulf War*, MR-305-AF, Santa Monica, Calif.: RAND Corporation, 1994.

Hourani, Albert. *A History of the Arab Peoples*. New York: Time Warner Books, 1992.

House, Jonathan M. *Toward Combined Arms Warfare: A Survey of 20th Century Tactics, Doctrine, and Organization*. Fort Leavenworth, Kans.: Combat Studies Institute, 1984.

Howard, Michael. *The Franco–Prussian War*. New York: Methuen, 1981.

Howard, Michael. *The Lessons of History*. New Haven, Conn.: Yale University Press, 1991.

Isenberg, David. "The Illusion of Power: Aircraft Carriers and U.S. Military Strategy." *Cato Institute Policy Analysis* no. 134 (8 June 1990).

Joe, Leland, John Grossman, Doug Merrill, and Brian Nichiporuk. "High Performance Units for *Force XXI*: Interim Briefing." *RAND Report DRR-1052-A*, Santa Monica, Calif.: RAND Corporation, April 1995.

Jones, L. R. "Management of Budgetary Decline in the Department of Defense in Response to the End of the Cold War." *Armed Forces and Society*, 19, no. 4 (Summer 1993).

Kagan, Donald. *On The Origins of War and the Preservation of Peace*. Anchor Books–Doubleday, 1995.

Keegan, John. *The Price of Admiralty: The Evolution of Naval Warfare*. New York: Penguin Books, 1988.

Keegan, John, ed. *Churchill's Generals*. New York: Grove Atlantic, 1991.

Keegan, John. *Six Armies in Normandy*. New York: Penguin Books, 1994.

Kennedy, Paul. *The Rise and Fall of the Great Powers*. New York: Random House, 1987.

Kiel, Douglas. *Managing Chaos and Complexity in Government: A New Paradigm for Managing Change, Innovation and Organizational Renewal*. San Francisco: Jossey-Bass, 1994.

Kimball, Jeffrey P. "The Stab-in-the-Back Legend and the Vietnam War." *Armed Forces and Society* 14, no. 3 (Spring 1988).

Kitfield, James. "Ships Galore! Federal Dollars Are Scarce. Belts Everywhere Are Being Tightened. But Thanks to Their Friends in Washington, Half a Dozen Yards That Build Ships for the Navy Are Doing Just Fine." *National Journal*, 10 February 1996.

Kugler, Richard L. *U.S.–West European Cooperation in Out-of-Area Military Operations: Problems and Prospects*. Santa Monica, Calif.: RAND National Defense Research Institute, 1994.

Kuhn, Thomas S. *The Structure of Scientific Revolutions*. Chicago: University of Chicago Press, 1970.

Lawson, Fred H. *Critical Issues: Opposition and U.S. Policy Toward the Arab Gulf States*. New York: Council on Foreign Relations Press, 1992.

Lebedev, Y. V., I. S. Lyutov, and V. A. Nazarenko. "The War in the Persian Gulf: Lessons and Conclusions." *Military Thought* no. 11–12 (November-December 1991).

Leffler, Melvyn P. "Was 1947 a Turning Point?" In L. Carl Brown, editor, *Centerstage: American Diplomacy Since World War II*. New York: Holmes and Meier, 1990.

Levite, Ariel. *Offense and Defense in Israeli Military Doctrine*. Boulder, Colo.: Westview Press, 1990.

Macgregor, Douglas A. "Future Battle: The Merging Levels of War." *Parameters* (Winter 1992–93).

Macgregor, Douglas A. "Setting the Terms of Future Battle for FORCE XXI." Land Warfare Paper No. 20. *Institute of Land Warfare*, Association of the United States Army, Washington, D.C. (June 1995).

Manchester, William. *American Caesar: Douglas MacArthur, 1880–1964*. New York: Bantam Doubleday Dell, 1983.

Massie, Robert K. *Dreadnought: Britain, Germany and the Coming of the Great War*. New York: Random House, 1991.

Mazarr, Michael J. *The Revolution in Military Affairs: A Framework for Defense Planning*. Carlisle, Penn.: U.S. Army War College Strategic Studies Institute Fifth Annual Conference on Strategy, April 1994.

McAuliffe, Amy. "Technology: Changing the Way the Army Does Business." *Military & Aerospace Electronics* (February 1996).

McCausland, Jeff. "Dual Track or Double Paralysis? The Politics of INF." *Armed Forces and Society*, 12, no. 3 (Spring 1986).

McCullough, David. *The Path Between the Seas: The Creation of the Panama Canal 1870–1914*. New York: Simon & Schuster, 1977.

McKearney, Terry J. "Rethinking the Joint Task Force." *Proceedings* (November 1994).

McNally, Brendan. "Czechs Ponder 'Stealth Tracker' Sale to Iran: Plane Comes After Government Eases Export Rules." *Defense News*, 12 July 1993.

McNamara, Robert S. *In Retrospect*. New York: Random House, 1995.

McPeak, Merrill A. *Selected Works 1990–1994*. Maxwell Air Force Base, Ala.: Air University Press, 1995.

Metz, Steven. "The Army and the Future of the International System." *Parameters* (Summer 1994).

Midgley, John J., Jr. *Deadly Illusions: Army Policy for the Nuclear Battlefield*. Boulder, Colo.: Westview Press, 1986.

Morgenthau, Hans J. *Politics Among Nations: The Struggle for Power and Peace*, 5th ed. New York: Alfred A. Knopf, 1973.

Motley, James Berry. *Beyond the Soviet Threat: The U.S. Army in a Post–Cold War Environement*. Lexington, Mass.: Lexington Books, 1991.

Nitze, Paul. *Securing the Seas: The Soviet Naval Challenge and Western Alliance Options*. Boulder, Colo.: Westview Press, 1979.

Nordlinger, Eric. *Isolationism Reconfigured: American Foreign Policy for a New Century*. Princeton, N.J.: Princeton University Press, 1995.

Odom, William E., and S. John Tsagronis. *Peru: Prospects for Political Stability*. Washington, D.C.: Hudson Institute, February 1992.

O'Hanlon, Michael E. *The Art of War in the Age of Peace: U.S. Military Posture for the Post–Cold War World*. Westport, Conn.: Praeger, 1992.

O'Hanlon, Michael E. *Defense Planning for the Late 1990s: Beyond the Desert Storm Framework*. Washington, D.C.: The Brookings Institution, 1995.

Olson, Mancur. *The Rise and Decline of Nations*. New Haven, Conn.: Yale University Press, 1983.

Osgood, Robert. *Ideals and Self-Interest in American Foreign Relations: The Great Transformation of the Twentieth Century*. Chicago: University of Chicago Press, 1953.

Owens, William. "The Quest for Consensus." *Proceedings* (May 1994).

Peay, J. H. Binford III. "The Five Pillars of Peace in the Central Region." *Joint Force Quarterly* (Autumn 1995).

Pfaltzgraff, Robert L., Jr., and Richard H. Shultz, eds. *The United States Army: Challenges and Missions for the 1990s*. Lexington, Mass.: Lexington Books, 1991.

Philips, Alan. "Dr. Strangelove Puts Peace in Doubt: Russia Sees NATO as Potential Enemy." *Daily Telegraph*, 13 February 1996.

Pimlott, John, and Stephen Badsey. *The Gulf War Assessed*. London: Arms and Armour, 1992.

Pogue, Forrest C. *George C. Marshall: Education of a General*. New York: The Viking Press, 1963.

Possony, Stefan T., and Jerry E. Pournelle. *The Strategy of Technology: Winning the Decisive War*. Cambridge, Mass.: Dunellen, 1970.

Post, Gaines, Jr. "Mad Dogs and Englishmen: British Rearmament, Deterrence, and Appeasement, 1934–35." *Armed Forces and Society*, 14, no. 3 (Spring 1988).

Prange, Gordon W. *At Dawn We Slept: The Untold Story of Pearl Harbor*. New York: McGraw-Hill, 1981.

Prina, Edgar L. "Sea Power from Over the Horizon to Over the Beach: Amphibs Move to Center Stage in Contingency Plans." *Seapower*, 13 November 1995.

Quinlivan, James T. "Force Requirements in Stability Operations." *Parameters* (Winter 1995).

Rauch, Jonathan. *Demosclerosis: The Silent Killer of American Government*. New York: Times Books–Random House, 1994.

Record, Jeffrey. *Revising U.S. Military Strategy: Tailoring Means to Ends*. Washington, D.C.: Pergamon–Brassey's, 1984.

Record, Jeffrey. *Hollow Victory: A Contrary View of the Gulf War*. New York: Brassey's, 1993.

Reimer, Dennis. "Leadership for the 21st Century: Empowerment, Environment and the Golden Rule." *Military Review* January–February, 1996.

Ridgway, Matthew. *Soldier: The Memoirs of Matthew B. Ridgway*. Westport, Conn.: Greenwood Press, 1974.

Rommel, Erwin. *The Rommel Papers*. Edited by B. H. Liddell-Hart. New York: Da Capo Paperback, 1953.

Roncolato, Gerard. "Methodical Battle: Didn't Work Then . . . Won't Work Now." *Proceedings* (February 1996).

Rosen, Stephen. *Winning the Next War: Innovation and the Modern Military*. Ithaca, N.Y.: Cornell University Press, 1991.

Rostow, Eugene. *A Breakfast for Bonaparte: U.S. National Security Interests from the Heights of Abraham to the Nuclear Age*. Washington, D.C.: National Defense University Press, 1993.

Rumsey, Michael G., Clinton Walker, and James H. Harris, eds. *Personnel Selection and Classification*. Hillsdale, N.J.: Lawrence Erlbaum Associates, 1994.

Scarborough, Rowan. "Perry Questions Plan to Defend Gulf Area: Sees Gap in Protection of S. Korea." *Washington Times*, 5 January 1996.

Schlacht, John, ed. *Second Indochina War Symposium: Papers and Commentary*. Washington, D.C.: Center for Military History, U.S. Army, 1984.

Schneider, James L. "The Theory of the Empty Battlefield." *RUSI Journal for Defence Studies* (September 1987).

Seabury, Paul, and Angelo Codevilla. *War: Ends and Means*. New York: Basic Books, 1991.

Sherry, Michael. *The Rise of American Airpower: The Creation of Armageddon*. New Haven, Conn.: Yale University Press, 1987.

Shy, John. *A People Numerous and Armed: Reflections on the Military Struggle for American Independence*. New York: Oxford University Press, 1976.

Simmons, E. H. "Getting Marines to the Gulf." *U.S. Naval Institute Proceedings* (May 1991).

Simon, Jeffrey, ed. *European Security Policy After the Revolutions of 1989*. Washiongton, D.C.: National Defense University Press, 1991.

Simpkin, Richard. *Deep Battle: The Brainchild of Marshal Tukhachevskii*. New York: Brassey's, 1987.

Skelton, Ike. "Inspiring Soldiers to Do Better Than Their Best." *Military Review* (January–February 1996).

Smith, William D. "Seapower: There Is No More Vital Research Than That Involving Defenses Against Theater Ballistic Missiles." *Defense News* (January 1996).

Solzhenitsyn, Alexander. *August 1914*. Translated by Michael Glenny. New York: Farrar, Straus & Giroux, 1971.

Spence, Floyd D. "What to Fight For? American Interests and the Use of Force in the Post–Cold War World." *The Brown Journal of World Affairs* (Winter–Spring 1996).

Spiller, Roger J., ed. *Combined Arms in Battle Since 1939*. Fort Leavenworth, Kans.: U.S. Army Command and General Staff College, 1992.

Spinney, Franklin C. "Defense Time Bomb: The Case of Tactical Aviation in the Air Force." Unpublished manuscript, 1996.

Spykman, Nicholas John. *The Geography of the Peace*. New York: Harcourt, Brace & World, 1944.

Stewart, William G. "Interaction of Firepower, Mobility, and Dispersion." *Military Review* (March 1960).

Taw, Jennifer, and Bruce Hoffman. "The Urbanization of Insurgency: The Potential Challenge to U.S. Army Operations." *Rand MR—398-A*, Santa Monica, Calif.: Rand Corporation, 1994.

Taylor, William C. "Control in an Age of Chaos." *Harvard Business Review* (November–December 1994).

Tilford, Earl. *Crosswinds: The Air Force's Set-up in Vietnam*. Ala.: Air University Press, Maxwell AFB, 1993.

Tillson, John C. F. "Force Planning for the 21st Century." *IDA Paper PP-2640*, Alexandria, Va.: Institute for Defense Analysis, 1992.

Toffler, Heidi, and Alvin Toffler. *War and Anti-War*. New York: Warner Books, 1993.

TRADOC PAMPHLET 525-5, *Force XXI Operations: A Concept for the Evolution of Full-Dimensional Operations for the Strategic Army of the Early Twenty-First Century. Fort Monroe, Va.: HQTRS TRADOC, 1 August 1994.*

Tucker, Robert W., and David C. Hendrickson. *The Imperial Temptation: The New World Order and America's Purpose*. New York: Council on Foreign Relations Press, 1992.

Turlington, John E. "Learning Operational Art." *Essays on Strategy IV*, Washington, D.C.: National Defense University Press, 1987.

Uehling, Steven. "The Case for the F/A-18E/F Just Doesn't Fly." *Navy Times* (September 1995).

Ullman, Harlan K. *In Irons: U.S. Military Might in the New Century*. Washington, D.C.: National Defense University Press, 1995.

Van Creveld, Martin. *Command in War*. Cambridge, Mass.: Harvard University Press, 1985.

Van Nizkirk, Phillip. "U.S. Flies Citizens out of a Liberia Torn by Civil War." *New York Times*, 10 April 1996.

Walsh, Mary Williams. "German Linked to Libyan Arms Deal." *Los Angeles Times*, 28 February 1996.

Weigley, Russell F. *Eisenhower's Lieutenants: The Campaign of France and Germany, 1944–1945*. Bloomington: Indiana University Press, 1970.

Weigley, Russell F. *The American Way of War: A History of United States Military Strategy and Policy*. Bloomington: Indiana University Press, 1977.

Weiner, Tim. "Cruise Missile Is Test-Fired from a Ship by Iran's Navy." *New York Times* 31 January 1996.

Weiner, Tim. "Smart Weapons Were Overrated, Study Concludes." *New York Times* 9 July 1996.

Welch, Jasper. "Why the Bomber Question Is So Controversial." *Strategic Review* (Winter 1996).

Wilkening, Dean, and Kenneth Watman. *Nuclear Deterrence in a Regional Conflict*. Santa Monica, Calif.: Rand Corporation, 1995.

Wilson, J. R. "Simulation Bites the Budget Bullet: Powerful Computers Bring New Levels of Reality." *International Defense Review* 1 April 1995.

Winton, Harold. *To Change an Army: General Sir John Burnett-Stuart and British Armored Doctrine, 1927–1938*. Lawrence, Kans.: University Press of Kansas, 1988.

Wood, David. "Navy Tries to Handle Mines." *The Plain Dealer*, 23 September 1995.

Zaloga, Steven. *Soviet Air Defence Missiles: Design, Development and Tactics*. London: Janes Defence Studies, 1989.

Zumwalt, Elmo. *On Watch: A Memoir*. New York: Quadrangle Books, 1974.

Index

About the Author

LIEUTENANT COLONEL (P) DOUGLAS A. MACGREGOR was commissioned in the U.S. Army in 1976 after one year at the Virginia Military Institute and four years at the U.S. Military Academy. After completing airborne and ranger training, Colonel Macgregor served in a variety of command and staff assignments including command of a Division Cavalry Squadron and one year in the War Plans Division of the Army General Staff. During Desert Storm, Colonel Macgregor was awarded the bronze star with "V" device for valor while leading combat troops in the 2nd Squadron, 2nd Armored Cavalry Regiment. He wrote *Breaking the Phalanx* while serving as the Army Fellow at CSIS in Washington, D.C. His other works include *The Soviet-East German Military Alliance*. Colonel Macgregor holds an M.A. in comparative politics and a Ph.D. in International Relations from the University of Virginia. He is assigned to the U.S. Army Combined Arms Center at Fort Leavenworth, Kansas.